GREGORY GEORGES

50 FAST PHOTOSHOP® CS TECHNIQUES

Wiley Publishing, Inc.

50 Fast Photoshop® CS Techniques

Published by
Wiley Publishing, Inc.
111 River St.
Hoboken, NJ 07030

www.wiley.com

Copyright © 2004 by Wiley Publishing, Inc., Indianapolis, Indiana

ISBN: 0-7645-4174-9

Manufactured in the United States of America

10 9 8 7 6 5 4 3 2 1

1K/RR/QS/QU/IN

Published by Wiley Publishing, Inc., Indianapolis, Indiana
Published simultaneously in Canada

For general information on our other products and services or to obtain technical support, please contact our Customer Care Department within the U.S. at 800-762-2974, outside the U.S. at 317-572-3993 or fax 317-572-4002.

Wiley also publishes its books in a variety of electronic formats. Some content that appears in print may not be available in electronic books.

Library of Congress Control Number: 2003116748

WILEY

Each time I complete a book, I grow increasingly aware of the contribution my wife has made to each and every one of them. Thank you, Linda.

PREFACE

If you are serious about digital photography, either as a passionate amateur, money-earning professional photographer or artist, or anywhere in between and you want to edit your photos digitally with Adobe Photoshop CS — this book is for you! It is for you regardless of your experience level with Adobe Photoshop CS or other versions.

Without a doubt, the more you know about Adobe Photoshop CS or an earlier version of Photoshop, the easier these techniques will be to complete. But, if you are new to Adobe Photoshop CS you can complete all of the techniques in the book by carefully following each of the steps and by reading the occasional detailed explanation. By the time you complete all or even most of the 50 techniques, you will have acquired a considerable amount of knowledge about Adobe Photoshop CS's most important features and will be well on your way to being able to competently edit your own digital photos.

The premise of this book is that the best way to learn how to use a complex software application such as Adobe Photoshop CS is to just use it. You will have successful results while working with fun photos, which will make the learning process enjoyable. If the learning process is truly enjoyable, time will fly by and the hours of effort will result in success. Success will result in more knowledge, which eventually will turn those that work hard to learn Adobe Photoshop CS into competent Adobe Photoshop CS users.

In contrast to those who say Adobe Photoshop CS is too complex for many potential users, I believe that inexperienced Photoshop users can create some outstanding results by learning how to use just a few features extremely well. This book includes many techniques that will help you to learn all about some of the more important features and how to use them extremely well to do what you want to do.

ACKNOWLEDGMENTS

Each time I write a new book, I fully recognize the growing number of people that have substantially helped me in one way or another learn more about the topics that I write about, and to write about them in better ways. For this book, special thanks to:

- Readers of my books, attendees of my workshops, students, and subscribers to my e-mail group who have contributed to my understanding of what topics need to be included and how they should be presented — an understanding that is essential for writing books that help readers and provide the value they should.
- The many contributors of specific techniques and photographs, which added considerable "genetic diversity" to this book. These contributors include Peter Balazsy, Phil Bard, Scott Dingman, Bobbi Doyle-Maher, Tammy Kennedy, Marc McIntyre, Arthur Morris, Lance Richardson, and Alan Scharf. Special thanks go to Maria and Preddy for allowing me to use their photos in this book.
- The entire Wiley team who helped to turn the 50 techniques in my head into a book that I hope will become invaluable to photographers of all skill levels. I would like to thank the following key people on the team, including Mike Roney, the Acquisitions Editor who acquired this book, many before it, and I hope many more to come; Amanda Peterson, for her excellent work as Project Editor; and Roxane Marini for her copy editing.

CONTENTS AT A GLANCE

CONTENTS

CHAPTER 2   CORRECTING AND ENHANCING DIGITAL PHOTOS   59

CHAPTER 3   WORKING IN BLACK AND WHITE   107

CHAPTER 4   ENHANCING PORTRAITS   145

Chapter 5   Combining Photos in Montages, Collages, and Composites   183

CHAPTER 6   FINE ART TECHNIQUES   205

CHAPTER 9   CREATING AN ONLINE PHOTO GALLERY   309

INTRODUCTION

I wrote this book — with its 50 step-by-step techniques and 50 sets of "before" and "after" images — to provide you with the knowledge, skills, and practice that you need to use Adobe Photoshop CS to edit your own digital photographs. All the techniques are applicable to images created with scanners or with digital cameras. They are for those just beginning to learn more about working in the "new digital darkroom." They are for those that have worked in a traditional darkroom for many years and now want to work digitally, as well as experienced Photoshop users who want to learn more about Adobe Photoshop CS and the digital photo techniques that can be found in this book.

ABOUT BOOT CAMPS AND CHAPTER 1

Many years ago, my father told me that all good things in life that are worth having require effort — having Adobe Photoshop CS skills is one example of this axiom holding true. Adobe Photoshop CS skills don't always come easy and so you'll have to work to get them; however, the techniques and the photos you will find in this book should make it a relatively painless process that you should enjoy.

In an effort to help you become successful with the last 44 techniques, the first 6 techniques in the first chapter have been written as "boot-camp" techniques. These techniques will help to get you and your equipment ready to complete the remaining techniques. I highly recommend that you complete all 6 of the techniques in Chapter 1 before trying any of the other techniques. After you've completed Chapter 1, you may choose to do the other techniques in any order that you want.

A FEW THINGS TO CONSIDER BEFORE BEGINNING THESE TECHNIQUES

Before jumping into the techniques, here are a few additional things to consider.

Color management is important

If your monitor is not properly calibrated, you will likely not see the results that are expected when you use the techniques and settings suggested in this book. Likewise, if you have not properly set up your printer, your prints will not turn out to look like the image viewed on your monitor or as intended. Completing Techniques 1, 2, and 3 will have you well on your way to working in a color-managed environment.

About the photos on the companion CD-ROM

Having ready access to the digital photos on the companion CD-ROM will save you time and make it easier to do each of the techniques. If you have room on your hard drive for these photos, I recommend that you copy the entire \techniques folder and sub-folders to your hard drive. **Please note that any time that you copy files from a CD-ROM to a hard drive using a PC or a Mac, the files will be tagged with a Read-Only attribute. This is okay if you want to keep those original files for later use without the possibility of over-writing them. However, if you want to save your work over those files, you will have to remove the Read-Only attribute. To do so in Windows, right-click a folder or file to get a pop-up menu. Select Properties to get the Properties dialog box — and then uncheck the Read-Only attribute. You can change attributes for a single image or an entire folder of images and/or folders all at once. On a Mac using Finder, select File ➢ Get Info and change Ownership & Permissions to Read & Write.**

To fit all the photos that are needed for the 50 techniques on the companion CD-ROM, some of the "after" images have been saved as compressed JPEG image files. To get the best possible prints or to view the best possible images on your screen, you should complete each technique and use the completed images instead of the JPEG versions of the "after" images found on the companion CD-ROM. In many techniques, when an original photo was taken using a RAW file format, the original RAW file is provided. However, a JPEG version is also available so that you do not have to have a RAW conversion tool to be able to work with the images.

Learn what you need to learn and ignore the rest

Adobe Photoshop CS is big! It can take years for professionals who work with it all day long, every day, to become proficient with it — and then, there are still many features that they do not know how to use, or may not even be aware that they are there! If I had to make a single recommendation about how to quickly learn to successfully use Adobe Photoshop CS, it would be to learn all about those few features that you need to use to get you work done — and ignore the rest.

WHAT COMPUTER HARDWARE AND SOFTWARE DO YOU NEED?

When it comes to digital image editing, the axiom "the more the better" applies. Editing digital images is an activity that can consume lots of disk space, RAM, monitor pixels, and computer processing cycles. Fortunately, the computer industry has been good to us these past few years as the cost of having power and storage to spare has dropped sharply. Powerful computers with lots of RAM, enormous hard drives, and quality monitors are getting less and less expensive. At a minimum, you'll need a computer that meets the requirements specified by Adobe for running Adobe Photoshop CS.

If you use a computer that matches Adobe's minimum requirements, you may find you'll enjoy doing the techniques in this book much more if you have 512MB or more of RAM, and 3GB or more of available disk space. The cost of adding additional RAM or adding an additional hard drive can be relatively inexpensive in today's competitive computer marketplace. An 80GB internal hard drive sells for under $120 and depending on the type of RAM you need, you can buy 128MB of RAM for as little as $50. If you have a relatively slow processor, adding additional RAM can significantly increase the processing speed and help you to avoid the long waits that can occur when editing digital images. If you spend much time editing digital photos, you'll find the investment in more RAM to be more than worthwhile. If you shoot using the RAW file format and use 16-bit images, having more RAM is more a necessity than it is a luxury.

Besides having a fast computer with enough RAM and hard drive space, a rewriteable CD-ROM or DVD-ROM can be one of the most useful (and in my view essential) peripherals for those doing digital image editing. A rewriteable CD-ROM allows you to easily back up your digital photos, to share them with others, and to make space on your hard drive. Rewriteable CD-ROM drives can be purchased for under $125. Remember that when you begin to store your digital photo collection on your computer hard drive, it is possible to lose everything if you have problems with your hard drive. If you value your digital photos, you need to back them up on to a removable storage device of some type such as a CD-ROM or DVD-ROM.

The monitor and graphics card you use is also very important to successful and enjoyable image editing. If you primarily work with images that are 1,600 x 1,200 pixels or smaller, you may find it acceptable (or possibly not) to work on a 14" or 15" monitor with 800 x 600 pixels. If you are working on larger images, you'll find that a 17" or larger monitor with at least a 1,024 x 768 pixel workspace is far more useful. While there are larger monitors than 19" monitors, I was extremely happy with the 19" monitor that I used until I got a 24" monitor! It is so wonderful to be able to view and edit images with the necessary tools and palettes on the screen and still be able to see most of the image. You can also buy special graphics boards and use two monitors at once, which is becoming increasingly common. Having two monitors enables you to put your images on one screen and all the palettes on the other screen.

For those of you wondering whether it is better to use a PC or a Mac, I'd say that the computer that you have or know how to use is the better one. Without a doubt, there are differences between the two platforms, but there aren't any clear-cut reasons why the PC or the Mac is better at doing mage editing. Therefore, have it your way and enjoy using the computer that you will be most comfortable and successful using — that will be the best one for *your* digital image editing. Or, if you are like me — you can use both!

NOTES TO MAC USERS

The great news for Mac users is that Adobe has historically offered both PC and Mac versions of all their products. The Adobe engineers work hard to keep the differences between the PC and Mac versions of Photoshop limited to the differences between the operating systems, user interfaces, and keyboards. The Mac screenshots will look slightly different from the PC screenshots shown in this book. Otherwise, this book is equally useful to PC and Mac users as all differences are covered in each technique when it is appropriate and keyboard shortcuts are shown for both the PC and Mac throughout the book.

WHAT IS NEW IN PHOTOSHOP CS?

What Photoshop CS features will you love? Besides offering lots of cool and useful new features, many of Photoshop CS's features have been enhanced for better results or so that they are easier to use. You'll want to get this new version right away — especially if you shoot in RAW file format using one of the large-pixel digital SLR cameras and you want to edit in 16-bit mode!

Some of the more important new features or enhancements that will be useful to photographers are as follows:

- Integrated Camera RAW converter
- New image resolution algorithms to get better-quality images when up- or down-sampling images
- Comprehensive 16-bit image editing support that allows you to take advantage of the extra image information found in RAW image files
- A powerful new Shadow/Highlight Correction feature that is wonderful for bringing back details in both shadows and highlights
- An always available Histogram palette that offers several different display modes to make it easier for you to track Histogram changes while editing
- Oodles of new and useful enhancements to the File Browser, which make it a truly useful tool that you ought to add to your workflow no matter which image manager you use.
- The useful Photomerge formerly only found in Adobe Photoshop Elements has now been included for merging photos seamlessly.
- Other new features such as Photo Filters, Lens Blur, Customizable Keyboard Shortcuts, PDF creation features, new Web photo galleries, Match Color, easy access to online digital printing services, ability to track your edits, and much more.

1

PHOTOSHOP CS FUNDAMENTALS

Doing more, doing it better, and doing it quicker are the objectives of just about everyone using Adobe Photoshop CS. Adobe Photoshop CS is an extraordinarily powerful application with rich functionality and its complexity and versatility often work against achieving these objectives. The good news is that if you know all that is contained in these first six techniques, you'll be able to work efficiently and effectively, which will allow most of your mental resources to be applied to the creative use of Adobe Photoshop CS rather than figuring out how to get done what you want to do.

Even if you are an experienced user of Adobe Photoshop CS, these first six techniques offer many practical tips that will be invaluable to anyone interested in digital photo editing. You must become the master of your tools, or they will master you and frustration will prevail! This is not a short chapter, but it is an important one worth doing step-by-step — even for those who consider themselves to be Adobe Photoshop CS experts.

CONFIGURING PHOTOSHOP CS

1.1

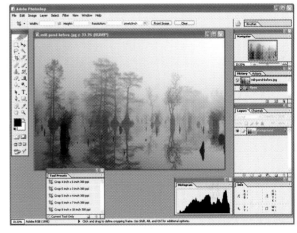

1.2

Evening at Merchant Mill Pond Canon EOS D30 mounted on a tripod, 28-70mm f/2.8, ISO 100, f/18 @ 1/25, RAW setting, 2,160 x 1,440 pixels, edited and converted to 0.96MB 2,048 x 1,365 .jpg

Adobe Photoshop CS has more than 550 menu items that can be accessed from the main menu bar. Additionally, it has 18 feature-rich tool palettes including the Toolbox, which has more than 65 tools. Plus, Adobe Photoshop CS offers a plethora of tool presets, color swatches, actions, styles, brushes, blend modes, and much more. Oh, yes — there are 67 menu items in the new File Browser, too. Wow, you might think: How am I going to learn all about *all* that stuff! The fact is that if you configure Adobe Photoshop CS properly and you learn to use the tools that you need to use, it really is possible to do all that you'd like to do, without having to learn about everything. This first technique covers all the necessary steps you should take to set up Adobe Photoshop CS — for you and what you want to do.

STEP 1: OPEN FILE

■ Select **File ➤ Open** (**Ctrl+O** PC, **Cmd+O** Mac) to display the **Open** dialog box. After locating the **\01** folder, double-click it to open it. Click **mill-pond-before.jpg** and then click **Open** to open the file.

STEP 2: CHOOSE SCREEN RESOLUTION AND COLOR QUALITY SETTINGS

Before you begin configuring Adobe Photoshop CS to best fit your working style, I ought to point out that monitor screen resolution and color quality settings can be changed. If you know about these settings and you know how to use them, then skip to Step 3. Otherwise, this is a step worth reading carefully. I know many competent computer users who were not aware that they could change these settings and were pleased to learn about them — especially those with aging eyes!

■ If you are using a PC, right-click anywhere on your desktop where there are no application windows or icons to get a menu. From the menu select **Properties** to get the **Display Properties** dialog box. Click the **Settings** tab to get a dialog box similar to the one shown in Figure 1.3. Toward the bottom-left of this dialog box, you will see a slider in the **Screen resolution** area. Depending on your display monitor and your graphics board, you will have one or more choices of screen resolutions as you move the slider.

■ If you are using Mac OS X, you can set screen resolution by selecting **System Preferences ➤ Displays** and click the **Display** tab to get the dialog box shown in Figure 1.4.

Choosing the best screen resolution setting depends on several factors such as monitor size, graphics card capabilities, available graphics card RAM, your eyesight, and current work at hand. Most new computers allow you to change screen resolution "on-the-fly,"

meaning that you do not have to reboot your PC each time you change screen resolution. If your computer allows "on-the-fly" changes to your display, then you may want to consider changing often to suit your immediate needs.

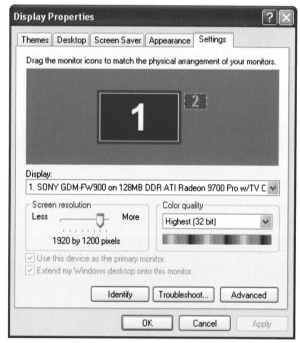

1.3

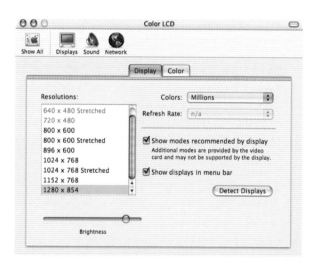

1.4

At lower screen resolutions such as 800 x 600 pixels, or 1,024 x 768 pixels, everything is relatively large including text, application menus, and application windows—making them easy to see and read. However, the downside is that you have less work-space. This means that you can see less of a large image, or if you have two or more applications open and viewable on your desktop at the same time, you'll have less room to display the applications. Even more importantly, you will see less of the image you are working on if you have lots of tools and palettes open as you work.

■ After you have decided what screen resolution to use, click the slider and drag it to the left or right until you get the setting you want. For most Adobe Photoshop work, you should use the largest screen resolution you can. Any screen size smaller than about 1,024 x 768 is too small for

TIP

Many photographers are now either adding a second computer screen to their computer or they are using one of the new "wide" computer screens such as the Sony Premierpro 24" FD Trinitron CRT GDM-FW900 (1,920 x 1,200 pixels) or the Apple 23" Cinema HD Display (1,920 x 1,200 pixels) if they are using a Mac.

If you want to use two screens, you will need to have a graphics card that can support two screens. When using two screens you can have an uncluttered image on one screen and all the tools and palettes (except for the File Browser) on the other screen and the cost of two screens is usually less than the $2,000 it costs for the wide screens mentioned above. Once you use two screens or a wide screen, you'll wonder how you ever worked with such limited desktop space before.

serious digital photo editing. Adobe supports this notion by requiring a minimum size of 1,024 x 768 pixels for the Adobe Camera RAW dialog box.

■ After setting screen resolution, make sure to check the **Color quality** setting—it *must* be set at **24 bits** or higher on the PC, or on the Mac set **Colors** to **Millions**. Anything less and you will have way too few colors to effectively edit digital photos. If your graphics board does not have enough video RAM to display 24 bits of color at a high screen resolution setting, then you may have to choose a lower screen resolution setting to use 24-bit color, or buy a new computer display.

■ Once your choice of screen resolution has been selected and you have **24-bit** or higher color qual-ity, click **OK** to apply the settings. You'll then likely see your display flicker as it changes to the new settings. If you get a dialog box saying that you have to reboot your PC, then first save any open documents, and then click **OK** to reboot your PC.

STEP 3: CHECK FOR AND INSTALL UPDATES

One of the many benefits we have in today's Internet-connected world is the capability to always use up-to-date software. Many of Adobe's new products such as Adobe Photoshop CS have a built-in update feature, called **Adobe Online Update**. It is a terrific feature that you ought to use!

■ First make sure that you have an open connec-tion to the Internet. Then, select **Help ➢ Updates** and follow the steps to download and install any new updates.

STEP 4: RESTORE PREFERENCES TO THEIR DEFAULT SETTINGS

Adobe engineers have made Adobe Photoshop CS easy to use by making sure that most features have default settings. This means you can just use features and not worry about having to select options each time you use them. The approach they took was to put most of these default settings into a single preference file, which can be accessed from a series of dialog boxes. We'll be going through each of these dialog boxes in the next step. Before then, I suggest that you first restore your preferences to their default settings.

If you have already set color management settings, or, for that matter any other settings that you do not want to change, then you may want to skip this step and go on to Step 5. Setting all the preferences to their default settings before completing Step 5 simply makes it easier for you to end up with the suggested settings.

- If you are using a PC you can restore the preferences file by pressing and *holding* **Alt+Ctrl+Shift** immediately after launching Adobe Photoshop CS. When using Mac OS, hold down the **Shift+Option+Cmd** keys at the startup of Adobe Photoshop CS to reset preferences to their default settings. If your timing is right, you will get a dialog box asking if you want to delete the Adobe Photoshop settings file. If you don't get the dialog box, close Photoshop after it loads and have another try. Click **Yes** when asked if you would like to delete the settings file.
- If you clicked **Yes**, after Adobe Photoshop CS is loaded, you will get another dialog box asking if you want to customize your color settings now. Click **No** to continue loading Adobe Photoshop CS as we will get to the color settings later in this chapter in Technique 6.

STEP 5: SET PREFERENCES

There are nine **Preferences** dialog boxes with lots and lots of changeable options. Not to worry! I am making a bold assumption that you are configuring Adobe Photoshop CS for editing digital photos and that your printer is a consumer-grade digital photo printer such as an Epson Stylus Photo 1280 or 2200, or a Canon

i9100 Photo Printer. We'll just cover those options that you are most likely to need to make sure they are set for these purposes. The rest we'll just skip over!

While you may not want to make any changes to the preferences file at this time, it will be worth the effort to take a quick tour through these screens to see what is available. A simple change in one of these settings will often make your work considerably easier and quicker, and in some cases remarkably better.

- Select **Edit ➤ Preferences ➤ General** (**Ctrl+K**) on a PC to get the **Preferences - General** dialog box shown in Figure 1.5. On a Mac, select **Photoshop ➤ Preferences ➤ General** (**Cmd+K**).
- Leave **Color Picker** set to **Adobe**.
- One of the useful new features of Adobe Photoshop CS is the option to choose one of several new or updated interpolation methods to use when resizing an image. When you use commands such as **Image Size**, the setting you've chosen for **Image Interpolation** is the default setting. I suggest that you set **Image Interpolation** to **Bicubic Smoother**, which is generally the best method to use for increasing image size. You can read more about increasing image size in Technique 41.
- **Leave History States** set to **20** for now. It is important to know that this feature can gobble

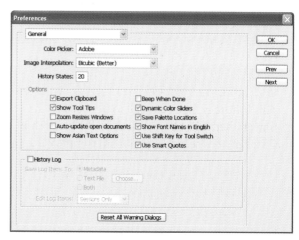

1.5

up RAM in huge bytes (or I should say bites!). In Technique 5 you will learn more about history states and how it impacts the use of RAM. Now you know where to come to change the setting for number of states should you find your computer is struggling with huge working files.

■ Click **Export Clipboard** to clear the box. This saves you from worrying about having a large image in the clipboard when you change application windows. It also saves RAM.

■ If you want to have **Tool Tips** pop up when you hover over various tools and options in the **Options** bar and other dialog boxes (even the **Preferences** dialog boxes) you should leave a checkmark next to **Show Tool Tips**. Otherwise, you can clear the box.

■ If you have a large screen you may want to turn on the **Zoom Resizes Window** feature. If this feature is unchecked, when you zoom in on an image, the image will zoom in, but the document window size will remain unchanged and so you will see a smaller portion of the image each time you zoom in. If the feature is on, the document window will increase in size up to the maximum size of your screen, when you zoom in on an image. I prefer to have this option turned on.

■ The **Beep When Done** feature is nice to use if you have a slow computer or you frequently work with large files. If you find yourself looking at the screen for long periods of time to see when Adobe Photoshop CS has finished a task, turn it on. Otherwise, turn it off so that you don't have what to some might be considered an annoying beep. This feature is smart enough to not beep all the time; rather, it just beeps when Adobe Photoshop CS takes a few seconds or more to complete an edit or open a file. I leave it turned on.

■ If you have **Save Palette Locations** turned on, each time you close Adobe Photoshop CS and then open it again, all palettes will be in the same location they were before closing Adobe Photoshop CS. If the option is off, palettes will be displayed in the default layout. This may not seem like a particularly good feature, but for those that use lots of palettes, having the tools show up where you left off last time is a very nice feature indeed.

■ Another of the exciting new Adobe Photoshop CS features to some photographers is the ability to have Adobe Photoshop CS keep a written log of your edit steps. A history of your edit steps can be wonderfully useful if you need to be able to document your work. If you want to turn this feature on, click in the box next to **History Log**. You can then select where the log is to be saved. You can save it as metadata in the image file, as a text file, or in the image file and in a separate text file. You can also choose how much detail is saved by selecting one of the options in the **Edit Log Items** box. You should at least try this feature once. Be aware that using this feature can increase the size of your image files. If you are working on an image to use on a Web page, you most likely will want to turn it off to minimize file size.

■ If you have set the preferences as suggested, your **Preferences** dialog box should now look like the one shown in Figure 1.6.

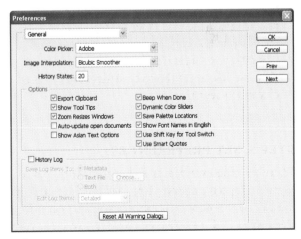

1.6

■ Click **Next** to get the **File Handling** dialog box shown in Figure 1.7. If you find that you frequently open previously opened files, which you have recently closed, you will want to set the **Recent files list contains** box at the bottom of the dialog box to an appropriate number. This setting determines the number of files that will appear in a menu when you select **File ➢ Open Recent.** I use this feature all the time so I set it for an even dozen files.

■ Click **Next** to get the **Displays & Cursors** dialog box shown in Figure 1.8. The default settings work for me in most cases. In particular, I suggest that

you leave the **Painting Cursors** setting to **Brush Size**. This is an exceedingly useful feature when you paint with the **Clone Stamp** tool or the **Brush** tool as it make it possible to see the size of the brush before you begin painting.

■ Click **Next** to get the **Transparency & Gamut** dialog box shown in Figure 1.9. These settings are generally fine just as they are.

■ Click **Next** to get the **Units & Rulers** dialog box shown in Figure 1.10. If you usually work on images for Web pages, you'll want to set **Rulers** to **pixels**; otherwise the best setting is **inches**.

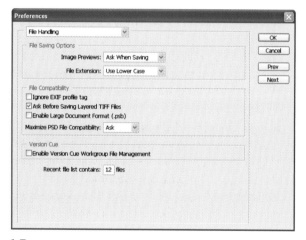

1.7

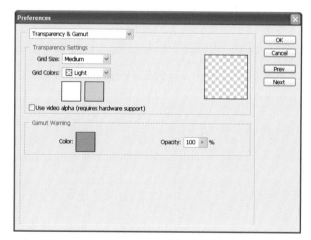

1.9

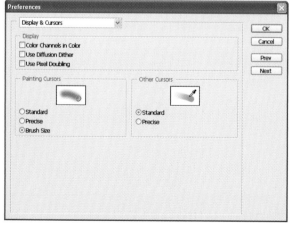

1.8

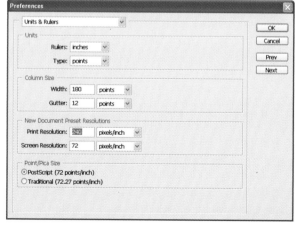

1.10

While we're on the subject, when you want to use rulers while editing an image, select **View** ➢ **Rulers** (**Ctrl+R** PC, **Cmd+R** Mac) to display rulers. To turn off the rulers, select **View** ➢ **Rulers** (**Ctrl+R** PC, **Cmd+R** Mac) again.

■ Setting **New Document Preset Resolutions** to the correct setting for the printer you use most often will save you from having to change the print resolution field each time you create a new document. As I most often use an Epson printer, I set **Print Resolution** to **240 pixels / inch**.

■ Click **Next** to get the **Guides, Grids, & Slices** dialog box shown in Figure 1.11. If you use grids, guidelines, or slices (for Web pages as shown in Technique 28) then this dialog box allows you to determine how they will appear in your document window. For example, if you are laying out images to be printed out as a photo album, guides and grids set in the appropriate intervals and in an easily viewable color can be very useful.

To show a grid in a document window, select **View** ➢ **Show** ➢ **Grid** (**Ctrl+'** PC, **Cmd+'** Mac). To add guidelines to a document you must first make the **Rulers** visible. To display the rulers select **View** ➢ **Rulers** (**Ctrl+R** PC, **Cmd+R** Mac). To make a vertical guideline, click inside the **Ruler** along the left side of

the document window and drag the guideline onto the document where you want it to be placed while watching where it is on the **Ruler** at the top of the document window. For horizontal guidelines do the same except click in the **Ruler** at the top of the document window. Drag it down while viewing the **Ruler** shown at the left side of the document to place the guideline where you want it. Should you want to snap precisely on one of the **Ruler's** marks, press and hold **Shift** while you are dragging the guideline. You'll notice that this causes the guideline to snap to the marks shown on the **Ruler**. You can also change the color of the grid so that it may be seen against the colors shown in your image.

■ Click **Next** to get the **Plug-Ins & Scratch Disks** dialog box shown in Figure 1.12. Using the correct (or incorrect) settings in this dialog box can dramatically impact the overall performance of your computer when editing images with Adobe Photoshop CS.

■ If you have installed plug-ins in a folder other than the default Adobe Photoshop CS compatible plug-in folder, and you want to use them in Adobe Photoshop CS, you can by selecting the **Additional Plug-ins Folder** box. This enables you to browse and select one additional folder that

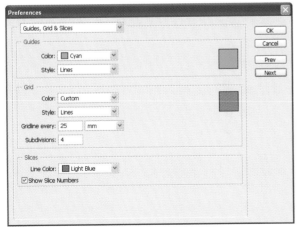

1.11

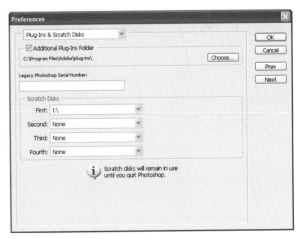

1.12

contains plug-ins that you want to use as a source folder for plug-ins. When a folder has been selected, the plug-ins appear in the plug-in menu in Adobe Photoshop CS the next time you open Adobe Photoshop CS.

■ If you have more than one hard drive, click in the **Scratch Disks** box, and set First to a drive other than the drive where you installed Adobe Photoshop CS, usually d:\ as the d:\ drive is usually the second hard drive. This will let Adobe Photoshop CS use one hard drive for the swap file and one for the scratch disk, which will maximize performance.

One caveat: Be careful not to set the swap file to one partition and the scratch file to another partition on the same hard drive. This makes the hard drive head jump around way too much to efficiently read and write to your image file or files while attempting to maintain the scratch file. You must have two hard drives — not just two different disk partitions — if you set one or more disks to different settings. If you have only one hard drive, just use the default settings — first set to **Startup**, all others to **None**.

TIP

If you have a large number of plug-ins installed in the default plug-in folder \Adobe\Photoshop CS\Plug-Ins, you may find that it takes considerable time to load Adobe Photoshop CS. To reduce the time it takes to load the plug-ins each time you load Adobe Photoshop CS, install them in a separate folder and use the **Additional Plug-Ins Folder** setting in the **Preferences, Plug-Ins & Scratch Disks** dialog box to "turn on" or "turn off" the plug-ins. For example, if you use a folder named **\Adobe\plug-ins2**, the folder can easily be found and can often be used with other image applications that support Adobe Photoshop-compatible plug-ins, too.

■ Click **Next** to get the **Memory & Image Cache** dialog box shown in Figure 1.13.

Cache Levels in the **Memory and Image Cache** dialog box has to do with how Adobe Photoshop CS saves (or doesn't save) images in RAM to facilitate the display of images onscreen. When **Cache Levels** is on (it has a value of **1** or more), Adobe Photoshop CS saves one or more lower resolution versions of the image so that your screen will update more quickly when zooming in or out to see more or less of an image. Besides taking up extra RAM, **Cache Levels** also takes up some extra scratch disk space as well. If you routinely work on large images and you have sufficient RAM and hard drive space, this is an indispensable feature — use it!

So how do you decide on the number of cache levels to use? You will need one cache level for each incremental zoom setting you plan on using. You can view the various zoom settings by clicking the **Zoom** tool in the **Navigator** starting from the one just below **100%** to get **66.67%, 50%, 33.33%, 25%, 16.67%, 12.5%, 8.33%,** and so on to numbers that are less than **1%**. Obviously, you would need a very large image to find much use in zooming to these lower levels, but they are available should you need them. For example, let's assume that we will zoom to **12.5%**. In this case, set **Cache Levels** to **6**.

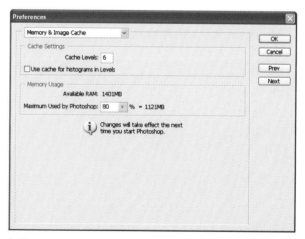

1.13

- If you have lots of RAM and hard drive space relative to the size of images that you typically edit, set **Cache Levels** to the appropriate number of zoom levels you expect to use.
- If you don't have much RAM and you normally edit large images, then set **Cache Levels** to **0** and have patience as Adobe Photoshop CS down- or up-samples the images to display.
- Make sure that the **Use cache for histograms** feature is turned off as turning it off ensures that your histograms will be accurate relative to the image file — not the displayed image.
- While the optimal percentage to use in the **Physical Memory Usage** box is dependent on whether you use a PC or Mac, and which operating system you use and the amount of RAM you have, you will generally be safe setting it to around **80%** if you have 256MB or more of RAM.
- Click **Next** to get the **File Browser** dialog box shown in Figure 1.14. The default settings are good as they are. You may want to check **Allow Background Processing** as it will allow you to continue working while the **File Browser** creates thumbnail images as a background task. If you have a slow computer or are very short on hard

drive space, you may want to consider clearing the **High Quality Previews** box.
- Click **OK** to close the **Preferences** dialog box.

That's it! We've covered all nine of the preferences dialog boxes and Adobe Photoshop CS is now configured for you. However, all of your settings have not yet been saved and applied so that they are in effect. To save them, you must close Adobe Photoshop CS, which will cause your newly created preferences file to be written to your hard drive. So, close Adobe Photoshop CS *now* to make sure your settings get saved.

STEP 6: RESET TOOLS AND PALETTES

While we are on the topic of resetting "things" to default settings I would be remiss to not cover the **Preset Manager**. It allows you to reset libraries of preset **Brushes**, **Swatches**, **Gradients**, **Styles**, **Patterns**, **Contours**, **Custom Shapes**, and **Tools**.

- To reset any of the preset libraries, select **Edit ➢ Preset Manager** to get the **Preset Manger** dialog box shown in Figure 1.15. Click the **Preset Manager** menu button (the tiny triangle just to the right of **Preset Type** box) to get a menu — then select **Reset [the name of the tool].** You'll then get a dialog box asking if you want to replace the library to the default library; click **OK**.
- When you have reset all the tools you want to reset, click **Done** to close the **Preset Manager.**

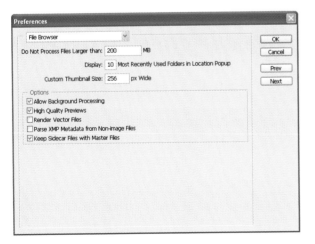

1.14

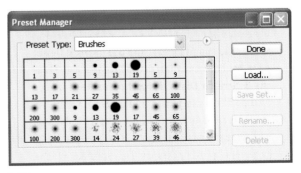

1.15

STEP 7: ORGANIZE AND CONTROL YOUR PALETTES

The key to working efficiently in a woodworking shop, an artist's studio, or any creative environment including Adobe Photoshop CS is to have an organized workspace, one where every tool can be found easily and yet is not in the way of you getting your work done. Adobe Photoshop CS palettes contain many of the most used features in Adobe Photoshop CS and while their use is essential, they can, if you allow them to, take up most of your desktop and block your view of the image that you are editing.

The clever Adobe Photoshop CS interface designers have, if you can believe it, come up with six different ways to help you manage palettes! Palettes collapse to the size of a dialog box title bar, they can be docked in the palette well, they all can be turned on and off with the **Tab** key, they can automatically be arranged in either a default or a pre-defined layout, and they can be grouped and even stacked.

If you are inclined to either skip, or just read the next few steps that show you how to manage palettes, I urge you to grab your mouse and move a few palettes around your desktop. The time and effort you take now to learn about palettes will save you much time and aggravation in the future.

- Once again open the **mill-pond-before.jpg** file, if it is not open, so that you have an image displayed.
- Let's use **Navigator** and the **Info** palettes to practice controlling palettes. If either the **Navigator** or **Info** palettes are not showing, select **Window** ➢ **Navigator**, or **Window** ➢ **Info** to display them.
- To make the **Navigator** palette use as little space as possible without closing it, double-click the **Navigator** tab bar and it will collapse to just the **Navigator** tab bar and dialog box. To expand it, once again double-click the **Navigator** tab bar and it will display full-size.

If you are using a display setting larger than 800 x 600 pixels, the **Options** bar shown just below the

main menu bar will feature a palette well for holding palettes such as the **Navigator** palette. The palette well can be found on the right side of the **Options** bar. If you are using a smaller screen resolution than 800 x 600 pixels, you will not find it because there is no room for it to display.

- To dock the **Navigator** palette in the palette well, click the **Navigator** tab and drag and drop it into the palette well as shown in Figure 1.16. You can remove it once again by clicking the **Navigator** tab and dragging and dropping it back onto the workspace.

  Alternatively, you can dock palettes by clicking the menu button (the tiny triangle icon in the upper-right corner) in the palette and selecting **Dock to Palette Well** from the menu.

The advantage to docking a palette is that it makes it easy to access — one click and it is accessible. The disadvantage is that any palette that is docked in the **Palette Well** will close as soon as any other tool is selected or when clicking an open image. For this reason, it is excellent for those palettes that you don't need to view when using other tools such as the **Brushes** or **Color** palettes. You click to open them, and then choose the color or brush you want. As soon as you use another tool, they close automatically leaving you with more visible desktop space or image.

- Palettes may also be stacked. To stack the **Navigator** palette with the **Info** palette, click the **Info** tab and drag it onto the **Navigator** tab to get

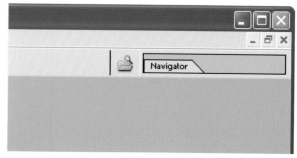

1.16

the stacked palette shown in Figure 1.17. To separate them, click one of the tabs and then drag and drop the palette back on the desktop.

■ Now let's *group* the **Navigator** with the **Info** palette into a single palette. This is something that I do frequently as I often use the **Navigator** and I am always using the **Info** palette. Click the **Info** tab and drag it slowly to the bottom of the **Navigator** palette. If you drag slowly, you'll see a dark line appear at the bottom of the **Navigator** palette. Release the mouse button and they will be grouped as shown in Figure 1.18.

■ At this point you should have at least two palettes open. I suggest you open up a few more along with the **Toolbox**, by selecting **Window** and any palette that does not have a checkmark next to it.

■ To hide all these palettes, press **Tab** and they will all disappear. Press **Tab** again and they will return to the desktop as before you first pressed **Tab**. You'll notice that this switch also hides the **Options** bar. This is a very valuable shortcut that results in a clear workspace. Press **Shift+Tab** to hide all palettes while leaving the **Toolbox** displayed.

That covers four of the six ways to organize palettes that I mentioned earlier. The last two ways will be covered in the next step where you'll learn how to personalize your workspace.

STEP 8: PERSONALIZE YOUR WORKSPACE

As you grow more familiar with Adobe Photoshop CS and you begin to learn how you work most effectively, you're likely to want to personalize your workspace. Adobe Photoshop CS allows you to reset palettes to a default workspace by selecting **Window ➢ Workspace ➢ Reset Palette Locations**. In Step 4, you learned how you can set Adobe Photoshop CS to open with the palettes in the same location as they were when it was last closed (using **Preferences**). You can also customize and save your own workspaces and set them up with a simple click of a menu.

Over time I have learned how I work most efficiently. Sometimes I like to use a 1,920 x 1,200 screen setting and other times I like to use the 1,024 x 768 setting when I want everything to be larger and easier to read. Depending on the screen resolution that I am using and if I am working on digital photographs or

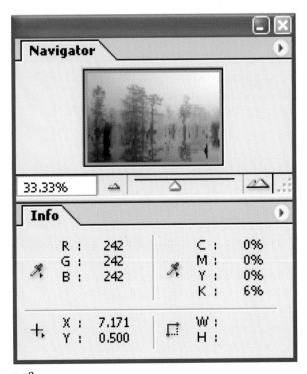

1.17

1.18

images for Web pages, I like to change my workspace. Every now and then I use a Wacom pen tablet and make digital paintings. At other times, I split my desktop between my word processor and Adobe Photoshop CS when writing content for books, magazines, or Web pages. In each of these cases, I use different workspaces. You can see the many variations that I use in Figure 1.19, which shows the **Window ➢ Workspace** menu as I have customized it.

My most used workspace is shown in Figure 1.20. I use this workspace when I am working in 1,920 x 1,200 mode and am making both global and selective adjustments to an image. As I frequently use the **Navigator** and the **Info** palette, they are grouped for ready access. The **History** palette is open because I am very much a "trial and error" kind of Adobe Photoshop person, so using **Snapshots** is invaluable. **Layers** and **Channels** are stacked, as I only need to see one at a time. Finally, I like having the **Actions**, **Tool Presets**, and **Color** palettes tucked neatly away in the well. This enables me to get to them in a click and once I've selected the action, tool setting, or color I need, the palette closes automatically.

■ To set up a workspace, arrange the **Toolbox** and palettes where you want them to be. Then select **Window ➢ Workspace ➢ Save Workspace** to get the **Save Workspace** dialog box. Type in the name you want to have show up on the menu and click **Save**. That's it!

Next time you want to use a customized workspace, just select **Window ➢ Workspace**; then click on your customized setting.

Besides using customized workspace settings, Adobe has created a default setting for you. To use this default setting, select **Window ➢ Workspace ➢ Reset Palette Locations** to get a workspace like the one shown in Figure 1.21, which is shown in a 1,024 x 768 pixel desktop.

I should mention that you might occasionally lose a palette. When you select **Window** you see a checkmark next to the palette you want to display, but it is not viewable on your desktop. The reason for this is that it has been moved off the desktop. This frequently happens when you resize your desktop. To make all the palettes and the **Toolbox** viewable, select **Window ➢ Workspace ➢ Reset Palette Locations**.

1.19

1.20

STEP 9: SELECT STATUS BAR TYPE

Useful information about the image, the active tool, image processing speeds, efficiency, and so forth may be displayed at the bottom of the Adobe Photoshop CS application window. This information is displayed in the **Status** bar. If you have the **Status** bar turned on, you will find it at the very bottom of the Adobe Photoshop CS application window (PC) as shown in Figure 1.22 or document window (Mac). If you don't see it, select **Window** ➢ **Status Bar** to display it. It always shows on a Mac.

■ The **Status** bar can be set to show **Document Sizes**, **Document Profile**, **Document Dimensions**, **Scratch Sizes**, **Efficiency**, **Timing**, or **Current Tool**. To select the information you want displayed,

click the menu button (the triangle icon) in the **Status** bar to get the menu shown in Figure 1.22.

I frequently set my **Status** bar to either **Scratch Sizes** to keep an eye on how large my images are getting or to **Efficiency** to determine if I am running low on RAM. If you want to learn more about these settings, consult Adobe Photoshop CS's Help or the printed User Guide.

STEP 10: CHANGE KEYBOARD SHORTCUTS TO INCREASE YOUR PRODUCTIVITY

New to Adobe Photoshop CS is the **Keyboard Shortcuts** feature, which enables you to modify existing keyboard shortcuts or to create new sets specifically for your intended purpose. For example, if you wanted to have keyboard shortcuts for rotating an image clockwise or counterclockwise, you could. Or, maybe you always wanted a keyboard shortcut for creating a drop shadow; if so, just select **Edit** ➢ **Keyboard Shortcuts** and use the **Keyboard Shortcut** dialog box shown in Figure 1.23 to create the keyboard shortcuts you want. You can create shortcuts for applications menus, palette menus, and tools.

1.21

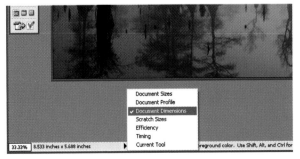

1.22

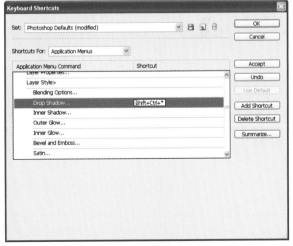

1.23

2

CALIBRATING YOUR MONITOR

2.1

2.2

Displaying accurate color on your computer display is essential if you want to be able to edit images with Adobe Photoshop CS and make prints that look like the images you saw on your computer screen. Without good calibration of your monitor, you are simply wasting your time trying to do any other tweaking to your workflow to get "good color."

There are two basic approaches for calibrating your monitor. You can use one of the free monitor calibration utilities or you can use a special hardware device called a colorimeter that can read the color on your screen. If you are using a PC, you can use the "free" (after you have purchased a copy of Adobe Photoshop CS) Adobe Gamma utility that gets installed when you install Adobe Photoshop CS. If you are using a Mac, you must use Mac OS X's ColorSync and Display Calibration utility because Adobe Gamma is not an option—it does not run under OS X and consequently does not get installed with Adobe Photoshop CS.

While it is possible to get reasonably good results with these free utilities, you are more than likely to get less than satisfactory results. The second choice you have is to buy a hardware monitor calibration package. Fortunately, increased interest by photographers in getting accurate color and innovation by vendors has resulted in a number of calibration tools that can help you calibrate your monitor and provide good color profiles for under $300 — much, much less than they were even a few years ago.

My recommendation is that you first try to get the best results that you can with the "free" utilities; then, if you aren't happy with your results, get MonacoOPTIX. MonacoOPTIX is a hardware calibration tool consisting of both hardware and software and it can be used to calibrate both CRT and LCD displays used on a computer running Microsoft Windows (Windows 98SE\ME\2000\XP), or Apple Mac OS 9.1–9.*x* or OS X. You will need a USB port to connect the colorimeter and your monitor and video card must support 24-bits or more and have LUT support. MonacoOPTIX is available for under $300 and its wizard-based interface makes the software simple and easy to use. You

can install the software, attach the colorimeter, and calibrate your monitor in less than ten minutes. Figure 2.3 shows the colorimeter attached to a CRT screen. If you want to learn more about MonacoOPTIX, visit `www.monacosys.com`. You can download the MonacoOPTIX user guide at `www.monacosys.com` to both learn more about color management and about using the colorimeter.

> **WARNING**
>
> A quality monitor is necessary to get accurate color. Toward the end of 2003, there was considerable debate over whether the high-end LCDs were better for color managed systems than the high-end CRTs. With the investment that vendors are putting into developing LCDs, it is a good bet that LCDs will ultimately prove to be the more accurate and stable monitors. However, in the short term, in spite of the claims by Apple that their Cinema Displays are superior to any CRT, many (but not all) experts believe that they are close to CRTs in terms of color accuracy, but not yet superior in all ways.
>
> One CRT that is frequently chosen by color management experts is the Sony Artisan. It can be used with a PC or a Mac. It comes with a hood, color sensor, and software that allow the sensor to communicate directly with the display. While the Apple Cinema and the Sony Artisan monitors may be considered to be the "ultimate" monitors, many other monitors provide good results for substantially less money. Be aware that many of the lower-priced LCDs can be very poor monitors to use when editing digital photos both in terms of image contrast and color. The moral of the story: Choose your monitor carefully!

2.3

TO CALIBRATE YOUR PC MONITOR WITH ADOBE GAMMA . . .

If you have not calibrated your monitor, then you really, truly, ought to do so. While this is just the first of many steps you can take to move into a "fully color managed workflow," your monitor ought to be calibrated even if you don't want to do much more. It is the one thing that needs to be done to ensure that you are reaping the benefits from your investment in equipment, time, and effort. It is straightforward and will take you less than ten minutes.

To calibrate your monitor, we'll use Adobe Gamma, which is a utility that does two important things. It helps you to calibrate or adjust your monitor so that you can see the most accurate colors it is capable of displaying, and it creates a color profile that is used by Adobe Photoshop CS and your PC's operating system to help display colors correctly. Both of these are very worthwhile functions providing that you take time to do them as well as possible.

Depending on your requirements, your hardware, and possibly some luck, you can do a pretty good job of calibrating your monitor with Adobe Gamma. The Adobe Gamma tool can be particularly useful for some people as they seem to have a knack for getting good settings each time. So, try this technique first, and then if you aren't happy with your results, do some research on current monitor calibration applications and hardware and try one of them.

STEP 1: GETTING READY TO CALIBRATE YOUR MONITOR

The success you will have using Adobe Gamma is dependent on lighting conditions. If you have direct sunlight from a nearby window or are wearing a white or bright colored shirt that is reflecting color or white light onto your monitor, you might as well not take the time to use Adobe Gamma. The best environment to calibrate your monitor and to make critical color adjustments is one with subdued light. As I work in a home office with nearly floor-to-ceiling glass on three of the four walls, I use a hooded monitor; I wear a black or dark shirt when working, and I do most critical color correction early in the morning, in the late evening, or in the dark hours of the night (all Photoshop book authors know these hours all too well). It also helps to view the Adobe Gamma utility against a medium gray desktop.

- Right-click your desktop and select **Properties** to get the **Display Properties** dialog box. Click the **Desktop** tab and choose the medium gray color by clicking the **Color** box at the bottom right of the dialog box. Click **OK** to apply the setting.

Your monitor should have been on for an hour or more before using **Adobe Gamma**. It takes awhile for monitor colors to stabilize after a monitor has been turned on. Also, monitor colors can drift over time. Depending on your monitor and how often it is used, you may want to run **Adobe Gamma** every few months to ensure that the profiles match its current display characteristics.

STEP 2: OPEN FILE

Before opening **Adobe Gamma**, I suggest that you open a digital photo in Adobe Photoshop CS to use as a "reality check." When you get to Step 10, you'll have an option to switch back and forth between "before" and "after" settings. If you already have a digital photo open, you'll be able to more clearly see if you have improved your settings.

- Select **File ➤ Open (Ctrl+O)** to get the **Open** dialog box. Double-click the **\02** folder to open it and then click the **sample-photos.tif** file to select it. Click **Open** to open the file.
- Double-click the image window title bar to maximize the document window. Resize the Adobe Photoshop CS application window to be about one-quarter of the size of your desktop.

After resizing, drag the Adobe Photoshop CS application window to the upper-left of your desktop where it will be out of the way of the small **Adobe Gamma** dialog box, which you will open in Step 3.

- Select **View** ➢ **Fit on Screen** (**Ctrl+0**) to make the entire open image visible.

STEP 3: LAUNCH ADOBE GAMMA

Adobe Gamma is a simple utility that can either be completed using a single dialog box, or a wizard that displays each of the nine steps in nine separate dialog boxes. Either way, the whole process of adjusting your monitor can take less than a few minutes once you've done it a few times.

- As **Adobe Gamma** gets installed in the **Control Panel** during the installation of Adobe Photoshop CS, you launch it by double-clicking the **Adobe Gamma** icon after opening the **Control Panel**.
- After launching **Adobe Gamma** you will get the dialog box shown in Figure 2.4. I suggest that you use the **Step By Step** wizard, which is the default selection. Click **Next** to confirm selection.

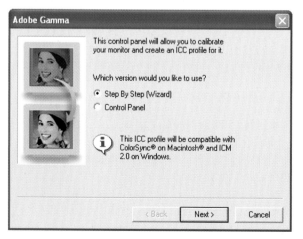

2.4

STEP 4: NAME NEW PROFILE

While it appears that you are simply naming the new profile that you are creating in this step, in fact, you are selecting the profile that will be used as the starting point for your calibrations too! Therefore it is important to select the best profile for your monitor if possible. In many cases, the default profile will not be the best choice to use as a starting point. Selecting and loading a profile yourself is the best approach.

- Figure 2.5 shows the dialog box where you can click the **Load** button to select and load the best profile that is available for your monitor.

STEP 5: ADJUST MONITOR'S CONTRAST AND BRIGHTNESS

- Click **Next** to display the dialog box shown in Figure 2.6. Set your monitor's contrast to the highest setting — usually **100%**. Then, use the brightness control to make adjustments until the center box is as dark as possible, but not quite black, while keeping the frame white.

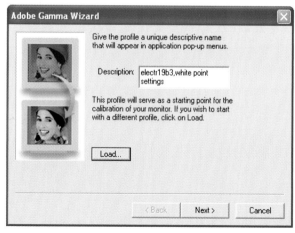

2.5

STEP 6: SELECT PHOSPHOR TYPE

■ Click **Next** to get the dialog box shown in Figure 2.7. It is best to read the documentation you got with your monitor to determine the correct setting to use for **Phosphors** type.

If you can't ascertain the kind of phosphor that your monitor has, then look to see if you can see light gray lines running horizontally across your monitor — one approximately one-quarter of the way down from the top, and one one-quarter of the way up from the bottom. If you see these lines, use the **Trinitron** setting. If you don't have a Trinitron, odds are good that you will have good results using the **P22-EBU** setting as two vendors manufacture the vast majority of monitors and these are the settings for those vendors.

STEP 7: ADJUST RGB GAMMA

■ Click **Next** and clear the box next to **View Single Gamma Only.** The dialog box should now have a red, green, and blue box as shown in Figure 2.8 allowing you to adjust each color independently. The goal here is to adjust each of the three sliders so that the center box fades into the patterned frame, thereby removing any color imbalance in the monitor.

While it seems easy, it takes some practice especially with the green one as it seems a little more difficult than the other two. If you squint your eyes and turn your head slightly, you should be able to repeatedly set each of the three sliders in the same position each time. It does take practice;

2.6

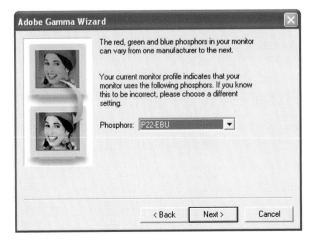

2.7

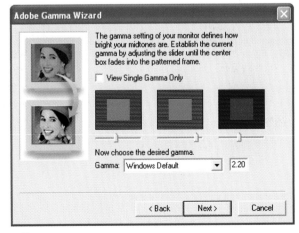

2.8

so try it a few times for each color until you have some confidence that you are setting them correctly. If you are way off, you'll know it and you can have another go at it!

■ Set **Gamma** to **Windows Default** and the value of **2.2** will be displayed.

STEP 8: SELECT HARDWARE WHITE POINT

■ Click **Next** to get the dialog box shown in Figure 2.9. Adobe Gamma usually sets this setting correctly itself. If your monitor allows a hardware white-point setting (usually accessed via an onscreen menu controlled from buttons at the bottom of the display), then check to see that this setting matches the setting of your monitor.

STEP 9: CHOOSE ADJUSTED WHITE POINT

■ Click **Next** to get the dialog box shown in Figure 2.10. In most cases, you will simply want to leave the **Adjusted White Point Setting** to **Same as Hardware**.

STEP 10: COMPARE "BEFORE" AND "AFTER" RESULTS

■ Click **Next** to get the dialog box shown in Figure 2.11. As you click the **Before** or **After** box, you'll be able to see the difference between the settings you had before you began using Adobe Gamma and the settings that you just selected. Should these before and after previews indicate that your settings are worse than they were before you began, click **Back** until you get to the settings

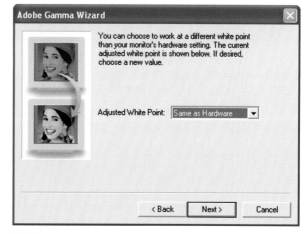

2.10

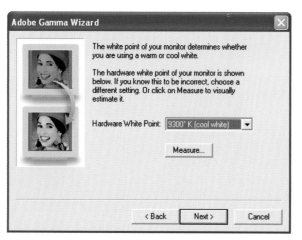

2.9

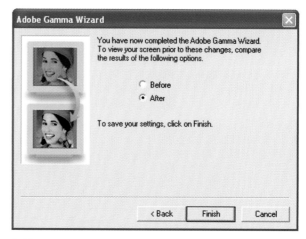

2.11

you need. Keep trying until you have the best settings you can get. Viewing the image you opened in Step 2 will help you to see the differences between "before" and "after" settings.

STEP 11: SAVE NEW PROFILE

■ Once you are satisfied with the results, click **Finish** to get the **Save As** dialog box. You will then be prompted to type in a name for the profile that you've just created. I suggest you use a name that is similar to the original filename you started with, but add your initials and a date. That way, you can recognize that it is a file that you created from a default file, and you can see the date so you know when you created it.

■ Click **Save** to save the file and you will have completed using Adobe Gamma.

Your monitor should now be calibrated and you have created a monitor profile.

TO CALIBRATE YOUR MAC MONITOR WITH COLORSYNC AND MONITOR CALIBRATOR...

Apple offers an excellent and free guide on ColorSync and using the Monitor Calibrator on its Web site at `www.apple.com/colorsync/`. The PDF file is titled **ColorSync in Mac OS X (May 2003)**.

Once you have calibrated your monitor — either by using one of the free utilities, or with a hardware calibration tool — you are ready to begin configuring Adobe Photoshop CS's color settings, which you learn about in the next technique.

CONFIGURING PHOTOSHOP CS'S COLOR SETTINGS

3.1

3.2

When I mention color management to photographers who use Adobe Photoshop, they usually have one of two different reactions. One is: What the heck is color management? The other: Oh no — what a nightmare! The fact is that color management is truly not a piece of the proverbial "piece of cake" for sure — but it is getting tastier with each new version of software, each new hardware calibration device, and increasingly sophisticated printers and printer drivers.

In simple terms, *color management* is a complete workflow that begins with the creation of a digital photo taken with a digital camera, and then moves to your computer display and to one or more output device you use — such as your own photo-quality printer, a high-end printer at a service bureau, or a film recorder.

While you may be happy (or unhappy) with your current results, you likely will have even better results if your workflow is color managed. Some (but not all) of the key steps to correctly setting up your workflow in a fully color managed environment are found in Techniques 1 and 2, this technique, and several of the techniques that can be found in Chapter 8.

As the goal of this book is to provide you with 50 practical techniques for digital photos with a primary focus on using Adobe Photoshop CS, complete coverage of how to set up color management is out of the scope of this book. However, without covering some of the basics of color management, you will not have the high level of success that I want you to have by the time you've completed all 50 techniques in this book. So, the lofty goal of this technique is twofold: to give you a basic understanding of management (while consuming just a few pages) and to help you configure Adobe Photoshop CS so that it is working with you to get the best results, rather than against you (which it can do if the wrong settings are used). While I will cover all of the important settings, I will avoid too much explanation about why you ought to use the suggested settings and I'll skip some of the lesser important settings altogether.

Before you begin clicking your mouse button and setting options, a conceptual understanding of color management will help you feel more comfortable with the settings you choose, and later on when you see dialog boxes pop up that ask you how you want to handle mismatched color profiles, you'll know why you are being asked such questions and have a better idea how to answer them.

Color management is a process whereby color will maintain a consistent appearance across all the devices you use in your digital photography workflow. In other words, when you shoot a sky-blue sky over a barn-red barn with a digital camera or with a film camera, in a properly managed color workflow, the sky will remain the same sky blue and the barn the same barn red when you view it on your computer's display or as a final print made by any one of many different types of printers you may choose.

That is the obvious intent for everyone for sure. However, the problems come from the many different devices that are used and how they display color.

Digital cameras, scanners, monitors, and output devices such as printers all have different ranges of colors they can reproduce — called a color gamut — and some have a wider range than others. It is these differences in color gamut and the need to precisely communicate color between devices that causes the need for color management. The approach used to solve both these problems is to use color profiles to define color gamut, embed these color profiles in image files, and then use a conversion engine to convert between two different profiles used for different devices.

Let's look at a real world example. Assume you were to use a Canon EOS 10D digital camera to take a digital photo. Let's also assume you have chosen the user-selectable color space setting of sRGB. After taking a photo, when you open up the file with Adobe Photoshop CS, Adobe Photoshop CS first checks to see if it has an embedded profile and it finds that it is sRGB. Assuming you have set up Adobe Photoshop CS's workspace to be Adobe RGB, the working space is a different color space from that of the image taken with the EOS 10D. So, Adobe Photoshop CS along with a little help from your computer's operating system converts one color space to the other color space. Your computer and operating system along with Adobe Photoshop CS once again work using the color profile you have chosen for your color monitor to display the image correctly. After completing any image editing, you can save the file (again with an embedded profile) or it can be printed out to a printer. When you print your image to a specific printer, you will once again need a color profile to describe as closely as possible the gamut that is possible with your printer and the specific ink and paper combination you use.

If everything is set up properly, and your color profiles are good, the workflow will be color managed and you will have consistent color from when you shot the photo, to when you viewed the photo on your computer screen, to the final print. As you can see, the role Adobe Photoshop CS plays in controlling color is a big one. It allows you to edit digital photos based upon the proper display profile, it allows you to convert profiles between different devices if you choose, and it lets you embed color profiles in files that you save.

My hope is that you now understand more about why in the last technique we covered the very important topic of calibrating your monitor. Later in this technique you will set options for working space profiles, color management policies, conversion engines, and other stuff! Then in Chapter 8, you'll learn how to make accurate color prints using color profiles. That in a nutshell (albeit a very tiny nutshell) is color management.

STEP 1: OPEN SAMPLE FILE

If you have an image open when you open the **Color Settings** dialog box, you can use the **Preview** feature later in this technique to see how changes to the working space settings affect the image. If you just want to set the settings without using **Preview**, skip to Step 2.

■ Select **File** ➢ **Open** (**Ctrl+O** PC, **Cmd+O** Mac) to get the **Open** dialog box. Double-click the **\03** folder to open it and then click the **gourds-before. tif** file to select it. Click **Open** to open the file.

STEP 2: OPEN COLOR SETTINGS DIALOG BOX

■ Select **Edit** ➢ **Color Settings** (**Shift+Ctrl+K**) on the PC to display the **Color Settings** dialog box

shown in Figure 3.3. On the Mac, select **Photoshop** ➢ **Color Settings** (**Shift+Cmd+K**). If you don't see the bottom portion of the dialog box that includes **Advanced Controls**, click **Advanced Mode.** Besides giving you **Advanced Controls,** you'll also get a few more choices in some of the pop-up menus. The settings shown in Figure 3.3 are the default settings you will get when first installing Adobe Photoshop CS.

■ As we are going to create new settings and save them under a new settings name, it doesn't matter what is currently shown in the **Settings** name box.

■ Click the **RGB** box in the **Working** spaces section to see the available options. Based upon our earlier assumption that you are primarily editing digital photos and will be printing them out on a consumer level printer such as those made by Canon, Epson, or HP, select **Adobe RGB (1998)**.

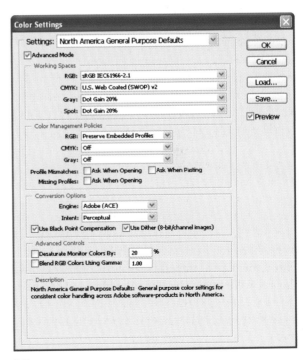

3·3

Notice that once you've made a selection, as you move your cursor over the pop-up menu, the **Description** box offers short descriptions of the profile that you've selected.

If you chose to open up the sample photo suggested in Step 1, look at it now while clicking the **Preview** on and off. **Preview** shows you the difference between the original setting and the setting that is currently selected. For example, if your original setting was Adobe RGB (1988) and your current setting is sRGB, you may be able to see that the sRGB space is a much narrower color space. If you experiment with these settings, make sure you set the RGB setting back to Adobe RBG (1988).

- As the **CMYK** setting is of no use for our agreed-upon purposes, you may leave the setting as it appears.
- The **Gray** setting is of particular importance if you are using a printer set up to print black and white prints such as Jon Cones' excellent Piezography BW print making system (`www.inkjetmall.com`). However, for now, you may leave these settings as they are.
- Leave the **Spot** setting to **Dot Gain 20%**.

You have now correctly set up your working space. The next section determines color management policies — in other words, how you want Adobe Photoshop CS to prompt you to handle files that you open up, if they have an embedded color profile that does not match your current working space.

- Set **RGB** to **Preserve Embedded Profiles**.
- While you are not likely to work in the **CMYK** or **Gray** settings, you might as well change them to **Preserve Embedded Profiles,** too, as it is the best setting for most purposes should you work in those color spaces.

- Make sure that the box for **Ask When Opening** is checked in the **Profile Mismatches** area. This will set Adobe Photoshop CS to ask you each time you open up an image file with an embedded profile how you want to handle any mismatch between your current working space and the file's profile.
- Turn on **Ask When Pasting.** This ensures that you are asked how you want to handle any mismatch between a copied image and the image that you want to paste it into.

Conversion Options is the next area in the **Color Settings** dialog box. This is where you define how you want Adobe Photoshop CS to convert your images when you have a profile mismatch. In other words, if you open a file with an embedded color profile and it does not match your working space, how should Adobe Photoshop CS convert colors?

- For the **Engine** setting use **Adobe (ACE).** This selects the **Adobe (ACE)** engine as the module that makes the conversions from one color space to another color space.
- Set **Intent** to **Perceptual**.
- Leave **Use Black Point Compensation** turned on. This option determines how the darkest image information will be handled during a conversion. If it is off, the darkest neutral colors will get mapped to black, thereby making the overall colors out of balance.
- Leave **Use Dither (8-bit / channel images)** on as it will blend and combine some values in digital photos better than if it is off.

STEP 3: SAVE COLOR SETTINGS

You are now done and your **Color Settings** dialog box ought to have the settings shown in Figure 3.4.

■ To save your **Color Settings**, click **Save** to get the **Save** dialog box. Adobe Photoshop CS automatically opens the color settings folder, which you ought to use because it allows you to easily select your settings file as it will be displayed along with the standard settings.

Use a filename that allows you to determine that it is your custom setting and when it was created. For example, I used **gg09-30-03-psCSbook.csf** to identify the settings I used for this book. The date lets me see when I created the settings.

■ When you click **Save**, you will get the **Color Settings Comment** dialog box shown in Figure 3.5. This dialog box allows you to add comments to further help you identify the purpose of the color settings file. After adding some descriptive text, click **OK** to save the file.

OPENING FILES WITH EMBEDDED PROFILE MISMATCH

You now have set your color policy settings to have Adobe Photoshop CS ask how you want to handle mismatched color profiles on an image-by-image basis. Because you have set **Working Space** to **Adobe RGB (1998)**, anytime you open up an image that does not have that space you will be presented with a dialog box giving you several choices.

■ You will find a copy of the gourd photo with an embedded **sRGB** profile in the **\03** folder on the companion CD-ROM. It is named **gourds-sRGB. jpg**. When you open the file, you will get the dialog box shown in Figure 3.6. **sRGB** is the most

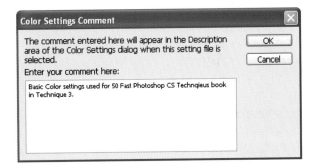

3.5

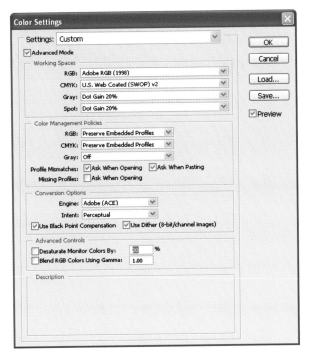

3.4

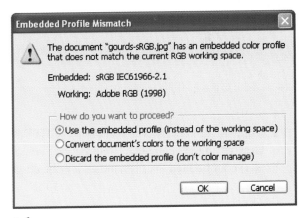

3.6

frequently used color space for many consumer-level digital cameras. Yet, **Adobe RGB (1998)** is a wider color space and is a favorite for those who edit digital photos. So, the mismatch must be resolved. In most cases, you will want to select the **Convert document's colors to the working space** option. In this case, it will be converted to **Adobe RGB (1998)** when that setting is chosen. Remember that we set the **Working Space** to **Adobe RGB (1998)** early in this technique in Step 2. Click **OK** to convert the profile.

■ After you have completed your editing and you are ready to save your file, remember to make sure you have checked the **ICC Profile** box (see Figure 3.7) to embed the **Working Space** profile in the image file, which, in this case, is **Adobe RGB (1998)**.

I grant you that you may have had to take my suggestions with a fair bit of trust. However, these settings are likely to be exactly what you ought to have for editing and printing digital photos on consumer-level printers. For those of you who want to learn more, I suggest that you consult the book **Real World**

Color Management by Bruce Fraser, Fred Bunting, and Chris Murphy.

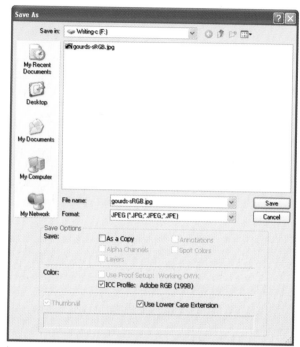

3.7

GETTING AROUND THE PHOTOSHOP CS WORKSPACE

4.1

4.2

After reading this technique's title, you may be ready to skip it and head to the next technique. But I've got a nickel here that says there is something worthwhile in this technique for everyone. Admittedly, I am a stickler for getting everyone to do all of the first six techniques in this chapter. If you do them in a step-by-step fashion, you are almost certain to learn a number of new things or, at the very least, you'll practice using the tips enough to make some of them become part of your regular work habits.

The six photos we will use for this technique are of a great blue heron flying in to land on a nest built one hundred feet or more up in a dead tree. I

31

have spent hundreds of hours watching these magnificent birds build nests and raise their young. One of the most spectacular events that I've seen is a young heron getting brave enough to take its first flight. They stand on a dead branch and look down almost like a small child getting ready to take a dive off a high dive into a pool for the first time. Sometimes they lean forward and they look like they are ready to jump, but at the last moment, they get scared and try to keep from falling. Usually prompted by a sibling in their nest, they finally make the jump and fly off.

STEP 1: OPEN FILES

■ Select **File ➢ Open** (**Ctrl+O** PC, **Cmd+O** Mac) to display the **Open** dialog box. After locating the

\4 folder, double-click it to open it. Press and hold **Ctrl** (**Cmd** on the Mac) and then click **heron1.jpg**, **heron2.jpg**, **heron3.jpg**, **heron4.jpg**, **heron5.jpg**, and **heron6.jpg** to highlight them. Click **Open** to open all six files in a cascaded stack in the workspace.

STEP 2: SIZE ADOBE PHOTOSHOP CS APPLICATION WINDOW

Most application windows can be resized or expanded to occupy the entire desktop and so can the Adobe Photoshop CS application window.

■ When using a PC, you can make the Adobe Photoshop CS application window fill the entire screen by double-clicking the Adobe Photoshop

4.3

4.4

CS application title bar. To return it to its previous size, double-click the application title bar once again. You may achieve the same results by clicking the **maximize button** in the upper-right corner of the application window on a PC. One click and the window will expand; click it again and the application window will return to its previous size. Mac OS X always displays the Adobe Photoshop CS application as a full-screen application with the application title menu at the top of the screen when it is the active application.

STEP 3: SIZE DOCUMENT WINDOWS

■ Document windows can be resized by clicking any corner of a document window; drag and drop to resize the document window as you like. Try resizing one of the heron photos.

When using Mac OS X, you resize a document window the same way except you can only click the lower-right corner of the document window.

■ You can also work in the **Standard Screen Mode** (**F**) view on a PC, by double-clicking any document window title bar, by clicking on the maximize icon in the upper-right corner of a document window, or by choosing **View ➢ Screen Mode ➢ Standard Screen Mode**. Click the maximize icon again and the document window returns to its previous size, or press **F**.

When using Mac OS X, you can work in **Standard Screen Mode** by choosing **View ➢ Screen Mode ➢ Standard Screen Mode**, or by pressing **F**.

4.5

4.6

■ When in **Standard Screen Mode**, you can easily change between any open documents by selecting **Window** and then selecting the document you want to view from the bottom of the menu. Click **Window** now and you will get a menu that lists the name of all six of the open heron image files. Alternatively, you can press **Ctrl+Tab** to cycle through all the open documents — even when you are in **Full Screen** mode with no menus.

The maximized document mode is particularly useful when you want to select all of, or part of, an image that includes one or more edges because it allows you to click outside of an image and then drag the selection marquee or crop marquee as you choose. When a document window is not maximized, it is hard — if not impossible — to select an image all the way to one or more of its edges.

STEP 4: CHANGE IMAGE ZOOM

■ To resize an image inside of a document window, use the **Navigator** palette as is shown in Figure 4.7. You can increase or decrease the image size by using the **Zoom Slider**, or by clicking the **Zoom In** or **Zoom Out** image icons on either side of the slider.

Image size within a document window can also be changed by using the **Status Bar** on the PC (on a Mac the **Status Bar** is *always* on and it is displayed at the bottom of each document window). On a PC, to turn on the **Status Bar** if it isn't already showing, select **Window ➢ Status Bar**. At the left end of the **Status Bar**, there is an image magnification setting, as shown in Figure 4.8. To change the level of magnification, simply type in the percentage of image size that you want and press **Enter** (**Return** on a Mac).

■ To view an image at full-size, type **100%** in the **Status** bar zoom magnification box and then press **Enter**. Or you can do one of the following: click the **Navigator Zoom In**, click the **Zoom Out** image icon until you get **100%**, select **View ➢ Actual Pixels** (**Alt+Ctrl+0** PC, **Option+Cmd+0** Mac), or double-click the **Zoom** tool in the **Toolbox** to get to **100%**.

■ Sometimes, you will want to make an image as large as possible while still being able to view the entire image in the workspace. To accomplish this, you can select **View ➢ Fit on Screen** (**Ctrl+0** PC **Cmd+0** Mac), or double-click the **Hand** tool in the **Toolbox**.

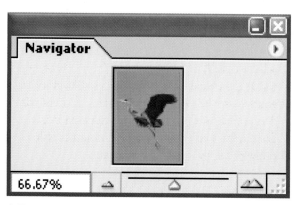

4.7

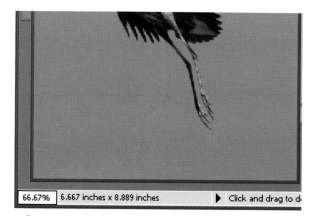

4.8

■ If you select the **Hand** tool (**H**), the **Options** bar will display buttons for **Actual Pixels**, **Fit On Screen**, and **Print Size**, which are handy if they are accessible.

STEP 5: ORGANIZE DOCUMENT WINDOWS

Some projects require that you have more than one image open at a time and consequently, there can be so much clutter your productivity decreases. Adobe Photoshop CS offers a number of ways to help you to organize document windows.

■ Document windows can be tiled by selecting **Window ➢ Arrange ➢ Tile**. This opens up all the windows and sizes them so they all fit on the screen like tiles.

■ Document windows can also be cascaded by selecting **Window ➢ Arrange ➢ Cascade**. When I need to work with two or three or more open images at once, I often tile document windows, and then switch back and forth between a maximized document window view and the tiled view. Remember you can move between the images by pressing **Ctrl+Tab**.

■ You may also minimize document windows by clicking the **Minimize** button in the upper corner of a document window, which automatically places them in neat rows at the bottom of the Adobe Photoshop CS workspace (PC only). Using Mac OS X, you can minimize a document window by shrinking it to the **Dock** by clicking the **Minimize** icon at top-left of a document window.

STEP 6: VIEW JUST WHAT YOU WANT TO VIEW

■ When you have a document window open and the image is scaled at a size that makes it larger than the document window, you can move the image around inside the document window to view the portion of the image that you want. To do so, click inside the **Navigator** palette inside the red "view" box. Drag the red box inside the thumbnail image in the **Navigator** palette until it shows the portion of the image you want to view.

Alternatively, you can select the **Hand** tool (**H**) in the **Toolbox**; then click inside a document window to drag the image around within the document window. The best way to select the **Hand** tool is to hold down the **Spacebar**, which selects the **Hand** tool; then it turns the cursor into the **Hand** tool icon. Click in your image and drag it to where you want it. When you release the **Spacebar**, the **Hand** tool will automatically revert back to the previously chosen tool.

■ Another approach to view just what you want to view without having to worry about selecting viewing percentages is to use the **Zoom** tool. While you can click the **Zoom** tool (**Z**) in the **Toolbox** to select it, I suggest you get used to selecting the **Zoom** tool by pressing **Ctrl+Spacebar** (**Cmd+ Spacebar** Mac) because this approach allows you to **Zoom** quickly and then automatically return to your previously selected tool. Once you have selected the **Zoom** tool, click and drag a marquee inside the image where you want to view it. When you release the mouse button, the document window will show the selected area centered in the document window — and the **Zoom** tool will revert to the previously selected tool.

■ Occasionally, you may find that you need to methodically examine or edit all of an image at a magnified level. For example, after taking a digital photo with a digital SLR, you may want to check the entire image for imperfections caused by dust particles and other unwanted things on the image sensor. To do this using keystrokes, press **Page Up** or **Page Down** (**Cmd+Page Up**, or **Cmd+Page Down** Mac) to have Adobe Photoshop CS scroll the image a little less than a page's worth of pixels up or down. To move right or left when you get to the top or bottom of an image, press **Ctrl+Page Up** or **Ctrl+Page Down** (**Shift+Cmd+Page Up**, or **Shift+Cmd+Page Down** on a Mac). Use the **Navigator** palette to keep track of where you are in the image. Pressing **Home** or **End** takes you to the upper-left, or bottom-right of the image respectively.

STEP 7: DISPLAY MULTIPLE VIEWS OF THE SAME IMAGE

There are many reasons why you may want to have more than one document window open at the same time that shows the same image. For example, I am always very picky about having a catch-light in eyes when shooting people, pets, and wildlife. A catch-light is a highlight in an eye; without one an image generally is far less successful than if it had one. To create a catch-light or enhance one, you may need to zoom in on an image to 200 percent or more to select and edit the eye. At this zoom level, it is hard to see how your enhancements fit with the overall image. The solution to this problem is to open up a second window.

■ Click the **heron2.jpg** file to make it the active image. Double-click the **Zoom** tool to make sure the image displays at **100%**.
Click the **heron2.jpg** document title bar and drag the document window to the left of your workspace.
■ To open up a second window showing **heron2. jpg**, select **Window ➢ Arrange ➢ New Window**

for [**filename**] (in this case the filename will be **heron2.jpg**). Click the document title bar of this new window and drag it to the right so that you can see the 100 percent view image on your left.

To zoom in on the heron's eye, press **Ctrl+ Spacebar** (**Cmd+Spacebar** on a Mac) to get the **Zoom** tool; then click inside the image and drag a marquee around the head of the heron to select the area you want to view.

You now have one window showing the heron at 100 percent and a second window showing the same image, only it is zoomed in to show the heron's head. You can now make edits in one window and see the results simultaneously in both windows at different scales, as is shown in Figure 4.9. Notice how the other heron photos have been minimized at the bottom of the workspace. (If you are working on a Mac and you have minimized the other images they will have been minimized to the **Dock** and hence they will not show at the bottom of the screen.)

STEP 8: MAXIMIZE VIEWABLE WORKING SPACE

When you open multiple palettes and multiple images, consider the space that goes to Adobe Photoshop CS's

4.9

application window, menu bar, **Options** bar, **Status Bar**, and window scroll sliders — you don't have much space to view and edit images. But, there are ways you can see it all!

- To turn off all palettes including the **Toolbox**, the **Status Bar**, and the **Options** bar press **Tab** — they are gone! To get them back, press **Tab** again. If you are using a Mac, pressing **Tab** will also change the screen mode to **Standard Screen**.
- For those types wanting an even more uncluttered view when using a PC, they can rid their screens of Adobe Photoshop CS's applications window, the application title bar, and menu bar by simply pressing **F**. The first time you press **F**, the application window will disappear and the active document window will expand to fill the screen with the image. You will now be in **Full Screen Mode with Menu Bar** mode. Press **F** again and the menu bar will go away, too, and you will be in **Full Screen Mode**.

Press **F** once more and your desktop will be restored to its previous state. Pressing **F** allows you to cycle through three modes — **Full Screen View with Menu Bar**, **Full Screen View** without menu bar — and return to previous screen state.

The other way to switch between these different modes is to use the view controls at the bottom of the **Toolbox**, just above the **ImageReady** button, as shown in Figure 4.10. The first button is for **Standard Screen View**, the second for **Full Screen Mode** (with menu bar) and the last is for **Full Screen View** (without menu). While you can use these buttons, I suggest that you learn to use **F** — it is faster and much more convenient than moving a mouse and doing a click. Plus, you can use the **F** key anytime — even when the **Toolbox** is not showing.

I should also point out that when you are in **Full Screen Mode**, you could still use the **Tab** key to turn on the **menu** bar, the **Toolbox**, and other palettes. Press **Tab** again to turn them off. If you want to move around your image, press the **Spacebar** and the **Hand** cursor will appear, enabling you to drag your image around to see what you want. Now you can see why it is so worthwhile to learn a few of the shortcuts that we covered earlier. Having such a clutter-free workspace allows you to concentrate more on your image, which ought to help you be more creative and get better results.

4.10

STEP 9: JUMP BETWEEN PHOTOSHOP AND IMAGEREADY

Adobe Photoshop CS comes with a powerful Web graphics application called Adobe ImageReady CS. If you use digital photos for Web pages, you will want to use the features in Adobe ImageReady CS.

■ To edit the active image in Adobe ImageReady CS, click the **Edit in ImageReady** icon at the bottom of the **Toolbox** shown in Figure 4.11 or choose **File ➢ Edit in ImageReady** (**Ctrl+Shift+M** PC, **Shift+Cmd+M** Mac).

This feature allows you to launch Adobe ImageReady CS with the image open. Jumping between applications allows you to easily use the full feature sets of both applications. Images updated in one application can be automatically updated in the other application by setting **Auto-update open Documents** in the **Edit ➢ Preferences ➢ General** dialog box.

■ Once you are in ImageReady and you have completed your tasks, click **File ➢ Edit in Photoshop** (**Ctrl+Shift+M** PC, **Shift+Cmd+M** Mac) to return to Adobe Photoshop CS with the updated image.

STEP 10: CLOSE DOCUMENT WINDOWS

■ To close a document window, click the **Close Window** icon at the upper-right of the document window on a PC (click the **Close** icon in the upper-left on a Mac), or click a document window that you want to close to make it active, and then select **File ➢ Close** (**Ctrl+W** PC, **Cmd+W** Mac).

■ To close all the open document windows, select **File ➢ Close All** (**Alt+Ctrl+W** PC, **Option+Cmd+W** Mac). If you have edited any of the images, you'll get a dialog box asking if you want to save changes before closing. If you do, click **Yes**; otherwise, click **No**. If you realize that you need to save the edited files under another name or want to cancel the **Close All** command, click **Cancel**.

You should now have a few tips and techniques in mind that you will want to use often. While we all find a good tip every now and then that we intend to use, it is only the diligent souls that actually put these tips into everyday use. It is those souls who ultimately become Adobe Photoshop CS experts—the rest merely remain known as Photoshop users. What are you going to be?

4.11

5

CREATIVE EXPERIMENTATION

5.1

5.2

Editing digital photos can often be a creative process requiring lots of experimentation. You try a few things. Then you back up one or more steps and try something different. Often that won't be what you want either so you'll want to back up to an even earlier step. Or, maybe you will want to just go back and adjust settings made in an earlier step. You might even go back and check out earlier steps and decide what you had was just fine, so you quit — satisfied with your results. This back and forth process is a way of life for experienced Adobe Photoshop users.

I believe so much in the creative exploration process and the features that are available in Adobe Photoshop CS to facilitate creative exploration, that this entire technique was created to both show you how, and to give you practice in the magical art of "Back and Forth." In fact, we'll cover eight different ways you can undo, step back, change settings, and go forward in your edit process until your image is just the way you want it. Learn to use all these techniques and life with Adobe Photoshop CS will be good.

STEP 1: OPEN FILE

■ Select **File ➢ Open** (**Ctrl+O** PC, **Cmd+O** Mac) to get the **Open** dialog box. Double-click the \05 folder to open it and then click the **packard-before.tif** file to select it. Click **Open** to open the file.

■ Before beginning any edits, open the **History** palette if it is not already on your desktop by selecting **Window ➢ History**. Move it to the right edge of your workspace. As you edit the image, notice how the **History** palette tracks each step.

STEP 2: CREATE NEW LAYERS

Conceptually, I have an idea about what to do to this image. It needs a better background with some kind of texture, richer colors, and I'd like to see the blue cast become more dramatic. My first idea is to create a new background layer and then find a good combination of a blur filter and layer blend mode. I'll warn you, however—we are not going there straight away. Rather, we are going to do a few things to show the Adobe Photoshop CS features that help you do some serious creative experimentation. So, start this technique when you have 20 minutes or more and can concentrate—it will be worth the time you invest.

■ If the **Layers** palette is not open, select **Window ➢ Layers** (**F7**). To create a new layer from the background layer, select **Layer ➢ New ➢ Layer from Background** to get the **New Layer** dialog box shown in Figure 5.3. Type **Textured Background** in the **Name** box and click **OK**.

5.3

The background layer is different from other layers in many ways—for one, it cannot be scaled without scaling the entire image. Therefore, because we will be scaling the image, I used **Layer ➢ New ➢ Layer From Background**, which transforms the background layer into an image layer.

■ We need one additional layer, so select **Layer ➢ Duplicate Layer**. When the **Duplicate Layer** dialog box appears, type **Ornament** in the **As** box and then click **OK**. You should now have two layers in the **Layers** palette as shown in Figure 5.4.

After creating a duplicate layer, notice that the **History** palette is keeping a record of each command you apply to the image. Each of these commands is called a "history state." You should now have a history state named **Make Layer** and one named **Duplicate Layer,** as shown in Figure 5.5.

STEP 3: EDIT BACKGROUND LAYER

Now let's begin editing the **Textured Background** layer. To do so we first need to hide the **Ornament** layer so that we can view the lower layer.

■ Using the **Layers** palette, click the **Layer Visibility** icon (the eye icon) in the left column in the **Ornament** layer to hide the **Ornament** layer.

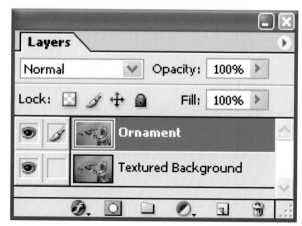

5.4

■ Click the **Textured Background** layer to make it the active layer. It should now be highlighted with a blue color.

To make the new background we are going to scale the image, add some blur, adjust saturation, and then add noise.

■ To make it easy to scale the image, reduce the size of the image using the **Navigator** so that the image fills about one-fourth of the workspace. Double-click the **packard-before.tif** document window title bar to maximize it (or press **F** if you are using a Mac). You should now have a small version of the image in the middle of a large gray workspace.

Select **Edit ➢ Transform ➢ Scale** to get a bounding box with nine handles. Press **Shift** and click the upper-left handle and drag it up and to the left. Pressing **Shift** while dragging the bounding box forces the proportions of the image to remain the same. The goal is to get an image that looks similar to the one shown in Figure 5.6. When you let up on the mouse button, you can click again inside the image and drag the image to position it. Depending on the size of your workspace, you may have to **Shift**+click the upper-left handle and drag it up and to the left again to scale it properly. Then, click inside the image to position it until it looks like Figure 5.6. Then press

Enter (**Return** on the Mac) or click the **Commit Transform** button on the **Options** bar.

■ Select **Filter ➢ Distort ➢ Diffuse Glow** to get the **Diffuse Glow** dialog box shown in Figure 5.7. Set **Graininess** to **8** by typing in **8** or by sliding the slider until **8** is displayed. Set **Glow Amount** to **10**, and **Clear Amount** to **18**; then, click **OK** to apply the settings.

■ To blend the two layers, click the **Ornament** layer in the **Layers** palette to make it the active layer. Set the **Blend** mode in the **Layers** palette to **Multiply**. You should now see the "ornament" image overlaid onto the **Background Texture** layer.

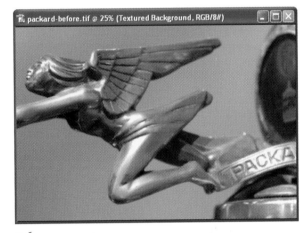

5.6

5.5

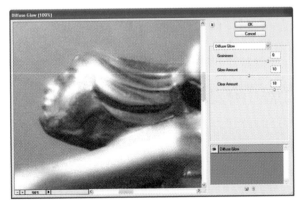

5.7

STEP 4: USE UNDO AND STEP BACKWARD/FORWARD

What do you think of the results? Not quite right for sure. I like the concept of adding grain; but we might get a better grain using another filter. I also think it might look cool to have some forward motion blur added. Plus, we need to lighten the background image so that the ornament stands out from the background. To do that we must back up two steps and then apply the **Motion Blur** filter to replace our earlier steps. There are several ways to go back, but let's first try using **Undo**.

- Select **Edit** ➢ **Undo Blending Change** (Ctrl+Z PC, **Cmd**+Z Mac) and the blend mode will be set back to normal. Now we need to go back one more step and undo the **Diffuse Glow** filter.

If you were to once again select **Edit** ➢ **Undo** (**Ctrl**+Z PC, **Cmd**+Z Mac), you would find that the menu would now read **Edit** ➢ **Redo Blending Change**! In Adobe Photoshop CS, the **Undo** feature is merely a *last step only* undo-redo feature — it cannot undo more than the last command. If you want to step back more than one step, you'll have to use another approach.

- Select **Edit** ➢ **Redo Blending** change (**Ctrl**+Z, **Cmd**+Z Mac) to re-apply the blend mode.
- This time, we'll step back two steps by selecting **Edit** ➢ **Step Backward** (**Alt**+**Ctrl**+Z, **Option**+ **Cmd**+Z Mac). Now the blend mode has been undone. Select **Edit** ➢ **Step Backward** (**Alt**+ **Ctrl**+Z PC, **Option**+**Cmd**+Z Mac) one more time and the **Diffuse Glow** has been removed. We are now back where we wanted to be.

STEP 5: USE THE HISTORY PALETTE

If you happened to watch the **History** palette, you noticed that each time you used the **Step Backward** command in the prior step, the **History** palette showed that you backed up one history state each time. The steps after the current history state are then grayed out.

Another approach and perhaps the easy way to go back one or more steps is simply to use the **History** palette.

- Click the **Free Transform** state in the **History** palette (see Figure 5.8) to make it the current state as it was the last state where we were happy with the results.
- Now select **Filter** ➢ **Blur** ➢ **Motion Blur** to get the **Motion Blur** dialog box shown in Figure 5.9. Set **Angle** to **–7 degrees** and **Distance** to **60 pixels**; then, click **OK** to apply the blur.

As soon as the **Motion Blur** filter was applied, all the states in the **History** palette past the selected state immediately vanished. Now you have seen how you can move forward and backward in the **History** palette as you please — checking to see the image as it was at each step. Once you have gone back where you want to be, you can then continue to edit your image and a new set of history states will be created from that point on.

5.8

STEP 6: COMPLETE EDITING OF BACKGROUND IMAGE

Okay, let's finish editing the background image.

■ Make sure that the **Textured Background** layer is highlighted to indicate it is the active layer. Also, make sure that the **Ornament** layer is not visible (the **Layer Visibility** icon is not visible in the left column).

■ Select **Image ➢ Adjustments ➢ Hue/Saturation** (**Ctrl+U** PC, **Cmd+U** Mac) to get **Hue/Saturation** dialog box shown in Figure 5.10. First click the box next to **Colorize** to turn it on. Then set **Hue**, **Saturation**, and **Lightness** to **40**, **20**, and **50** respectively. Click **OK** to apply the settings.

■ Now add grain once again, only this time by selecting **Filter ➢ Noise ➢ Add Noise** to get the dialog box shown in Figure 5.11. Set **Amount** to **10%**, **Distribution** to **Gaussian**, and turn on **Monochromatic**. Click **OK** to apply the filter.

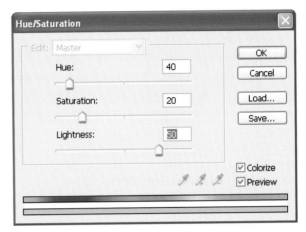

5.10

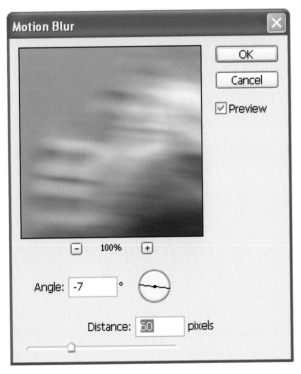

5.9

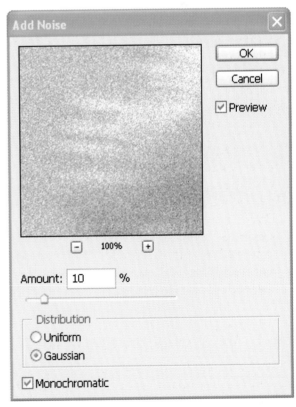

5.11

STEP 7: EDIT ORNAMENT LAYER

Before we edit the **Ornament** layer and blend the two layers, we first need to create a layer to edit and later use when we begin painting color back into the image.

- Click the **Ornament** layer in the **Layers** palette to make it the active layer; then select **Layer** ➢ **Duplicate Layer** to get the **Duplicate Layer** dialog box. Type **Paint Layer** in the **As** box and click **OK**.

Next we will blend the bottom two layers, make an adjustment, and flatten just those two layers.

- Click the **Layer Visibility** icon in the **Paint Layer** layer to hide the layer.
- Click the **Ornament** layer to make it the active layer. The **Layers** palette should now look like Figure 5.12.
- In the **Layers** palette, select **Multiply** as the **Blend** mode.
- Select **Layer** ➢ **Merge Down** (**Ctrl+E** PC, **Cmd+E** Mac) to merge the **Ornament** layer with the **Textured Background** layer.
- Select **Image** ➢ **Adjustments** ➢ **Hue/Saturation** (**Ctrl+U** PC, **Cmd+U** Mac) to once again get the **Hue/Saturation** dialog box. Click the **Colorize**

box to turn it on. Set **Hue** to **22**, **Saturation** to **8**, and leave **Lightness** set to **0**. Click **OK** to apply the settings.

We now have a monochromatic image where the ornament somewhat stands out against a grainy background, as shown in Figure 5.13.

STEP 8: CREATE SNAPSHOTS

Using the **History** palette as a "multiple undo/redo" feature alone makes it a valuable feature, but it offers far more capabilities. Next we'll look at how it can be used for making snapshots. Snapshots are nothing more than temporary copies of your image at a specific history state; however, they can be very useful.

If you scroll up to the top of the **History** palette as is shown in Figure 5.14, you'll find one there now titled **packard-before.tif**. If you don't see one, then your **History** palette settings are not set to **Automatically Create First Snapshot**. To set this option, click the menu button in the upper-right corner of the **History** palette to get a pop-up menu, and then select **History Options**. Click in the box next to **Automatically Create First Snapshot** and then click **OK** to apply the settings. The next time you open up an image, a

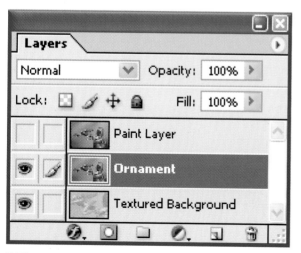

5.12

5.13

"first" snapshot will automatically be created for you. If you do not have a snapshot now, don't fret as it will not be needed for this technique

Next we will make some adjustments to the **Paint Layer** layer and make a snapshot that can be used in the next step.

- Click in the **Paint Layer** to make it the active layer.
- As we want richer colors, select **Image ➢ Adjustments ➢ Hue/Saturation** (**Ctrl+U** PC, **Cmd+U** Mac) to get the **Hue/Saturation** dialog box. Set **Hue** to **0**, **Saturation** to **40**, and **Lightness** to **0**. Click **OK** to apply the settings.

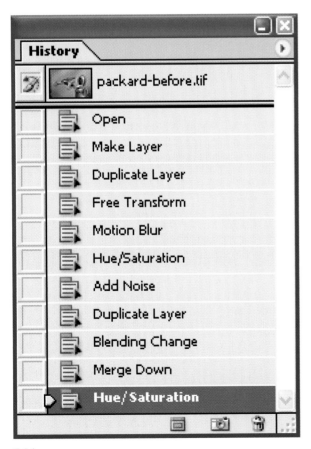

5.14

You should be aware that we could have created an **Adjustment Layer** for applying the **Hue/Saturation** command. This would let us go back later in the edit process and make adjustments to the **Hue/Saturation** settings. However, for now let's keep this technique as simple as possible and wait for Step 10 to investigate the use of **Adjustment Layers**.

- Right-click in the last history state (it should be **Hue/Saturation**) in the **History** palette to get a pop-up menu. Select **New Snapshot** to get the **New Snapshot** dialog box. Type **Rich Colors** in the **Name** box and click **OK**.

If you scroll to the top of the **History** palette, you should now see two snapshots, as shown in Figure 5.15, one named **Rich Colors**, which we just created, and one named **packard-before.tif**, which was created when the file was opened.

You might now be wondering what you can do with the snapshot we just created. **Snapshots** are similar to a history state in the **History** palette, except you can

5.15

name them, they don't get deleted when you run out of the maximum number of history states set in **Preferences**, and they show up at the top of the **History** palette with a thumbnail of the image at that particular state. If you saved a number of snapshots during an editing process, you could then flip through them to find the best one. Plus, you can use a **Snapshot** with the **History Brush** tool and the **Art History** brush as we will do in the next step.

STEP 9: USE THE HISTORY BRUSH TOOL

To add some color back into the image, we are going to use the **History Brush** to paint the ornament back into the image by using the **Rich Colors** snapshot. Not only will this add some color, it will eliminate all the grain that was put into the ornament when we blended layers.

■ To select the **Rich Colors** snapshot for painting purposes, click the **Sets the Same Source for the History Brush** box next to the snapshot at the top of the **History** box, as shown in Figure 5.16. Clicking this box sets the history state as the source for the **History Brush** tool.

To see what is shown in the **Rich Colors** snapshot, click inside the thumbnail. You can now see the rich colors we selected earlier.

To compare the saturated version with the original image, click the **packard-before.tif** thumbnail. This is a great way to compare two different images.

To go back to the current history state, scroll all the way to the bottom of the **History** palette and click in the last state — it should be **Hue/Saturation**. You should now be viewing a saturated version of the original image.

The source image for painting with the **Art History** brush is now the **Rich Colors** snapshot. Next we need to select the layer where we will paint. We could paint directly on the **Textured Background** layer, but this would make it difficult to correct over-painting. If we

were to paint on a transparent layer, these mistakes could be fixed, plus we would have tremendous control over how the painted layer looks and is blended with the "texture background" layer.

■ To make it easy to correct our paint strokes and to give us some extra control over the results, click the **Paint Layer** layer in the **Layers** palette to make it the active layer.

■ Select **Select** ➢ **All** (**Ctrl+A** PC, **Cmd+A** Mac) and then **Edit** ➢ **Clear** (**Backspace** PC, **Delete** Mac) to clear the layer to transparency.

■ Select **Select** ➢ **Deselect** (**Ctrl+D** PC, **Cmd+D** Mac) to remove the selection marquee.

We now have a transparent layer where we can paint the saturated ornament while allowing the **Textured Background** layer to show where we don't paint with the **History Brush** tool.

■ Select the **History Brush** tool (**Y**) by clicking it in the **Toolbox**.

5.16

■ Click the **Brush Preset Picker** (the second box from the left in the **Options** bar) as shown in Figure 5.17. Then select a brush size from the drop-down palette shown in Figure 5.18. I suggest starting off with a soft brush around **45 pixels** in size. As you paint, you will want to change brush settings.

■ I now suggest that you maximize your working space and make it as clutter-free as possible by pressing **F**, **F**, and **Tab**.

■ To begin painting, press the left mouse button and begin painting inside of the ornament. As you move your cursor, you will see that you are painting the saturated ornament onto the background image.

If you make a mistake and paint outside of the boundaries of the ornament, you can select **Step Backwards** or **Undo**, or you can select the **Background Eraser** tool from the **Toolbox** and touch up anywhere that is needed.

If you click the mouse button often while painting, you can step back a stroke when needed and not have to erase too much of your work. Also, remember that you can press **Spacebar** to get the **Hand** tool, which allows you to drag your image when you need to view more of it. Plus, you can zoom in to a size that makes it easiest for you to paint accurately. Using these tips, you should find it a real joy to paint on the image that is totally void of all tool palettes, menus, scroll bars, and so on.

Besides painting with the **History Brush** tool, you may want to experiment with the **Art History Brush** tool. It is like the **History Brush** tool, but it paints with a variety of random brushstrokes much like those seen on paintings done by an Impressionist era painter.

STEP 10: USE ADJUSTMENT LAYERS

As we took the time to create a layer specifically to paint on, you can now begin your experimentations with different blend modes and any other filters and commands you'd like to try. My final bit of editing on this image was to use an **Adjustment Layer** and **Levels**. Like many of the other "go back and do it again" features we have used, **Adjustment Layers** figure prominently in the list of these important features. While there are many advantages to using **Adjustment Layers**, suffice it to say that one of the biggest is that you can go back at any time and change the settings without causing any picture data loss.

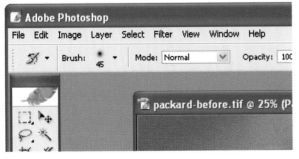

5.17

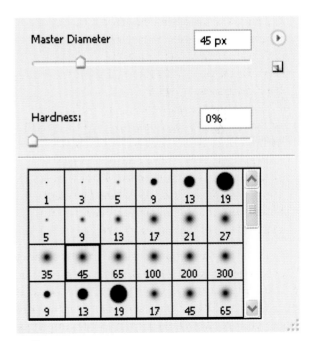

5.18

■ Select **Layer ➤ New Adjustment Layer ➤ Levels** to get the **New Layer** dialog box. Click **OK** to get the **Levels** dialog box. Try setting **Input Levels** to **40**, **1.00** and **255**; click **OK** to apply the settings. You should now have an adjustment level layer in the top of the **Layers** dialog box, as shown in Figure 5.19.

■ Should you not be happy with the results, you can go back anytime and make changes to **Levels** by clicking on the thumbnail image in the **Adjustment Layer**. Make your changes and click **OK** to apply them.

The main advantage of using **Adjustment Layers** is that you can go back and change settings that you made earlier rather than apply another **Levels** command, which would cause more loss of picture information.

Once your painting is complete and you've adjusted **Levels** as you want, you should have an image that looks similar to Figure 5.2.

One additional benefit of creating an **Adjustment Layer** is that you automatically get a **Layer Mask** created with it. A **Layer Mask** allows you to paint on the mask and either reveal or hide the "adjustment" selectively where you want it.

STEP 11: USE REVERT

But suppose that after all the work that you have done so far in this technique, you just don't like it all! Well then, use the **Revert** tool.

■ Select **File ➤ Revert** (**F12**) to reload the most recently saved version of a file, clearing any edits made since then.

The good news: **Revert** will show up as a **History** state, meaning that if you **Revert** and realize that you should not have written over the file, you can use the **History** tool to back up and un-**Revert**!

Admittedly, this was not an easy technique and it was a bit contrived so that you could learn as many ways as possible to jump around in your editing process to get the results you want. Hopefully, you however will have learned some techniques that will help you to easily create the images you want.

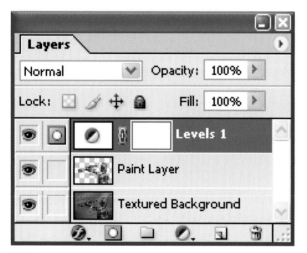

5.19

AUTOMATING TASKS

6.1

6.2

ABOUT THE IMAGE

Multihued Iris Canon EOS D30, Canon 300mm f/2.8, 533 x 800 pixels, 1.25MB .tif files, cropped and edited with Pictographics iCorrect Professional

Not long after you start using Adobe Photoshop CS to digitally edit photographs, you will become aware of the need for a way to automate many tasks that are either repetitive or boring — or just to get them done as fast as possible. Adobe Photoshop CS's response to this need is a trio of powerful features: **Actions**, **Droplets**, and **Batch** automation.

The process of creating properly sized photos and thumbnails for Web galleries can involve doing the same things over and over and over and over until you go crazy! For this reason, we'll use a folder containing six iris photos to show you how you can get more done quicker, using Adobe Photoshop CS's trio of go-faster features. Besides just sizing these six photos, we'll also create an automated frame **Action** to make them look better on a Web page.

STEP 1: USE A PREDEFINED ACTION

Before we create our own action, let's first use one of the many predefined **Actions** that come with Adobe Photoshop CS. That way, you'll understand exactly what you are doing when you get to Step 2. Plus, you'll have an opportunity to see what **Actions** the inventive folks at Adobe created for you.

■ Select **File** ➤ **Open** (**Ctrl+O** PC, **Cmd+O** Mac) to display the **Open** dialog box. Double-click the **\06** folder to open it and then click on the **iris1.tif** file to select it. Click **Open** to open the file.

■ If the **Actions** palette is not showing, select **Window** ➤ **Actions** (**Alt+F9** PC, **Option+F9** Mac) to display the palette. Click the **Actions** palette menu button (the tiny triangle in the upper-right corner of the dialog box) and select **Clear All Actions** to start off with an empty palette. Click **OK** when asked **Delete all the Actions?**

Click the **Actions** palette menu button once again. You should see at least six different sets of **Actions** at the bottom of the menu. At this time, click **Frames** to load the **Actions** palette with actions for creating frames. The **Actions** palette should now look like the one shown in Figure 6.3.

■ The **Drop Shadow Frame** is a useful frame to use when creating images for Web galleries, so click the **Drop Shadow Frame** to make it the active action. If you click the triangle to the left of the **Drop Shadow Frame** action, the **Action** will open up and you can see each step it will take. At the bottom of the **Actions** palette, you'll find the **Play Selection** icon — the triangle icon. Click it to run the selected action. Your image should now have a drop shadow as shown in Figure 6.4.

If you want to undo the **Action**, select **File** ➤ **Revert** (**F12**). You can also use the **Snapshot** feature in the **History** palette. To learn more about using the **History** palette, read Technique 5.

As you can see, **Actions** are recorded sets of commands and keystrokes that can be played back to repeat an edit process. This is really a powerful automation tool, especially when you learn to use some of the other features it offers, too.

STEP 2: CREATE YOUR OWN ACTION

In the last step, we ran a predefined **Action**. In this step, we are going to create an **Action** that adds our own customized border to an image for use in a Web gallery. Creating such a border manually can require many steps and be rather time-consuming. So, let's see how we can automate the entire process to get it done error-free and best of all — quickly.

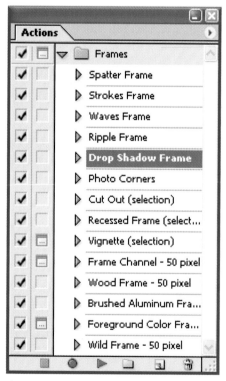

6.3

■ Select **File ➢ Open** (**Ctrl+O** PC, **Cmd+O** Mac) to display the **Open** dialog box. Double-click the **\06** folder to open it and then click the **iris1.tif** file to select it. Click **Open** to open the file.

Our first step is to reduce the size of the image so that when it is framed, it fits within a 640 x 640 pixel square. Next we will add a black line around the photo; then hand-select a color from the image to use for a wider outside frame. Finally, we'll add a drop shadow using the predefined action that we used in Step 1.

■ The **Actions** palette should still be set up as it was earlier in Step 1. It should show only the **Frames.atn** action set. Click the **Actions** palette menu button and select **New Set** to get the **New Set** dialog box. Type **Web Page Size & Frame** in the **Name** box and click **OK**. You should now see

the new **Action Set** at the bottom of the **Actions** palette, as shown Figure 6.5.

■ To create a new **Action** for the custom frame, click the **Create New Action** icon at the bottom of the **Actions** palette to get the **New Action** dialog box shown in Figure 6.6. Type in **Frame for Iris Photos**; then click **Record** to begin recording your steps.

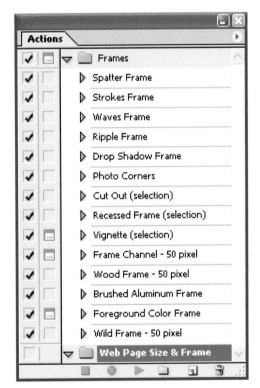

6.5

6.4

6.6

I've done the math and have found that the image needs to be 582 pixels tall. Using 582, we can add on the extra space and frames and still end up with an image that fits inside a 640 x 640 pixel square.

■ Select **Image ➢ Size** to get the **Image Size** dialog box shown in Figure 6.7. First, make sure there is a checkmark in the box beside **Constrain Proportions**, and then set **Height** to **582 pixels**, which forces **Width** to change to **388**. Because Adobe Photoshop CS has a new interpolation algorithm that is especially useful for down-sampling images for Web sites, let's use it. Make sure that there is a checkmark next to **Resample Image**; then, click in the box and select **Bicubic Sharper**. Click **OK** to resize the image.

■ To add a 7-pixel white border around the image, select **Image ➢ Canvas Size** to get the **Canvas Size** dialog box shown in Figure 6.8. Set **Width** to **402** (388 + 14) pixels and set **Height** to **596** (582 + 14) pixels. Make sure **Canvas extension color** is set to **White**; click **OK** to add white canvas.

■ Choose **Select ➢ All** (**Ctrl+A** PC, **Cmd+A** Mac) to select the entire image.

■ Select **Edit ➢ Stroke** to get the **Stroke** dialog box shown in Figure 6.9. Set **Width** to **2 pixels** to create a 2-pixel wide black border. Make sure that **Location** is set to **Inside** and then click **OK**. You should now see a 2-pixel black line all around the image.

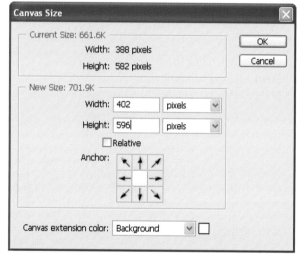

6.8

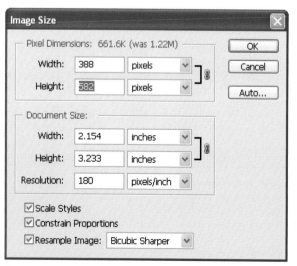

6.7

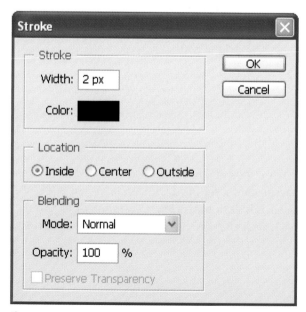

6.9

- Now we'll add some more white canvas by again selecting **Image ➤ Canvas Size**. Set **Width** to **446 pixels** and **Height** to **640 pixels** to create a 22-pixel wide white border. Make sure **Canvas extension color** is set to **White**. Click **OK** to create extra canvas.

- To create the outside border, select **Select ➤ All** (**Ctrl+A** PC, **Cmd+A** Mac). Select **Edit ➤ Stroke**. This time, we don't want to use black for the line; instead we want to pick a color from the image itself. Click inside the color box in the **Stroke** dialog box and you will get the **Color Picker**. Move the **Color Picker** so that you can see the image, and then click inside the image to get the color you want. Keep clicking until you find something that will look good as a border color. I chose a green color that has **R**, **G**, and **B** values of **56**, **124**, and **97** respectively. Click **OK** in the **Color Picker** dialog box to close it. Then make sure that **Width** is set to **6 pixels** and click **OK** to apply the colored border.

- Now we will add a drop shadow so that it appears to float over a white Web page. We'll do this by simply adding the **Drop Shadow Frame Action** that we used in Step 1. Scroll up the **Actions** palette until you find the **Drop Shadow Frame Action**. Click it to make it the active **Action**, and then click the **Play** button at the bottom of the **Actions** palette. Adobe Photoshop CS then does all the work necessary to create a drop shadow. We have just now added one **Action** to another **Action**.

If you look at the image, you'll notice that it has a background layer filled with white. If your intention is use this **Action** to create frames and drop shadows on images that are to go on a Web page that is any color but white (or has a pattern), you can modify this **Action** to make the **Background Layer** have the same color and texture as your Web page. This drop shadow makes the image appear as if it hovers over the page as the image will blend seamlessly with the Web page background.

- Before saving the image, select **Layer ➤ Flatten Image**.
- To save the image for use on a Web page, select **File ➤ Save for Web** (**Alt+Shift+Ctrl+S** PC, **Opt+Shift+Cmd+S** Mac) to get the dialog box shown in Figure 6.10. Set **Settings** to **JPEG Medium** and click **Save** to get the **Save Optimized As** dialog box. After naming your file and selecting an appropriate folder (for example c:\temp\iris\ photos), click **Save** to create a JPEG file.
- As your **Action** is now complete, turn off the recording function by clicking the **Stop Playing/ Recording** button at the bottom of the **Actions** palette — it is the square icon.

6.10

Your image should now have a narrow black line plus a wider color outside frame plus a drop shadow like the one shown in Figure 6.11.

If you want to save your **Action** to your hard drive for future use, click the **Web Page Size & Frame Actions Set** in the **Actions** palette to highlight it (it will turn blue). Then, click the **Actions** palette menu button and select **Save Actions**.

STEP 3: DO THINGS IN BATCHES

If you want, you could now open up one or more images and run the **Frame for Iris Photos Action** on each photo individually. The only problem is that it will run without getting any input from you. This means that you'll have no option to select border

colors and so every one of your images will have the green frame! Go on—try it. Open up one of the other iris photos and run the **Action**.

Lucky for all of us, there is a feature that allows you to stop any **Action** on any command that uses a dialog box. If you look at the **Actions** palette shown in Figure 6.12, there are two columns running down the left side of the dialog box. The first column allows you to turn on, or turn off, a specific step. The second column indicates whether the step has a dialog box associated with it or not. If it does, it shows a gray box. If you look down the column, you'll see that there is a gray box next to the **Stroke** command. The **Stroke** command step is where we need to select a color. If you were to click a specific step to make it the active step, you could then click the **Toggle Dialog**

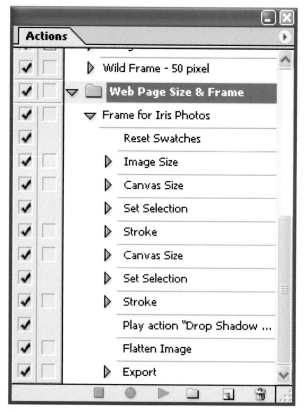

6.11

6.12

on/off box to show the dialog box when the **Action** is run. Then, as the **Action** runs it would stop at that step after opening up the dialog box, and would wait for you to choose a new color before the **Action** continued. Pretty cool, huh—let's try it.

- Look for the second **Stroke** command, as the first **Stroke** command creates the thin black line and we want to use a thin black line on all the images. Click the second **Stroke** command to make it active; then, click inside the **Toggle Dialog on/off** box to show the **Stroke** dialog box when this step is played back when the **Action** is run.
- Now open another iris image and run the **Action** again. Remember you must click the name of the **Action** you want to run to make it the active **Action**—in this case, the **Frame for Iris Photos Action**. This time, when the script gets to the second **Stroke** command, it will open the **Stroke** dialog box and wait for you to select the color for the stroke. Only when you have made any and all changes to the **Stroke** dialog box and have clicked **OK**, will the **Action** continue doing work for you!

Our goal was to create an **Action** and run it on an entire batch of images. As our **Action** has been completed and fully tested, we can now run it on the entire folder of iris images. All we need to do once the **Action** is running is to select the right border color for each of the images. Now that's what I call automation!

- One of the peculiar things about the **Batch** command is that it does not allow you to create new images in the same folder as the original images, or in a folder that is a sub-folder of the folder where the original images are stored. So, we first need to create a destination folder where our new images will be placed after the **Action** has been run. I suggest that you create a temporary folder on your hard drive such as: **c:\temp\iris photos**.

- Select **File ➢ Automate ➢ Batch** to get the **Batch** dialog box shown in Figure 6.13. If you have not selected other **Actions** since the beginning of this technique, **Set** should show **Web Page Size & Frame** and the **Action** should be **Frame for Iris Photos**. If not, select them using the menu boxes.
- Set **Source** to **Folder** and click **Choose** to choose the source folder containing the six iris photos. If you followed the suggestions in the Introduction, the source folder should be **\06**.
- If you have set your color management policies to **Ask When Opening**, then you will want to also check **Suppress Color Profile Warnings**. This allows the script to ignore any color profile conflict alerts.

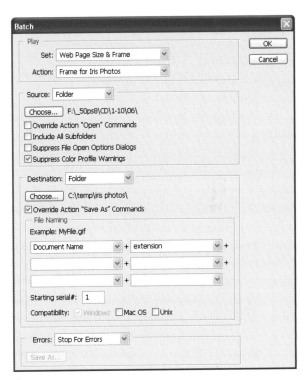

6.13

■ **Destination** should be set to **Folder**. Click **Choose** to select the temporary folder you set up for this exercise (for example, **c:\temp\iris photos**). Click **Override Action "Save As" Commands** to force the **Action** to write the files to the folder selected in the **Destination** folder. Click **OK** to run the **Action** and choose border colors.

Having seen all those steps flash before your eyes for just six digital photos just imagine how long and how crazy you might be creating the images needed for a Web gallery of around 50 or so photos without the **Batch** command.

If you want to, you can now go back and edit the **Frames for Iris Photos.atn Action** and add steps to add copyright information, overlay a layer that includes a signature or contact information, or even do some basic image correction. Now that you understand how to create and use the **Batch** command, stop and think for a minute how it can be used to make your Adobe Photoshop CS work easier. Then create the necessary **Actions** and let Adobe Photoshop CS do the work for you.

STEP 4: SAVE AN ACTION AS A DROPLET

A **Droplet** — now pray tell, exactly what is a **Droplet** you might ask? Well it is Adobe's name for a cool feature that makes it easy to run an **Action**. While we could use any **Action**, let's make one that you can use often. If you like to send digital photos as an attachment to e-mail, you'll find this one to be quite handy.

Before creating a **Droplet**, you must first have an **Action**. The **Action** we will create takes any image and reduces it to fit within a 640 x 640 pixel square and then saves it in a compressed JPEG format to a specific folder created especially for digital photos that are to be e-mailed.

■ Select **File ➢ Open** (**Ctrl+O** PC, **Cmd+O** Mac) to display the **Open** dialog box. Double-click the **\06** folder to open it and then click the **iris5.tif** file to select it. Click **Open** to open the file.

■ Create a folder for saving digital photos that you want to e-mail. I suggest using a name such as **c:_photos to e-mail**. The underscore will make sure the folder is listed at the top of your directory so that it will be easy to find.

■ Click the **Web Page Size & Frame Action Set** to highlight it. Click the **New Action** icon at the bottom of the **Actions** palette to get the **New Action** dialog box. Type in **E-mail photo converter** in the **Name** box and click **Record** to begin recording.

■ Select **File ➢ Automate ➢ Fit Image** to get the **Fit Image** dialog box shown in Figure 6.14. Set both **Width** and **Height** to **640 pixels**; then click **OK** to resize the image.

■ Select **File ➢ Save for Web** (**Alt+Shift+Ctrl+S** PC , **Opt+Shift+Cmd+S** Mac) to get the **Save for Web** dialog box. Make sure that **Settings** is set to **JPEG Medium** or **JPEG Low** if you want smaller files. Click **Save** to get the **Save Optimized As** dialog box. After locating the folder (for example, **c:_photos to e-mail**) where you want to save your photos, click **Save** to save the file.

6.14

■ Click the **Stop Playing/Recording** button at the bottom of the **Actions** palette and your action is complete.

■ To create a **Droplet**, select **File ➢ Automate ➢ Create Droplet** to get the **Create Droplet** dialog box shown in Figure 6.15. Click **Choose** to get the **Save** dialog box. After locating the folder where you want to save files (for example, **c:_photos to e-mail**), name the file with a name that makes it easy to know what it does, such as **Photo Converter**.

To avoid having to respond to a color management policies dialog box, make sure you check **Suppress Color Profile Warnings.** Then, click **OK** to create the **Droplet**.

Toward the middle of the **Create Droplet** dialog box you will find **Destination**; choose **Save and Close**.

Click **Save** to save the droplet. I suggest saving it to your desktop so that it is readily accessible.

You have now successfully created a **Droplet**. If you saved it to your desktop, you can drag and drop a file from Windows Explorer on the PC or the Finder on a Mac, or other file management program such as a thumbnail image application, and drop files onto the **Photo Converter** icon — with or without Adobe Photoshop CS being open. When you drag and drop a file onto the icon, Adobe Photoshop CS automatically loads if it is not already open and then converts the file. The file is then saved to your chosen folder ready for you to use as an e-mail attachment.

Droplets may be shared with anyone who has a copy of Adobe Photoshop CS. You just have to make sure that you have not referenced a folder that does not exist on their PC.

So what do you think of these automation tools? The trick to getting things done quickly is learning how to quickly use these automation tools. Then, each time you have a repetitive task: automate it. As I shoot many sporting events such as soccer and lacrosse games, I often run an **Action** against a folder of digital photos. Using the **Web Gallery** feature (we'll cover that later in Technique 47) I can have a Web page uploaded within a few minutes with none of the tedium that would put me off from sharing my photos.

That's it for the Adobe Photoshop CS boot camp! If you have gone through each of these techniques in a step-by-step fashion, you are ready to go do any of the other techniques in the book in any order that you choose. You should head off with the confidence that you have the skills to help you survive and even thrive in the exciting world of digital photography now that you're armed with the most powerful weapon on the planet: Adobe Photoshop CS!

6.15

CHAPTER 2

CORRECTING AND ENHANCING DIGITAL PHOTOS

While Chapter 1 is considered to be the "boot camp" chapter, I highly recommend that you complete all of (or most of) this chapter before doing any of the other techniques in this book. The first technique offers you a way to quickly edit your digital photos for use on a Web page or for making digital prints. You learn all that you need to know to convert RAW image files with Adobe Camera RAW in the next technique. Editing in a nondestructive manner and in 16-bit mode is the important topic covered next. You'll then learn how to use the new **Highlight/ Shadow** feature to reveal detail in shadows and highlights. You'll next learn several useful ways to sharpen images. The following technique demonstrates how to get good color when using a **GretagMacbeth ColorChecker** chart. The last technique helps you to effectively use metadata.

7

QUICK IMAGE CORRECTION

7.1

7.2

ABOUT THE IMAGE

Carolina Butterflies All three photos were taken with a Canon EOS D30 or EOS 1D digital camera with a 100mm f/2.8 macro lens or a 300mm f/2.8 lens with a 25mm extension tube, original .jpg files

Many photographers complain about the quality of prints made at one-hour processing labs. While images often are not printed as well as they could be, such labs are quick and inexpensive. The poor quality is often the result of the limited amount of time that is spent correcting each photo and the processing lab technician's lack of skill. If you shoot with a digital camera, you likely experience the same conflict between making the best possible images you can, which requires considerable editing time, or taking the "quick and dirty" approach to image editing and just getting the job done.

This technique offers two customizable Adobe Photoshop CS **Actions** that help you to quickly edit folders of images. The first **Action** enables you to create Web images that fit in a 640 x 640 pixel square. The second **Action** enables you to create images that can be used to make 4" x 6" prints at 240 dpi. Before I created these **Actions**, I frequently did not share my photos because it took too much time to "process" them all. Using these **Actions**, I can now shoot photos, run an **Action** on a folder, and have images that are

61

ready to be uploaded to an online print service or posted to a Web site in just a few minutes.

If you need a quick and not-always-perfect edit process, this technique is for you. You might call this the "one-hour film processing technique" versus the "professional color lab processing technique," which we get to in Techniques 8 and 9.

STEP 1: LOAD ACTION SET

On the companion CD-ROM you can find an **Action** set that contains two **Actions**: one for creating Web images and one for creating 4" x 6" 240 dpi prints. After opening this **Action** set, you can select the **Action** you want and run it on as many images as you like.

■ If the **Actions** palette is not showing, choose **Window** ➢ **Actions** (**Alt+F9** PC, **Option+F9** Mac). To reset the **Actions** palette, click the menu button on the **Actions** palette and choose **Clear All Actions** from the pop-up menu. Click **OK** when presented with a dialog box asking if you want to delete the current actions.

■ You are now ready to load the **One-Hour Processing.atn** action set. Assuming that you copied files from the companion CD-ROM as suggested in the Introduction, you can load the **Action** set by clicking the menu button in the **Actions** palette and choosing **Load Actions** to get the **Load** dialog box. After locating the **\07** folder, choose the file named **One-Hour Processing.atn**. Click **Load** to load the **Action** set. The **Actions** palette should now look like the one shown in Figure 7.3 with one **Action** for 640 x 640 pixel Web images and one for 4" x 6" 240 dpi prints.

If you plan on using these **Actions** often, you may want to copy the **One-hour Processing.atn** file to the **\Adobe\Photoshop CS\Presets\ Photoshop Actions** folder where it will be readily accessible from the **Actions** palette menu.

STEP 2: OPEN FILE

■ Choose **File** ➢ **Open** (**Ctrl+O** PC, **Cmd+O** Mac) to display the **Open** dialog box. Double-click the **\07** folder to open it and then click the **butterfly1-before.jpg** file to select it. Click **Open** to open the file.

■ Select **View** ➢ **Fit on Screen** (**Ctrl+0** PC, **Cmd+0** Mac). On a PC double-click the document title bar to maximize the window. On a Mac, type **F** to change to **Full Screen Mode with Menu Bar**.

STEP 3: RUN 640 X 640 PIXEL WEB IMAGES ACTION

■ Now run the action for Web images. Click the triangle to the left of the **One-Hour processing 640 x 640 Web images** action to open it up. Click the minimize button once in the upper-right corner of the **Actions** palette to open up the **Actions** palette to show all the steps, as shown in Figure 7.4. You can click the lower-right corner of the **Actions** palette and drag it out toward the right so that you can view all of the steps.

■ Click the **1-hour processing 640 x 640 Web images** action to make it the active **Action**.

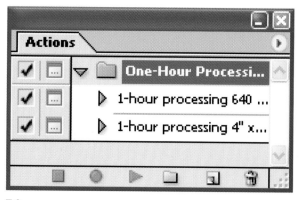

7.3

■ Click the **Play Selection** button (the triangle icon) at the bottom of the **Actions** palette to run the **action.** You then get the message dialog box shown in Figure 7.5. As the image needs to be straightened, click **Stop.** When working with an image that does not need to be straightened, click **Continue** to continue running the **Action.**

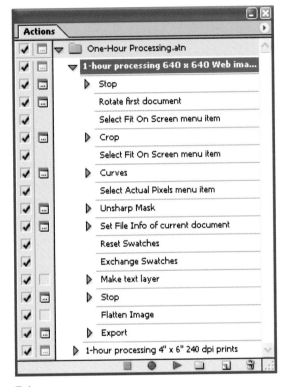

7.4

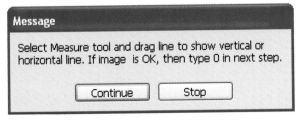

7.5

STEP 4: STRAIGHTEN IMAGE

Many photos need to be straightened. Buildings or horizons may look tilted, or as is the case with the image of the butterfly, the "specimen photo" needs to be slightly rotated toward the left. Straightening an image can be a trial-and-error process, unless you know about the incredible **Measure** tool, which has been built into the **Action.**

■ Click and hold your cursor on the **Eyedropper** tool in the **Toolbox** until you get a pop-up menu; choose **Measure** tool.
■ Click once in the image just above the center of the butterfly's head and drag down toward the tail of the image, as shown in Figure 7.6.
■ To restart the **Action** click on the **Play Selection** button at the bottom of the **Actions** palette. You will then get the **Rotate Canvas** dialog box shown in Figure 7.7. Notice that a value automatically is

7.6

7.7

placed in the **Angle** box and that **CCW** (Counter Clock Wise) is selected. This value is for the degrees of rotation needed to straighten the image. Click **OK** and you have a perfectly straight image on the first try.

STEP 5: CROP IMAGE

■ You will now see a selection made on the image. This was made with the **Crop** tool. When this **Action** was made, the settings in the **Options** bar were set to automatically create a 640 x 480 pixel Web image as is shown in Figure 7.8.

■ The objective now is to adjust the selection marquee to crop the image as is shown in Figure 7.2. Click inside the selection marquee and drag it up and to the left. To make the selection marquee larger, click on the bottom-right handle and drag it down and to the right. To center the butterfly in the selection marquee, you can click inside the marquee box and drag it to where you want it, as shown in Figure 7.9. You can also increase or decrease the size of the selection marquee box by clicking one of the four handles and dragging it until the box is sized as you want. For more precise position of the selection marquee box, you can press the **Up**, **Down**, **Right**, and **Left** arrow keys to move the selection marquee box one pixel at a time. To move the box 10 pixels at a time, press and hold the **Shift** key while pressing the arrow keys.

■ After the selection marquee box is as you want it, choose **Image ➢ Crop**, click the **Commit Current Crop Operation** icon in the **Options** bar, or press **Enter** on a PC (**Return** on a Mac) to crop the image and restart the **Action** to get the **Curves** dialog box.

STEP 6: CORRECT TONAL LEVELS AND ADJUST COLORS

Adjusting overall tonal range of an image and making color corrections are often two of the most time-consuming steps in processing digital photos. With the Adobe Photoshop CS **Auto Color** tool, these steps are reduced to a single-click command. However, you ought to be aware that even though this tool is an improvement over previous "auto" functions, the results can be somewhat less effective than you may want. Certain images can also fool the automatic logic and make it misbehave. It is worth knowing how the underlying mechanism works so you can make the necessary corrections manually if need be.

■ To choose settings for the **Auto Color** tool, click **Options** in the **Curves** dialog box shown in Figure 7.10.

■ You can now choose settings in the **Auto Color Correction Options** dialog box shown in Figure 7.11. For this technique, I suggest that you click **Enhance Per Channel Contrast** in the **Algorithms** area and clear the checkmark in the

7.9

7.8

box next to **Snap Neutral Midtones** to turn it off if it is already on. Click the box next to **Save as defaults** to place a checkmark in that box. Click

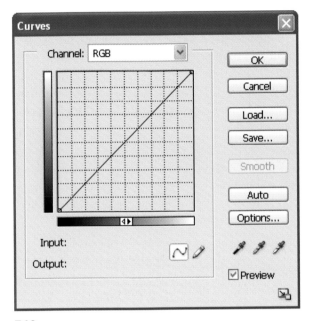

7.10

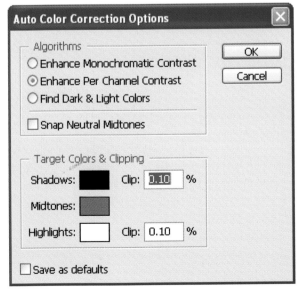

7.11

OK to save the settings. The next time you run the **Action**, you can either change these settings if needed or skip opening this dialog box.

■ To apply the **Auto Color** settings, click the **Auto** box in the **Curves** palette and then click **OK** to apply the settings. The **Action** will now display the **Unsharp Mask**.

STEP 7: SHARPEN IMAGE

■ After adjusting color, the **Action** zooms the image to 100 percent and opens the **Unsharp Mask** dialog box shown in Figure 7.12, so that you can choose settings to sharpen the image. I suggest that you set **Amount** to **150%**, **Radius** to **0.7 pixels**, and **Threshold** to **2 levels**. Click **OK** to sharpen the image and run the **Action**.

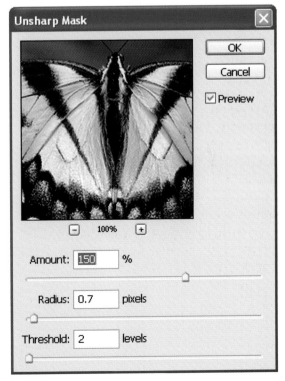

7.12

STEP 8: ADD METADATA

The latest versions of JPEG, TIFF, PSD, EPS, and PDF files all allow a wide range of information or data (known as metadata) to be added to picture files. Depending on the application, this data can be viewed, added, or modified for a wide variety of uses. For example, if you enter a title, caption, copyright information, credits, or other information to an image file, the Adobe Photoshop CS **Web Photo Gallery** feature can use this information to create HTML pages that display the metadata. To learn more about creating Web galleries read Techniques 46 and 47.

■ Once again, the **Action** automatically opens the next dialog box — the **File Info** dialog box shown in Figure 7.13. Type **Eastern Tiger Swallowtail** in the **Document Title** box and **Papilio Glaucus Linnaeus** (the scientific name of the butterfly) in the **Description** box. Click in the **Copyright Status** box and choose **Copyrighted** from the pop-up menu. Press and hold **Alt** while typing

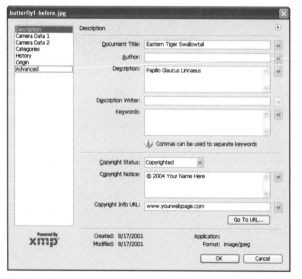

7.13

0169 to put a copyright symbol in the **Copyright Notice** box when using a PC. When using a Mac, you create the copyright symbol by pressing **Option+G**. Then, type **2004** and your name to complete the copyright notice. If you want to add a URL, type the URL in the **Owner URL** box.

■ Click **OK** to save the information in the image file and run the **Action**.

STEP 9: ADD COPYRIGHT INFORMATION TO IMAGE

Besides adding copyright information inside the file, you may also want to put your name, a company name, or a Web address and a copyright date on each image. This **Action** is set up to automatically place *your* name and a copyright on each image automatically.

■ After the **Action** places the copyright information on the image, it will display a dialog box asking if the copyright text needs to be moved on the image. If so, click the **Stop** button to stop the action. To move the copyright notice, click the **Move** tool (**V**) in the **Toolbox** and click the text and drag it until it is where you want it to be.

■ To restart the **Action**, click the **Play Selection** icon at the bottom of the **Actions** palette.

■ If you don't need to move the text, click **Continue**.

STEP 10: FLATTEN IMAGE AND SAVE FILE

■ The **Action** automatically flattens the image and then opens up the **Save for Web** dialog box shown in Figure 7.14. Click in the **Settings** box and choose **JPEG Medium**. Click **Save** to get the **Save Optimized As** dialog box. Select the folder where you want to save your image and click **Save**.

■ The **Action** has now completed all the steps and moved the active step highlight back to the beginning so that you are ready to open another image and run the action on another image!

Now try running the **1-hour processing 4" x 6" 240dpi prints Action** on the **butterfly2.jpg** and

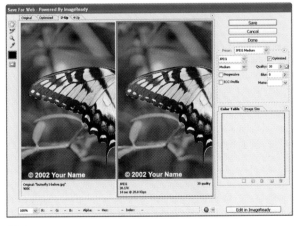

7.14

butterfly3.jpg images as a batch. This **Action** is very similar to the first **Action**, except it automatically creates images suitable for printing on an inkjet printer. If you have an inkjet printer that has a roll paper option, you can batch process an entire folder of images and then print them out by using a 4" wide roll of inkjet paper.

You have just run one of the two **Actions** in the **One-Hour Processing Action Set.** Just as easily, you could run an **Action** on any image to complete quick image processing to make a 4" x 6" 240 dpi print by simply selecting the other action (**1-Hour processing 4" x 6" 240 dpi prints**) in the action set.

Additionally, you can customize either of the two **Actions** by turning on or off any of the steps in the **Actions** by clicking a box in the left side of a step in the **Actions** palette. If you want to add steps or modify any of the existing steps, you can click in the **Action** where you want to make changes, click the **Begin Recording** icon at the bottom of the **Actions** palette, and complete the step you want to add or modify. After you have completed the step, click the **Stop Recording** button. You may then need to delete the step you replaced. To make changes to settings like those found in the **File Info** dialog box, double-click the step to open any dialog boxes that the step might include; in this case, you double-click the **Set File Info** to get the **File Info** dialog box. Type in your changes and click **OK.** Next time you run the **Action** you use the new settings.

Finally, I should mention that if you removed or turned off those steps that include the **Stop** command, you can automatically run either one of the **Actions** against an entire folder of images by choosing the **File ➤ Automate ➤ Batch** command. Using this feature, you don't even have to select, open, save, and close the images.

> **TIP**
>
> Using Adobe Photoshop CS's **File Browser**, you can select one or more images that you want to process using the **Actions** found in Technique 7 and run them against a batch of images. If some of the images are in portrait mode and the **Action** you have run is for images that are in landscape mode, you can use the **File Browser** to rotate the vertical images so that you can process all the images in one batch.

CONVERTING RAW IMAGES WITH ADOBE CAMERA RAW

8.1

8.2

Bald Eagle at Carolina Raptor Center Canon EOS D30 mounted on a tripod, 300mm f/2.8 IS, ISO 800, f/14 @ 1/100, RAW file setting, 2,160 x 1,440 pixels, 3.1MB .CRW

I f you shoot with a digital camera using the RAW file format, you will love the results you get using the new Adobe Camera RAW plug-in, which is a RAW file conversion tool that comes bundled with Adobe Photoshop CS. In this technique, you will be using a RAW file that features a beautiful bald eagle that was rehabilitated at the Carolina Raptor Center in Charlotte, North Carolina (www. birdsofprey.org). The photo was taken in November of 2001 when there were no *good* tools available for converting RAW files. Now, by following the steps in this technique, you will be able to get an absolutely outstanding image of this wonderful bald eagle. If you are photographer, you just have to love all this new technology!

STEP 1: OPEN FILE

■ Select **File** ➢ **Open** (**Ctrl+O** PC, **Cmd+O** Mac) to display the **Open** dialog box. After locating the **\08** folder, double-click it to open it. Click the **bald-eagle-before.CRW** file to select it; then, click **Open** to open the file. The file will then be previewed in the **Camera RAW** dialog box shown in Figure 8.3.

Before we begin choosing settings, let's first be clear about how the image is to be used so that we can choose optimal settings specific for that purpose. Let's assume that our end-objective is to make the

> **TIP**
>
> The Adobe Camera RAW dialog box has been created to be used with a minimum display size of 1,024 x 768 pixels. If your display is smaller than this, you may have a difficult time choosing settings and viewing the image. Read Technique 1 to learn more about display settings and how to change them if you can't view the entire Adobe Camera RAW dialog box.

8.3

largest possible print without increasing image resolution. Let's also assume the print will be made on an Epson inkjet printer that needs a minimum 240 dpi. Because the image was taken in the RAW file format, we will definitely want to take advantage of the extra picture information that is available in a 16-bit image. Also, we will want to be careful to not "blow-out" any highlights, to convert the image to the Adobe RGB color space, and to maintain the current image resolution. Great effort was taken to photograph this bird in rich fall colors in ideal light conditions, so any changes we make to the color should be done so that the intentional and desirable color cast is not removed. Now let's see what we can do with Adobe Camera RAW.

STEP 2: CHOOSE CAMERA RAW IMAGE SETTINGS

■ As the image was taken in portrait mode, click the **Rotate Image Counter Clockwise** (**L**) icon that is just to the bottom right of the preview window to rotate the image.
■ Click in the **Space** box and select **Adobe RGB (1998)** so that the converted image will be in the **Adobe RGB (1988)** color space.
■ Click in the **Depth** box and select **16 Bits/Channel**. This will double the size of the image over the **8 Bits/Channel** options, and it will increase the computer processing power requirements that will be needed to edit the image. But, that is a minor downside considering that we will be able to edit the image with commands such as **Levels** and **Curves** and still end up with a perfectly smooth histogram. Such a histogram means that no parts of the image will have been posterized due to "too much" editing.
■ Click in the **Size** box and choose **2160 x 1440** — the original size of the image.
■ Type **240** in the **Resolution** box and make sure **pixels/inch** is the increment setting.

STEP 3: ANALYZE IMAGE AND MAKE A PLAN

Before you begin making changes to settings it is wise to first analyze the image and make a plan. Ideally, it would be nice to be able to increase exposure to reveal more detail in the eagle's dark feathers. However, if we increase exposure to lighten the shadows, what will happen to the highlights? Also, what color cast is there that we ought to remove?

■ One of the first things you want to check is the **Histogram** that is shown in the upper-right corner of the **Camera RAW** dialog box. From the **Histogram**, we can see that there is excellent tonal range and that it is well-exposed. No details in either the shadows or highlights have been lost.

■ Click in the **White Balance** box in the **Adjust** tab and choose **As Shot** to preview the image without any white balance settings.

■ Click the **Zoom** tool (**Z**) in the upper-left corner of the **Camera RAW** dialog box. Click once above and to the left of the eagle's head and drag the marquee around the eagle's head to zoom in.

■ Click the **White Balance** tool (**I**) in the upper-left corner of the **Camera RAW** dialog box. Drag the **White Balance** tool over the brightest spots on the eagle's head while watching the **R**, **G**, and **B** values just below the preview image. Some of the lightest tones have **R**, **G**, and **B** values that are **185**, **206**, and **229** respectively. This means that exposure can be increased slightly without "blowing out" the highlights (for example, pushing the RGB values to 255). From those numbers, we have also learned that in spite of the fact that the image has a rich warm glow to it, there is a considerable blue cast as the **blue** values are substantially larger (**220**) than that of the **red** (**185**) and **green** (**206**) values.

STEP 4: REMOVE BLUE COLOR CAST

■ There are several ways that you can remove the blue cast in the eagle's white feathers. First, you can choose a different **White Balance Setting** in the **Adjust** tab. Before doing that, however, use the **Zoom** tool (**Z**) to zoom in on the eagle's head while leaving some of the trees and background visible, as shown in Figure 8.4. Try the following settings: **Auto**, **Daylight**, **Cloudy**, and **Flash**. What do you think? I like the **Flash** setting as it removes the blue cast without making the image too warm in tone. From that setting, you can make further adjustments with the **Temperature** and **Tint** sliders — try them.

■ To reset the image, press **Alt** on the PC, or **Option** on the Mac and the **Cancel** button changes into a **Reset** button; click **Reset** to reset the image.

■ Another approach for removing color casts is to use the **White Balance** tool (**I**). After clicking the **White Balance** tool (**I**) in the upper left-corner of the **Camera RAW** dialog box, click one of the

8.4

white feathers at the top of the eagle's head to remove the blue color cast. This correction looks very close to what we got earlier with the **Flash, White Balance** setting.

■ To reset the image once again, press **Alt** on the PC or **Option** on the Mac and the **Cancel** button changes into a **Reset** button; click **Reset** to reset the image.

■ If you have a properly calibrated monitor and you have a "good eye for color," you may also get excellent results by using the **Temperature** and **Tint** sliders. Try setting **Temperature** to **5300** to remove the blue color cast. Then, add back in a little yellow to the overly white eagle feathers by setting **Tint** to **–4**. Double-click the **Zoom** tool to make the image full size. Click the **Hand** tool (**H**) and click and drag the image so that you see almost nothing but the eagle's head. I like this setting the most, so let's continue on with it.

STEP 5: ADJUST EXPOSURE

Now that we are happy with the color settings, let's see if we can't improve the exposure so that we see more details in the dark feathers. In doing this, we need to make sure that we don't lose detail in the white feathers.

■ Click inside the **Zoom Level** box, which is just below the preview image on the left. Select **Fit in View** to show the entire image. To increase exposure, click the **Exposure** slider and drag it toward the right about one full stop (**+1.0**). As you slide the slider, watch the image and the **Histogram** carefully. As the right side of the **Histogram** is pushed off the end of the scale, you will notice that feathers on the eagle's head become pure white and detail is lost. To get a more accurate understanding of where you are losing detail,

press **Alt** on the **PC** (**Option** on the Mac) while clicking and moving the **Exposure** slider. You will see the clipped colors in the preview window, which should look similar to the one shown in Figure 8.5. You may want to zoom in on the eagle's face once again to get a more precise view of the image as you move the **Exposure** slider. I like the **Exposure** setting of **+0.35**, which is about one-third of a stop. It opens up some of the dark feathers while keeping detail in the white feathers.

STEP 6: ADJUST SHADOWS, BRIGHTNESS, CONTRAST, AND SATURATION

■ If you want to darken the shadows a small amount, slide the **Shadows** slider to the right to **3**.

■ Using the **Brightness** slider is the same as adjusting the middle-tones using the **middle-tone** slider in the **Levels** tool. To slightly lighten the image, set the **Brightness** to **55**.

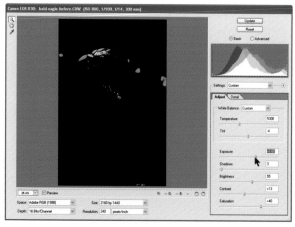

8.5

■ You can increase contrast with the **Contrast** slider. In this case, the default setting is fine.

■ To adjust color saturation, use the **Saturation** slider. Many photographers new to digital image editing have a tendency to over-saturate an image. Be careful to keep your images looking realistic, but use your own judgment to get the creative results you want. Boosting **Saturation** to **+40** gives you about as much rich orange colors in this image as you would get if you had taken a photo with Fuji's Provia or Velvia slide film.

STEP 7: SHARPEN THE IMAGE

If you click the **Detail** tab in the **Adobe Camera RAW** dialog box, you will get sliders for **Sharpness**, **Luminance Smoothing**, and **Color Noise Reduction**, as shown in Figure 8.6. While these sliders can be used to sharpen an image, I recommend that you not sharpen an image until it has been completely edited and has been sized for its final use. To learn more about image sharpening, read Techniques 11 and 39.

If you click **Advanced** in the **Adobe Camera RAW** dialog box, you will get **Lens** and **Calibrate** tabs, which offer additional "advanced" conversions features. In most cases, you will not need these features. You can learn more about these settings in the **Help** file.

Click **OK** to convert the image using the selected settings and open it in a document window in Adobe Photoshop CS. Figure 8.2 shows the results of the final conversion process. You are now ready to perform additional editing steps if you choose.

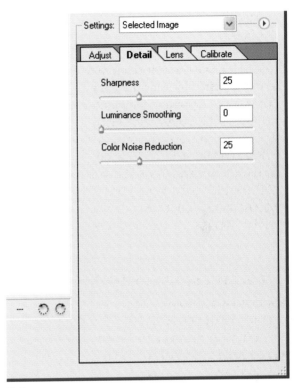

8.6

9

EDITING NONDESTRUCTIVELY IN 16-BIT MODE

9.1

9.2

White House Ruins in Canyon De Chelly Canon EOS 1D, 28-70mm f/2.8 at 28mm, ISO 200, f/16.0 @ 1/80, RAW file setting, 1,440 x 2,160 pixels, 5.2MB .tif (RAW)

If you shoot with a digital camera using RAW files, you should find Adobe Photoshop CS's new comprehensive 16-bit editing capability to be invaluable as you can unquestionably get better results than when using 8-bit images. For this reason alone, the cost of upgrading to the new version is worth every penny. Why? Because you can now convert a RAW image into a 16-bit image using the **Adobe Camera RAW** plug-in and use most of the core Adobe Photoshop CS features including **Levels**, **Curves**, **Layers**, **Hue/Saturation**, and brush tools on the 16-bit image. All this was not possible before Adobe Photoshop CS. When you combine this comprehensive 16-bit editing capability with **Adjustment Layers** and **Layer Masks** you can perform just about all of the most important digital photo editing steps on a 16-bit image, and then, when needed, go back and click an **Adjustment Layer** or **Layer Mask** and adjust any of your earlier settings without losing any picture information that would cause you to get a less than perfect image.

You might be wondering why editing in 16-bit mode is so important. What do you get with a 16-bits per channel image that you don't get with an 8-bits per channel image? Besides getting a file that is more than twice as large in size (okay—an unwanted downside), you also get 65,536 tonal ranges for each color instead of 256! The mathematics behind this is simple: 2^8 gives you 256 possible shades of gray versus 2^{16}, which gives you 65,536 shades of gray or 256 times more shades *per* color channel.

In more practical terms, this means that you have a greater dynamic color range to work with. When using 16-bit images you can make more drastic edit changes using tools such as **Curves** that discard some image data in the process of compressing some of the tonal range, while extending other parts. For example, if you were to apply the simple **Curve** shown in Figure 9.3 to the image shown in Figure 9.1 when it is in 16-bit mode, you would end up with the smooth histogram shown in Figure 9.4. If you first converted the image shown in Figure 9.1 to 8-bit mode and then applied the same curve, you would end up with the histogram shown in Figure 9.5. Notice how there was not sufficient image data to make this tonal correction without leaving parts of the image posterized as there are now gaps in the tonal range. Now imagine applying several more "destructive" commands such as **Levels**, **Hue/Saturation**, or maybe a blend mode such as **Multiply** or **Screen**—all of which would cause you to lose more image data. If you started with a 16-bit image, you are much more likely to end up with a smooth histogram and a smooth tonal range, which will make your image look better.

Okay—I know this is not a math class and that proving such points is not necessary. However, I wanted to stress how important it is for you to shoot in RAW

mode, convert your images to 16-bit mode, and then, edit in 16-bit mode. In the rest of this technique, you will learn how you can perform "nondestructive image editing in 16-bit mode." We'll be working with a digital

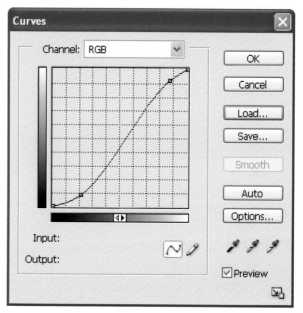

9.3

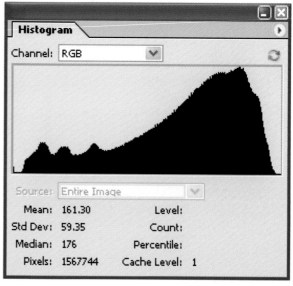

9.4

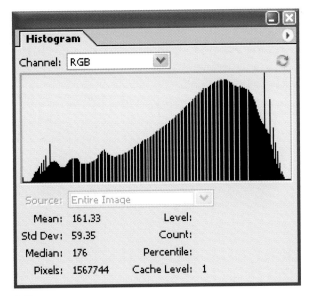

9.5

photo of the White House ruins in Arizona that was taken on a very hot day with bright sun. We'll make our edits to make the image look like it looked on that day rather than trying to make it look better than it did when the photo was taken.

STEP 1: OPEN FILE AND CONVERT IT WITH ADOBE CAMERA RAW PLUG-IN

■ Choose **File ➢ Open** (**Ctrl+O** PC, **Cmd+O** Mac) to display the **Open** dialog box. Double-click the **\09** folder to open it and then click the **white-house-before.tif** file to select it. Click **Open** to open the file in the **Adobe Camera RAW** plug-in.
■ As the use of the Adobe Camera RAW plug-in is covered in detail in Technique 8, just set your settings to match those shown in Figure 9.6. Make sure to set **Depth** to **16-Bits/Channel**. Click **OK** to open the image in a document window in **Adobe Camera RAW**.

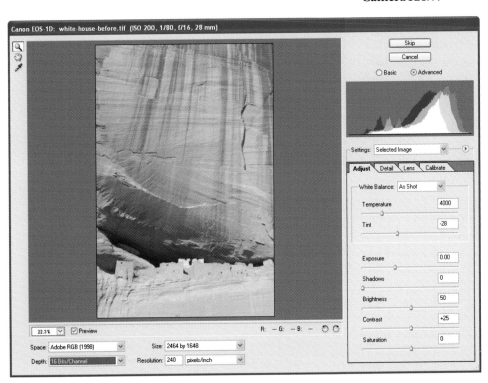

9.6

STEP 2: PERFORM QUICK ASSESSMENT OF IMAGE

As the primary intent of this technique is to show you how you can edit in a nondestructive manner while using 16-bit images, let's just agree to make a few simple edits using **Levels**, **Curves**, and **Hue/Saturation**. We'll also do a little selective editing using a **Layer Mask**. Once you understand this process, you can open up the image and take your time to improve it as you want it. If you save your steps as an **Action**, you can see just how valuable it is to work in 16-bit mode by running the **Action** on the same image in 8-bit mode. Compare the histograms of the two after you have completed your edits.

STEP 3: DUPLICATE LAYER

When editing most images, I find that I often want to be able to see the original image, or to use the original image in the edit process once I have taken several edit steps. For this reason, my first editing step is usually to duplicate the **Background** layer. I then use this new **Layer** as the image to edit. If you are working on large images, or you have limitations on memory or hard drive space, you may *not* want to duplicate the **Background** layer. In this case, you can still use a **Snapshot** in the **History** palette to compare your current edited image with the original image.

■ To duplicate the **Background** layer, select **Layer** ➤ **Duplicate Layer** to get the **Duplicate Layer** dialog box. Type **Image** in the **As** box and click **OK** to create a new layer. The **Image** layer will now be the active layer and it will be highlighted in the **Layers** palette.

STEP 4: TAKE ADVANTAGE OF THE HISTOGRAM PALETTE

One additional new feature in Adobe Photoshop CS worth using is the **Histogram** palette, which can be left open in the Adobe Photoshop CS workspace while you work.

■ If the **Histogram** palette is not visible, select **Window** ➤ **Histogram**. By default, the **Histogram** opens up in **Compact View**. Click the menu button in the **Histogram** palette and select all **Channels View** to get separate histograms for each of the three color channels plus one for the **RGB** channel. As this image is monochromatic, click the menu button and choose **Expanded View** to get a **Histogram** palette that shows a larger histogram than that of the **Compact View** along with some additional statistical information, but only a single histogram as shown in Figure 9.7.

STEP 5: FIND DARKEST AND LIGHTEST POINTS AND SET COLOR SAMPLER POINTS

When your overall edit intent requires that you exercise care over shadows and highlights in an image, you can take a minute or two and set **Color Sampler** points in your image and then monitor them during each step of the edit process by keeping your eye on their values in the **Info** palette.

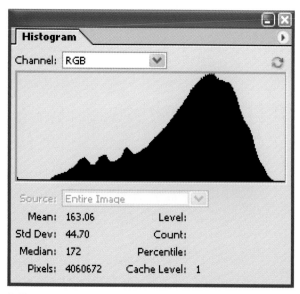

9·7

- If the **Info** palette is not visible, select **Window** ➢ **Info** (**F8**). The default view shows **RGB** and **CMYK** values. I prefer having the **RGB** values and a **Grayscale** value, which ranges from **0%** to **100%**, where **0%** is pure black and **100%** represents pure white. To show the **Grayscale** value, click the menu button in the **Info** palette and choose **Palette Options** to get the **Info Options** dialog box shown in Figure 9.8. Click in the **Second Color Readout Mode** box and select **Grayscale**; click **OK** and your **Info** palette should now look like the one shown in Figure 9.9.

- Now let's set two **Color Sampler Points** — one in the brightest area to monitor the highlights, and one in the darkest area to watch shadow values. Click the **Eyedropper** tool (**I**) in the **Toolbox**. Click in the **Sample Size** box in the **Options** bar and select **3 by 3 Average**.

- To easily find the brightest and darkest areas in the image, select **Image** ➢ **Adjustments** ➢ **Threshold** to get the **Threshold** dialog box. Click the slider and slide it all the way to the right; then, slowly drag it back to the left while watching the image to see what area changes from black to white first. Using the **Eyedropper** tool, press **Shift** and click in the white area to set a point. You should now see the **#1** point values in the **Info** palette.

- Do the same thing to set a point in the darkest area. Click the slider in the **Threshold** dialog box and slide it all the way to the left; then, slowly drag it back to the right until you see a sold black area emerge from the all-white image. Using the **Eyedropper** tool, press **Shift** and click in the black area to set a second point. You should now see the **#2** point values in the **Info** palette. Click **Cancel** to close the **Threshold** palette without applying the changes. The **Info** palette should now look like the one shown in Figure 9.10.

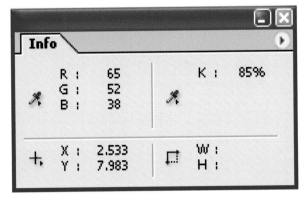

9.8

9.9

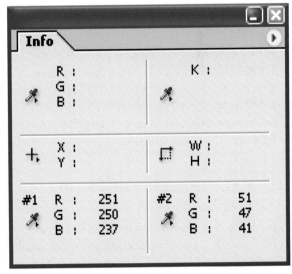

9.10

Rearrange your workspace so that you can see the image, the **Info** palette to monitor the values of the shadows and highlights, and the **Histogram** to see "before" and "after" tonal changes — all while you are performing edit steps. During the editing process you are likely to be glad you took the time to set up your workspace with the two **Color Sampler Points** and the **Histogram** palette. Once you get used to these features, editing without them is like driving a car without a speedometer and water temperature gauge.

STEP 6: INCREASE IMAGE CONTRAST

■ Now let's increase contrast a slight amount using **Levels**. While it is possible to select **Levels** and make any adjustments you want and apply them, you really ought to make the changes on an **Adjustment Layer**, which will enable you to go back and make any changes to your settings you want to make later in your edit process. To create a **Levels Adjustment Layer**, select **Layer** ➤ **New Adjustment Layer** ➤ **Levels** to get the **New Layer** dialog box; click **OK** to get the **Levels** dialog box.

■ Click the **Shadow** slider (the left-most slider) in the **Levels** dialog box and drag it toward the right where the left-most **Input Levels** box shows **34**. Now, click the **Highlight** slider (the right-most slider) and drag it toward the left until it just passes the right end of the histogram. The right-most **Input Levels** box should now read **244**. If you now look at the **Info** palette you can see that the point we set earlier in the darkest shadow area (**#2**) shows that the **RGB** values have moved from **244**, **243**, and **221** to **254**, **253**, and **227** respectively. You can also see what changes have occurred to the highlight point before you apply the settings. Also, take a look at the **Histogram** palette to see the **Histogram** before your settings are applied. Click **OK** to apply the settings.

STEP 7: ADJUST TONAL RANGE

■ To adjust the tonal range with **Curves**, we will use an **Adjustment Layer** for the same reasons discussed previously. Click on the **Image** layer to make it the active layer. Select **Layer** ➤ **New Adjustment Layer** ➤ **Curves** to get the **New Layer** dialog box; click **OK** to get the **Curves** dialog box. To lighten the area that is in shadow just over the ruins, drag your cursor over the dark area while watching the point slide up and down the curve in the **Curves** dialog box. This shows you where you need to set one or more points to lighten this area. Click once in the curve in the **Curves** dialog box and set a point with **Input** and **Output** values of **74**, and **82** respectively. Click **OK** to apply the settings.

■ To view the results of the **Curves** adjustment, click once on the **Layer Visibility** icon that is to the left of the **Curves 1** layer to see the **"before-Curves 1"** as is shown in the layers palette and once again to view the **"before-Curves 1"** image.

STEP 8: ADJUST COLOR

■ The image is currently much richer in color and more yellow than it was when I took the photos, so let's make some quick changes using **Hue/Saturation**. To adjust the color we will once again use an **Adjustment Layer**. Click on the **Image** layer to make it the active layer. Select **Layer** ➤ **New Adjustment Layer** ➤ **Hue/Saturation** to get the **New Layer** dialog box; click **OK** to get the **Hue/Saturation** dialog box.

■ To reduce color saturation, click the **Saturation** slider in the **Hue/Saturation** dialog box and slide it toward the left to about **−34**. To reflect the effects the bright sun had on the sun-washed rock, slide the **Lightness** slider toward the right to about **+15**. Click **OK** to apply the settings. The image is now looking much more like it was on that very hot, bright day when I visited.

STEP 9: SELECTIVELY CONTROL IMAGE DENSITY

One of the downsides to lightening the image is that we are losing detail in the hieroglyphics that are on the brightest part of the rock below the ruins. To bring back some of this detail, we can selectively increase image density in just this area. We'll accomplish this by creating an additional layer and changing the blend mode to **Multiply**, which will darken the image. Then we'll hide the results with a **Layer Mask** and paint back just the parts we want at the level we want. Don't worry: It isn't half as hard as it sounds — work with me.

■ Click the **Image** layer in the **Layers** palette to make it the active layer. Select **Layer ➢ Duplicate Layer** to get the **Duplicate Layer** dialog box. Type **hieroglyphics** in the **As** box and click **OK** to create a new layer. The **Layers** palette should now look like the one shown in Figure 9.11.

■ To darken the image, click in the **Blend** mode box in the **Layers** box and choose **Multiply**. The image will now be much too dark. Click in the **Opacity** box and slide the slider to about **30%**. Alternatively, you can use the new "scrubby slider" feature. Click the **Opacity** text and the cursor will turn into a two-headed arrow. As you slide your cursor to the right or the left the **Opacity** values will change. How's that for the trick of the day?

■ The problem now is that the entire image is darker than it was when I visited. To hide this entire layer, select **Layer ➢ Add Layer Mask ➢ Hide All** and the image will once again be light. Notice that there is now a black layer mask icon to the right of the thumbnail image in the **hieroglyphics** layer, as shown in Figure 9.12.

■ Now you can selectively paint in that darker layer to make the hieroglyphics more visible. Select the **Brush** tool (**B**). Click the **Brush**

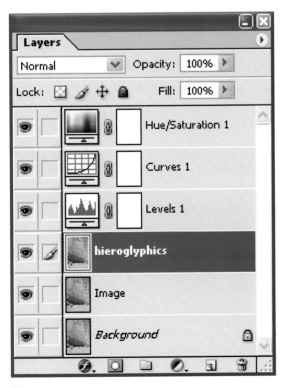

9.11

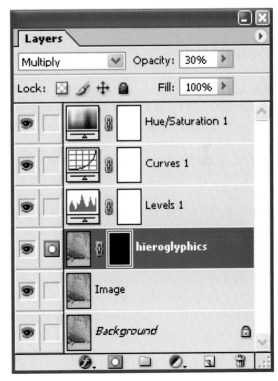

9.12

Preset Picker in the **Options** bar and select the **Soft Round 300 Pixels** brush. Press **D** to set **Foreground** color to **white**. Make sure **Mode** is set to **Normal**, **Opacity** to **25%**, and **Flow** to **100%**. As **Opacity** is set to **25%**, you will have to paint over the mask four times to darken the image up to the maximum tonal level we had before hiding the darker **hieroglyphics** layer with the **Layer Mask**.

■ I suggest that you now use the **Zoom** tool (**Z**) and the **Hand** tool (press and hold the **spacebar** while clicking and dragging an image) to arrange the image in your workspace so that you can easily paint the lower area of the wall to bring out the details in the hieroglyphics. If you make a mistake, or you want to lighten an area that you overpainted, you can switch to black and paint the mask back. To view your work, click the **Layer Visibility** icon to the left of the **hieroglyphics** layer to view the "before" and "after" effects.

STEP 10: MAKE FINAL ADJUSTMENTS

"And now—the rest of the story," as Paul Harvey is fond of saying and I enjoy hearing. Because we took our time to work to convert the RAW file to a 16-bit image we now have a wonderfully smooth histogram, as you can see in Figure 9.13, in spite of all the editing steps we have taken. We can also quickly look at the values of the extreme shadows and highlights by looking at the values of the two points we set in the **Info** palette. Plus—and this is a **BIG PLUS**—we can double-click any one of the layers in the **Layers** palette to pull up the associated dialog box and make any adjustments to our original settings. We can turn any **Adjustment Layer** off entirely. We can also turn any layer on and off to view "before" and "after" effects. Go on—try it. Double-click the **Curves 1** layer to get the **Curves** dialog box. Make a change to

the curve and click **OK** to apply it. This technique really shows the strength of Adobe Photoshop CS when you shoot in RAW mode, convert to a 16-bit image, and edit in 16-bit mode with **Adjustment Layers**. The results are incredible flexibility and higher-quality images. You will be a better photographer if you shoot in RAW mode and follow the steps in this technique.

> **TIP**
>
> When there is a tiny triangular warning symbol in the Histogram palette, the histogram represents the cache instead of the document's current state. Using the image cache, the histogram is displayed much faster, but it is only based upon a small sampling of the pixels in the image. To get an accurate view, double-click anywhere in the histogram or on the **Cached Data Warning** icon.

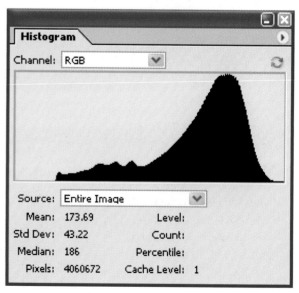

9.13

REVEALING DETAIL IN SHADOWS AND HIGHLIGHTS

10.1

10.2

ABOUT THE IMAGE

Loon on a Lake in Alaska
Canon EOS 1Ds, 500mm f/4.0 with 1.4 tele-extender, ISO 250, f/5.6 @ 1/2000, RAW setting, 2,160 x 1,440 pixels, edited and converted to 0.96MB 2,048 x 1,365 .jpg

The incredibly challenging photo shown in Figure 10.1 was taken by Arthur Morris, bird photographer extraordinaire. At first glance, I foolishly questioned the exposure that was used. However, after some careful studying of this photo using Adobe Photoshop CS, I found that Artie was "absolutely spot on" with all of his camera settings. I was even more surprised to learn that this sharply focused photo was taken from a raft with a heavy 500mm f/4.0 telephoto lens! The challenge now becomes one of using Adobe Photoshop CS to enhance the image by bringing out the detail in the dark areas of the loon while avoiding any loss of important detail in the highlights — the classic problem with wide tonal range images that feature both dark and near white detail.

83

STEP 1: OPEN FILE AND CONVERT IN ADOBE CAMERA RAW

■ Select **File ➤ Open** (**Ctrl+O** PC, **Cmd+O** Mac) to display the **Open** dialog box. After locating the **\10** folder, double-click it to open it. Click the **loon-before.TIF** file; then, click **Open** to open the file in Adobe **Camera RAW**.

As this technique will be primarily focused on using the new **Shadow/Highlight** feature, we won't spend much time here looking at the Adobe **Camera RAW** plug-in. However, to get the best results with the **Shadow/Highlight** feature, you must first convert the RAW image properly. To learn more about the Adobe Camera RAW plug-in, read Technique 8.

■ Click in the **White Balance** box in the **Adjust** tab in the **Adobe Camera RAW** dialog box and select **As Shot**. That setting gives us reasonable color.

■ When this image is opened in 16-bit mode, it will be nearly 63MBs. While you are learning how to use the **Shadow/Highlight** feature, you may want to click in the **Size** box and select **2048 x 1363** or even **1539 x 1024** to save processing time

and reduce the need for disk space. Make sure that **Space** is set to **Adobe RGB (1988)** and that **Depth** is set to **16 Bits/Channel**.

Earlier we agreed the challenge was going to be to increase exposure in the dark feather area of the loon without losing the detail in the white feathers. If possible, increasing exposure with a RAW file using **Adobe Camera RAW** is preferable over doing it later in Adobe Photoshop CS. But, we can't increase exposure *selectively* in Adobe **Camera RAW** as we can in Adobe Photoshop CS using masks, the new **Shadow/Highlight** feature, and other selective adjustment tools. So, let's take a look at what happens when we increase exposure from the initial one-third stop camera exposure compensation.

■ Press **Alt** (**Cmd** on a Mac) while clicking and dragging the **Exposure** slider to the right to increase exposure. At a **0** setting, you can see how precisely Artie had set the exposure — had he exposed even one-third stop more, he would have pushed the white feathers on the chest of the loon into pure white, which is a no-no when shooting digitally. As you slide the slider toward the right, you see more of the white areas being pushed into

ARTHUR MORRIS

With his images and articles published regularly in books, magazines, and calendars around the world, Arthur Morris is widely recognized as North America's premier bird photographer. He is a columnist for *Popular Photography*. His how-to book, *The Art of Bird Photography*, is *the* classic work on the subject. He has been a Canon contract photographer since 1995, having been selected as one of the original group of 55 in their Explorers of Light program. For more

than 20 years, Morris has simply taken a walk with a long telephoto lens on his shoulder and produced stunning images of free, wild, and unrestrained birds. While teaching seminars and leading his BAA/Instructional Photo-Tours, he has taught thousands of others to do the same. You can learn more about Artie and his workshops, seminars, online Bulletins, prints, and hard-to-find photographic accessories at www. birdsasart.com.

pure white, which removes important detail. So, let's convert this image with the **Exposure** set exactly as it was taken.

■ We could lighten the image by clicking and moving the **Brightness** slider to the right to about **75**. However, this slider works the same as the middle-tone slider in the **Levels** tool. We're better off lightening only parts of the image, so let's leave **Brightness** set to the default value of **50**.

■ At this point, we have not made any changes to the default settings. Click **OK** to convert the image and open it in a document window in Adobe Photoshop CS.

STEP 2: SET COLOR SAMPLER POINTS

■ To make it easy to monitor the lightest highlight and the darkest shadow, let's set two color sampler points. Click the **Eyedropper** tool (**I**) in the **Toolbox**. Click in the **Sample Size** dialog box in the **Options** bar and select **3 by 3 Average**.

■ If the **Info** palette is not already showing, select **Window** ➢ **Info** (**F8**).

■ Select **Image** ➢ **Adjustments** ➢ **Threshold** to get the **Threshold** dialog box. Click the slider and slide it all the way to the right; then, slowly move it back toward the left while watching the image. At a **Threshold Level** of around **232**, you should see a white area on a totally black background. This is the brightest highlight. Press **Shift** and click inside the white area to set a color sampler point for monitoring the highlight. Notice that the **RGB** values are around **240** (not near **255**, which is pure white) as it was well-exposed. The **Threshold** dialog box should now look like the one shown in Figure 10.3. The image should look like the one shown in Figure 10.4.

■ Click the **Threshold** slider once again. Only this time, slide it all the way to the left; then slide it

slowly back to the right while watching the image and the **Histogram** to see where the darkest shadows are on the image. Stop when the **Threshold** setting is around **30**. Press **Shift** and click once in the dark area in the loon's neck to set a second

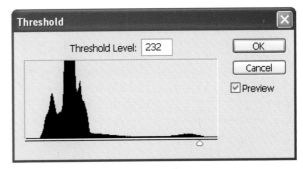

10.3

10.4

point to about **30**. The image should now look like the one shown in Figure 10.5 and the **Threshold** dialog box should look like the one shown in Figure 10.6. The largest dark area on the neck of the loon is a good place to set a shadow point. Press **Shift** and click inside the nearly black area to set a second **Color Sampler** point. Once again notice the **RGB** values, which range from about **14** to **20** indicating that no detail has been lost in pure black.

10.5

10.6

- Click **Cancel** in the **Threshold** dialog box to close it without applying the settings. You should now be able to see both color sampler points in the image and the **Info** palette should look like the one shown in Figure 10.7.
- Besides adding a couple of **Color Sampler** points to the image, you may also want to open the **Histogram** palette and set it to **Expanded View**. If you open it now you'll be able to watch it as you make changes to the settings in the **Shadow/Highlight** dialog box.

STEP 3: REVEAL DETAIL IN THE SHADOWS

- Using the **Zoom** tool (**Z**) and the **Hand** tool (**H**), zoom in and move the image so that it is as close to **100%** as possible while you can still see the entire loon and some of the reflections in the water just below the loon's chest. A near-100% zoom level will help you to avoid settings that create halos around dark areas that have been lightened. Admittedly, this may be impractical as this is a huge image that was taken with an

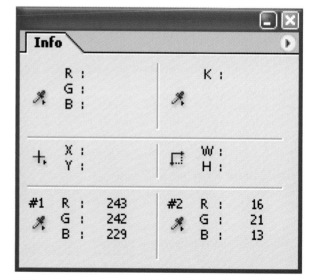

10.7

eleven-megapixel camera. So, you may have to settle for zooming in and out as needed.

■ Select **Image** ➢ **Adjustments** ➢ **Shadow/ Highlight** to get the all-powerful new singing and dancing **Shadow/Highlight** tool shown in Figure 10.8. If all the options are not visible, click in the box next to **Show More Options**, which is at the bottom of the dialog box. Make sure there is a checkmark in the box next to **Preview**. Check to make sure your settings match those shown in Figure 10.8.

The **Shadow/Highlight** filter is one of the more complex and yet powerful Adobe Photoshop CS features. Without this feature, you would need to worry about creating a number of **Adjustment Layers** and **Layer Masks** to dodge and burn the loon photo. All this requires considerable time and skill to avoid ending up with an image that has halos around different parts of the image. Once you understand how to choose the optimal settings with the **Shadow/ Highlight** filter, you can produce outstanding results. Let me warn you in advance that the **Shadow/ Highlight** filter is not an easy filter to use—unless you understand each of the eight sliders. When you understand what they do and how to get good setting—you'll love this feature.

In simple terms, the **Shadow/Highlight** filter enables you to adjust image contrast in shadows, or highlights, or both—all, without significantly altering the contrast in other tonal regions. First, we will work with the three **Shadow** sliders. Once you understand them, you will also understand the three **Highlight** sliders because they work the same way.

■ The default values of **50**, **50**, and **30** for **Amount**, **Tonal Width**, and **Radius** are good "start" values for most images. Larger **Amount** values provide more lightening of shadows. In other words, the **Amount** slider controls the amount of change that occurs in each pixel. A value of **0** means there is no change to the image at all. As we don't want to overly lighten the loon's dark black iridescent head, let's slide **Amount** down to **35%**. Notice that the **R**, **G**, and **B** values for point **#2** in the **Info** palette have moved from around **20**, **23**, and **18** to **49**, **55**, and **47** respectively.

■ The **Tonal Width** slider controls how much of the tonal range gets changed. For example, a small **Tonal Width** setting puts most of the change into the darker regions of the image. As the **Tonal Width** is increased, change occurs to a wider tonal range of the shadows. Because we just want to bring back detail in the darkest areas of the image, or the dark part of the loon, set **Tonal Width** to about **36%**.

■ The last **Shadow** slider is the **Radius** slider and it is the most difficult to understand. It enables you to control how much a pixel is modified depending upon how dark or light its neighboring pixels are—got that one? Don't worry, I struggled too at first. Let's look at it another way: If the

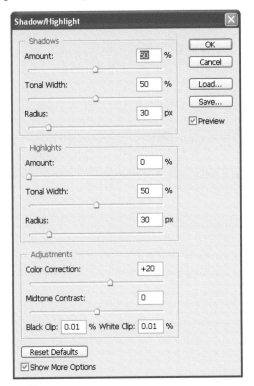

10.8

Radius is too small you lose contrast in your darker subject. If the **Radius** is too large you will lighten the entire image as opposed to just the shadowed subject. The rule of thumb for this slider is to set it approximately equal to one-half the width of the shadowed subject. In this case the dark face of the loon is about **360** pixels wide (use the **Measure** tool to measure it), so **Radius** should be set to around **180**.

■ To bring back in the rich iridescent color in the loon's head where we have been working, set the **Color Correction** slider to **+45**.

■ Click **OK** to apply the settings. The image should now look like the one shown in Figure 10.9.

10.9

STEP 4: MAKE FINAL ADJUSTMENTS

I like the way the image is beginning to look. You can see detail in all parts of the image. Looking at the **Info** palette and our two points, you can see that we have not pushed pixels into "detail-less space." A quick look at the **Histogram** palette and you see that we still have a nice smooth curve — that is just one of the many reasons to shoot in RAW mode and edit in 16-bit mode. However, my view is that we can add a bit more contrast to the image and possibly lighten the mid-tones somewhat. Let's see what we can do by applying a few final adjustments with **Levels** and **Curves**.

■ To enable settings to be changed, let's use an **Adjustment Layer** for **Levels**. Select **Layer** ➢ **New Adjustment Layer** ➢ **Levels** to get the **New Layer** dialog box; click **OK** to get the **Levels** dialog box. Click the **Shadow** slider and slide it to the right to about **44**. Click the **Midtone** slider and move it to about **1.15** to open up the midtones. Any adjustments we make to the highlights are going to cause some of the highlights to be pushed into the pure white range (**255**). However, we need to brighten the whites a small amount if we can. Press the **Alt** key (the **Option** key on the Mac) and click the **Highlight** slider and slowly move it to the left while watching how much of the highlights on the loon's chest get clipped. As any adjustment begins to clip large areas of the loon's chest, stop and leave it set to **255**. Click **OK** to apply the settings.

■ Now create a **Curves Adjustment Layer**. Select **Layer** ➢ **New Adjustment Layer** ➢ **Curves** to get the **New Layer** dialog box; click **OK** to get the **Curves** dialog box. Click once on the curve and set a point at **40, 46**. Click the curve again and set a point at **114** and **145**. Click once more on the curve and set a point at **211** and **220**. The **Curves** dialog box should now look like the one shown in Figure 10.10. Click **OK** to apply the settings. The final image should now look like the one shown in Figure 10.2. Figure 10.11 shows the detail in the head and in the white feathers on the loon's chest.

TIP

In Technique 10 you learn how you can bring back detail in the shadow area of an image by using the Shadow/Highlight filter. Using the same steps, you can also bring back detail in highlight regions of an image providing that they are not in a pure white tone (a tonal value of 255). You can even use the Shadow/Highlight filter to reveal detail in the shadows and in the highlights of the same image.

Of all the photographers who have inspired me to work harder to take better photos, Arthur Morris is at the top of my list. His book, *The Art of Bird Photography,* got me interested in bird photography and it was how I first learned about some of the best places to take bird photos. I also got equipment tips that later proved to be invaluable. When I met Morris in person and learned how he feels about birds, nature, and life, and I learned of his techniques for lying down in the cold water on sandy seashores so that he can be eye-level with his favorite subjects, I finally began to understand why it is that his bird photography is truly art — and why so many others merely take photographs of birds. Join him in one of his workshops and you'll understand.

10.10   10.11

SHARPENING DIGITAL PHOTOS

11.1

11.2

One of Many Barnyard Friends Canon EOS 1Ds, 28-70mm f/2.8 at 70mm, f/8.0 @ 1/50, 400 ISO, RAW file setting, 2,704 x 4,064 pixels, 10.4MB .tif (RAW). Converted, edited, and cropped to an 8-bit 1,920 x 2,400 pixel .tif

Nearly all digital images need to be sharpened — period. Well, I better qualify that somewhat. Those images that you intend to be sharp need to be sharpened as soft edges are just one of the characteristics of digitized photos no matter whether they have been created with a scanner or with a digital camera. The black and white goat photo in Figure 11.1 was chosen for this technique because most sharpening techniques require a tradeoff between sharper edges (on edges that ought to be sharpened) and getting undesirable effects, such as enhanced grain, halos, excessively pronounced textures, and other unwanted effects. This goat image has a variety of edges, plus lots of different kinds of textures that are useful for learning about the **Unsharp Mask** filter, a key tool for making images look sharper.

While this technique isn't particularly exciting, it is an essential one to make your photos look as good as they can. For this reason, in this technique you learn three different approaches to sharpening images, and you get more information on the "hows" and "whys" than most techniques in this book. The three different approaches covered are:

- Using **Unsharp Mask** on the entire image
- Sharpening one or more channels instead of the entire image
- Convert image to **LAB** mode and sharpen only the **Lightness** channel

I should point out that the best way to get sharp images is to use a high-quality, high-resolution digital camera with a sharp lens — then you usually still need to sharpen the image digitally. Although it would be nice, I am sad to report you can not sharpen an out-of-focus digital photo. In fact, when using the following sharpening techniques, you'll quickly realize that we are not really *sharpening* them at all. Instead, we are creating the illusion that they are sharp by digitally emphasizing "edges" in the image by making one side of an edge lighter and the other side darker.

As you soon discover, the illusion effect we use to make an image appear sharp is resolution dependent. This means that you should not apply sharpening effects to an image until you know what your final output will be. A sharpened high-resolution image won't have the optimal amount of sharpening if it is down-sized to be used as a low-resolution image on a Web page or vice-versa. Consequently, sharpening ought to be one of the last steps in your workflow. One other reason to leave sharpening as one of the last steps in your workflow is that the "sharpening effect" will likely be removed or damaged, if you first sharpen your image and then use a variety of other commands and filters.

USING UNSHARP MASK ON THE ENTIRE IMAGE

STEP 1: OPEN FILE

- Choose **File ➢ Open** (**Ctrl+O** PC, **Cmd+O** Mac) to display the **Open** dialog box. Double-click the **\11** folder to open it and then click the **goat-before.TIF** file to select it. Click **Open** to open the file.

A few minor adjustments have already been made to this image using **Curves** and **Hue/Saturation** to enhance the image so that this technique can be devoted to sharpening — a most important topic for digital photographers.

STEP 2: DUPLICATE LAYER

Before taking any steps to sharpen an image, first duplicate the layer. Not only does this duplicate layer make it easy for you to switch between "before sharpening" and "after sharpening" images so that you can view the differences, but it also allows you the option of "painting" back in some of the original image, or using a mask or selection to limit what is or isn't sharpened. Additionally, you can blend the **Background** layer with the sharpened layer by using one or more of the **Blend** modes to further improve the sharpness of the image.

- Choose **Layer ➢ Duplicate Layer** to get the **Duplicate Layer** dialog box. Type **Sharpened** in the **As** box and then click **OK**.

STEP 3: SET UP IMAGE VIEW

Any time you use the **Unsharp Mask**, view your image at **100%** to get an accurate view of the effects.

- Choose **View** ➢ **Actual Pixels** (**Alt**+**Ctrl**+**0** PC, **Option**+**Cmd**+**0** Mac).
- Press the **Spacebar** to get the **Hand** tool and click and drag the image until you can see the goat's face where the image is most sharply focused. This is the key area to watch as you apply effects.

STEP 4: APPLY UNSHARP MASK

Now we get to this seemingly misnamed filter — the **Unsharp Mask**. If you have never used the **Unsharp Mask** because you always want to sharpen an image when you select the **Sharpen** menu — not *un-sharpen* your image — you are not the first to *avoid* using one of the most valuable tools for *sharpening* images! The name comes from a pre-digital darkroom technique where a blurry version of a contact negative was layered with the original contact negative. The result of combining these two "layers" was a pronounced edge contrast, making the image appear to be sharper. As the **Unsharp Mask** works in the same way, it is appropriately named and it is the best tool for the job — period!

- Choose **Filter** ➢ **Sharpen** ➢ **Unsharp Mask** to get the **Unsharp Mask** dialog box shown in Figure 11.3.

The **Unsharp Mask** has the following three settings:

- **Amount:** This control determines how much the contrast increases in percentage terms ranging from **0%** to **500%**. This setting might also be considered as the *intensity* or *effect strength* setting.
- **Radius:** Measured in pixels, **Radius** determines how wide the "sharpening effect" is. You can choose a setting between **0** pixels and **250** pixels and even in parts of a pixel, which is important when you are using values under 5 pixels, which you do most of the time.

- **Threshold:** This control lets you set the starting point for when sharpening occurs. You can choose from **0** to **255** levels difference between two touching shades. When **Threshold** is set to **0**, everything gets sharpened. When **Threshold** is set to **255**, nothing gets sharpened. Using the optimal **Threshold** setting, you can usually prevent grain, scanner noise, or important image texture from being sharpened.

The **Unsharp Mask** is actually creating a halo effect around edges. It creates a lighter shade on one side of what it thinks is an edge, and a darker shade on the other side, thereby creating the illusion of a sharp edge. **Amount** determines how bright the halo is, **Radius** determines how wide the halo is, and

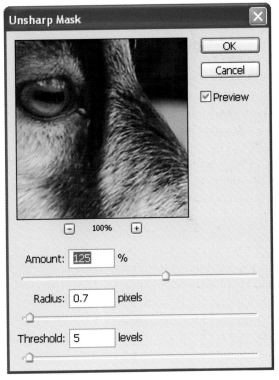

11.3

Threshold is the minimum shade difference required before a halo is created.

A good approach for getting optimal settings when working with high-resolution images is to set **Amount** to **175%**, **Radius** to **2**, and **Threshold** to **0**. Most high-resolution images require an **Amount** setting in the range of **150%** to **200%**. Generally, **Radius** values are less than **2.0** and each tenth of a pixel can be significant. Setting **Threshold** to **0** means that every edge gets sharpened and for now that is okay as it is the easiest setting to adjust after the other two settings are determined. The tricky part is determining the right combination of **Amount** and **Radius**.

- Set **Amount** to **175%**, **Radius** to **2**, and **Threshold** to **0**.
- Depending on the image, it may be better to define the edges with a narrower, but brighter halo. Other images may look better with a wider, but less bright halo. See what you think looks best for this one by sliding the **Amount** from **100%** to **200%** and lower **Radius** to around **.5** to **1.0**. These settings can dramatically alter how realistic the bristly hair on the goat looks. Sadly, in spite of how good you think the sharpening effect looks, the best way to determine the success of your settings if you are going to be making a print is to make a print. Once you get used to the settings that make good prints, you will be able to more accurately judge the settings you see on a computer screen.
- As you change settings, click the **Preview** box in the **Unsharp Mask** dialog box to view the image with and without the sharpening effect. Also, click inside the **Preview** box to get the **Hand** tool. Click and drag the image around to view areas where you want to make sure the settings work.
- As soon as you have a good combination of settings for **Amount** and **Radius**, look around the

image for an area where there is other fine texture. You can now slowly slide the **Threshold** slider toward the right until you remove the unwanted sharpening effect on the smoother areas.

- For this image, I set **Amount** to **125%**, **Radius** to **.7**, and **Threshold** to **0**. Any larger values for **Amount** and **Radius** seemed to more than double the width of the sharply focused hairs on the goat's neck. A quick print confirmed that these were pretty good settings.
- Click **OK** to apply the settings.
- Because you did all the sharpening in the **sharpened** layer, you can now click the **Layer Visibility** icon (the eye icon) in the left column of the **Layers** palette to view the difference between the original image and the sharpened image.
- If you want to reduce the effects, choose **Edit ➢ Fade Unsharp Mask** (**Shift+Ctrl+F** PC, **Shift+Cmd+F** Mac) to get the **Fade** dialog box shown in Figure 11.4. As you slide the **Opacity** slider toward the left, the sharpen effects fade. Besides using **Normal**, you should also try using the **Luminosity** blend mode.
- Click **Cancel** to cancel the **Fade** settings.

At this point, our dear old goat friend looks much better than he did before the **Unsharp Mask** was applied. In this example, we have applied the **Unsharp**

11.4

Mask to the entire image. Occasionally, you may work on an image where you don't want the entire image to be sharpened. Using the **Quick Mask**, a **Layer Mask**, or a selection tool of your choice, you can easily select and remove or even change the **Opacity** of the sharpened layer, leaving the unsharpened layer below as part of the viewable image.

Now that you have a good understanding of how to use the **Unsharp Mask**, here is one other approach to sharpening an image that is worth trying.

SHARPENING INDIVIDUAL CHANNELS

Some lower-end or older model digital cameras produce enough digital noise that it becomes difficult to sharpen an image without also sharpening and accentuating the unwanted noise, too. There are also images where it is hard to differentiate between important image texture or detail and the "edges" that you want to sharpen. In these and other cases, you want to take a look at each of the color channels to see if you can find one that holds most of the edges that you want to sharpen, but not much of the unnecessary detail. Typically, the lightest channel is the one that you want to sharpen, as it is also the one with the least amount of noise.

Some images have two channels that you may want to sharpen. If so, beware that applying different settings can cause some rather unusual things to happen. My suggestion is to use the same settings if you are going to sharpen two channels.

SHARPEN LIGHTNESS CHANNEL IN LAB MODE

Another sometimes useful approach to sharpening an image is to first convert the image to **Lab Color** mode by selecting **Image ➤ Mode ➤ Lab Color** mode. To view the **Channels** palette if it is not already showing, select **Window ➤ Channels**. The **Lab Color** mode allows you to separate the color information in an image from the black and white image information. When viewing an image that is in **Lab Color** mode, the **Channels** palette will show a **Lightness** channel, and an **a** and **b** channel, as you can see in Figure 11.5. As the **Lightness** channel only contains black and white image information it makes an excellent channel for applying the **Unsharp Mask** filter. Once you have applied the setting you want, you can change the mode back to **RGB** by selecting **Image ➤ Mode ➤ RGB Color**.

To learn more about image sharpening, read Technique 39.

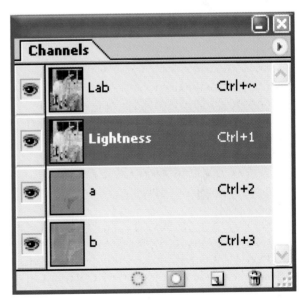

11.5

12

CORRECTING COLOR WHEN USING A GRETAGMACBETH COLORCHECKER

12.1

12.2

ABOUT THE IMAGE

Veritable Benedictine and Martel Cognac Canon EOS 1d mounted on a tripod, 70-200mm f/2.8 IS, ISO 200, f/9.0 @ 1/6, RAW setting, 2,160 x 1,440 pixels, edited and converted with Camera RAW to 266K 1,531 x 1,024 .jpg

When getting accurate color is essential and you know that requirement in advance, you should first take a photo that includes a GretagMacbeth ColorChecker Color Rendition Chart (see Figure 12.1) under similar lighting conditions as your final shots. Then, using Adobe Photoshop CS you can easily determine what setting adjustments you need to make to "color correct" the entire set of digital photos.

In this technique, you will learn how to use Adobe Photoshop CS's **Levels** command and the **Info** palette along with the GretagMacbeth ColorChecker to determine the **Levels** settings to be applied to the Benedictine and Cognac photo shown in Figure 12.3 to get excellent color, as shown in Figure 12.2.

STEP 1: OPEN FILE

- Select **File ➤ Open** (**Ctrl+O** PC, **Cmd+O** Mac) to display the **Open** dialog box. After locating the **\12** folder, double-click it to open it. Press **Shift** while clicking the **Macbeth-chart.tif** and **bottles-before.tif** images to select them both. Click **Open** to open both files in Adobe Camera RAW. Click **OK** to open both images using the default values.

> **NOTE**
>
> GretagMacbeth ColorChecker 8" x 11.4" charts are available at most professional photo stores. One good online source is www. bhphotovideo.com. The full-size chart costs around $70. There is also a smaller version, too.

12.3

STEP 2: CHECK COLOR

- It now appears that both of these images suffer from a blue color cast that needs to be removed. To learn more about the color cast, click the **Eyedropper** tool (**I**) in the **Toolbox**. In the **Options** bar, select **5 by 5 Average** as the **Sample size** to get a good average reading.
- If the **Info** palette is not already visible select **Window ➤ Info** (**F8**) to display the palette. To be able to easily read the tonal value in percentage grayscale, click the menu button in the **Info** palette and select **Palette Options** to get the **Info Options** dialog box. Click in the **Mode** box beneath **Second Color Readout** and choose **Grayscale**. Click **OK** to apply the settings. The **Info** palette will now show **RGB** values and a **K** value for grayscale ranging from **0%** as pure white and **100%** as pure black.
- Click once on the **Macbeth chart.jpg** image to make it the active image. Drag the **Eyedropper** tool over the white square, which is the bottom-left square in the chart. The **Info** palette will show you values similar to the ones shown in Figure 12.4. **R** (red) should be **246**, **G** (green) should be **252**, and **B** (blue) should be **255**. You may get slightly different values depending on the placement of the cursor. This means that there is much more green and blue in the image than there is red; hence, the color

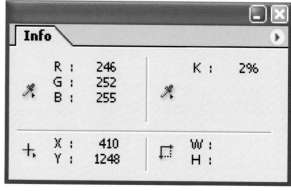

12.4

cast. The goal is to have the white square show equal values of red, green and blue.

STEP 3: SET COLOR SAMPLER POINTS

■ To be able to read "before" and "after" values in both the white and black areas of the image when using the **Levels** command, we need to set a **Color Sampler** point in both the black and white squares. To set a point in the white square, press **Shift** and click in the white square with the **Eyedropper** tool (**I**). To set a point in the black square, do the same — press **Shift** and click in the black square. Notice that you now have two **Color Sampler** points in the image: one in the white square and one in the black square.

■ Your **Info** palette should now look like the one shown in Figure 12.5. You now have two additional points: **#1** and **#2**.

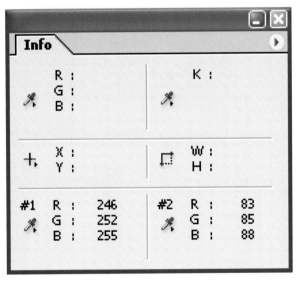

12.5

STEP 4: CORRECT COLOR USING LEVELS

■ We are now going to use the **Levels** command to remove the color cast. Select **Image ➢ Adjustment ➢ Levels** (**Ctrl+L** PC, **Cmd+L** Mac) to get the **Levels** dialog box.

■ Our objective is to set each of the **R**, **G**, and **B** values to be equal to the highest value in the white zone, and the lowest value in the black zone. Looking in the **Info** palette in the **#1** readings area, you will now find two values next to **R**, **G**, and **B**. These values are the before and after adjustment values. As these readings are for the white zone, we want to make adjustments with **Levels** to make the **R** value equal to **255**, the highest value, and **G** to also be equal to **255**.

■ To make the **R** value equal to **255**, click in the **Channel** box in the **Levels** dialog box and select **Red** (**Ctrl+1** PC, **Cmd+1** Mac). Click the **highlight slider** (the white slider; the white triangle slider just beneath the histogram on the far right. Drag the **highlight slider** toward the left until you see the second value following **R** in the **Info** palette reads **255**.

■ To make the **G** value equal to **255**, click in the **Channel** box in the **Levels** dialog box and select **Green** (**Ctrl+2** PC, **Cmd+2** Mac). Click the **highlight slider** and drag it toward the left until you see the second value following **G** in the **Info** palette reads **247** or very close. That completes the color corrections in the white zone.

■ We now need to do the same thing in the black zone, except this time we will be setting each value to be equal to the lowest value found in the black zone. Looking at the **Info** palette in the point **#2** area, you will find that the lowest value is now **83** in the red channel, whereas green is **85** and blue **88**.

■ To make the **G** value equal to **83**, click in the **Channel** box in the **Levels** dialog box and select **Green** (**Ctrl**+2 PC, **Cmd**+2 Mac). Click the **Shadow Slider** and drag it toward the right until you see that the second value following **G** in the **Info** palette reads **83** or very close. To make the **B** value equal to **83**, click in the **Channel** box in the **Levels** dialog box and select **Blue** (**Ctrl**+3 PC, **Cmd**+3 Mac). Click the **Shadow Slider** and drag it

WARNING

Using a GretagMacbeth ColorChecker Color Rendition Chart and Technique 12 is a quick and accurate way to remove color casts so that a photo accurately reflects the original colors. However, you may not always want to remove a color cast. If you intentionally shot a photo in early morning or late evening light, or in candlelight, or in other desirable lighting conditions — you will generally have a color cast. In these and other cases, such color casts may be desirable and you therefore will not want to correct the color as you will remove the colorcast while attempting to accurately reflect the original colors.

toward the right until you see that the second value following **G** in the **Info** palette reads **83** or very close. That completes the color corrections in the black zone.

■ Before closing the **Levels** dialog box, we will save these adjustment settings so that they can be easily applied to the photo with the two bottles to make a quick and accurate color correction. Click **Save** in the **Levels** dialog box to get the **Save** dialog box. Type **bottles** in the **File Name** box and click **Save**. The image now accurately reflects the color of the original scene. Click in the **Preview** box to see the difference between the "before" and "after" images. Click **OK** to apply the settings.

STEP 5: APPLY COLOR CORRECTION SETTINGS TO OTHER IMAGES

■ Click once on the **bottles-before.tif** image to make it the active image. Select **Image** ➢ **Adjustments** ➢ **Levels** (**Ctrl**+L PC, **Cmd**+L Mac) to get the **Levels** dialog box. Click **Load** and select the **bottles.alv** levels correction settings file that we created in Step 4; click **OK** to apply the settings. This image has now been color corrected. Figure 12.2 shows the results of making a few additional changes with **Levels** and **Curves** to increase tonal range and to brighten the image.

USING METADATA

13.1

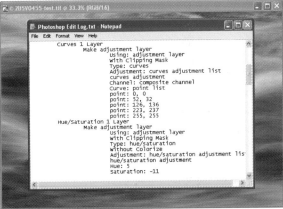

13.2

Swift River in White Mountain National Forest Canon EOS 1Ds mounted on a tripod, 200mm f/2.8 with 3-stop ND filter, ISO 100, f/22 @ 1 second, RAW setting, 4,064 x 2,704 pixels, 8.2MB .CRW

One of the luxuries of working with digital files is that there is a growing list of ways in which the image itself can be enhanced by textual content that is written into the image file itself, or saved in a separate but matched file in the same folder. While your initial reaction may be, "So what!" this technique will show you just a few ways in which you can read the shooting data and view, create, and edit metadata to make your digital photos even more valuable. Finally, you will learn how to have Adobe Photoshop CS document your edit steps for you in a textual file format.

STEP 1: LEARN HOW TO READ "SHOOTING" DATA

One of the most valuable features of digital cameras is that they write "shooting" data about each camera setting into each image file. If you are used to shooting with a film camera, you'll appreciate just how valuable it is to be able to take lots of pictures without making any notes about your camera settings, and then sit down in the comfort of your home or office and view each photo you've taken along with all the camera settings that were used for each of the photos! Adobe Photoshop CS provides you with three different ways to read the "shooting" data, which is technically called EXIF data. The easy way is to open Adobe Photoshop CS's **File Browser**. To do so, you can either select **Window ➤ File Browser**, or you can click the **File Browser** icon in the middle of the **Options** bar. Once the **File Browser** is open, you will find that it has four different windows. One window is the **Folders** window where you can find and open folders. Below the **Folders** window is the **Preview** window, which allows you to preview any image that you have selected in the **thumbnail** window. There is also a window that has tabs for **Metadata** and for **Keywords**. You can see all of these windows in Figure 13.3.

■ To view the **EXIF** data, click the **Camera Data (Exif)** arrow to expand the view. If you select the \13 folder and click the **swift-river.TIF** image, you will be able to read all the camera settings that Kunio Owaki used to take a picture of the Swift River in New Hampshire. A quick look shows that you can see the **Camera make**, **model**, **serial number**, **date,** and **time** the photo was taken, **shutter speed**, **aperture**, **ISO setting**, **focal length**, whether a **flash** was used or not, and much more. If you want to become a better photographer, reading and studying your photos while viewing the shooting data is an excellent way.

■ To tailor the list of information that you want to read (and to avoid having to view information you don't often want) click the menu button in the **Metadata** tab to get a pop-up menu; choose **Metadata Display Options** to get the **Metadata Display Options** dialog box shown in Figure 13.4. Here you can choose each of the different types of information that you want to read. Clicking the **Hide empty fields** box at the bottom of the dialog box makes the list even easier to read when you have empty fields. After choosing the information types you want, click **OK** to apply the settings.

■ Once you have selected a file in the **Thumbnail** window, you can also view **Metadata** specific to

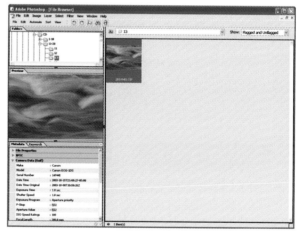

13.3

KUNIO OWAKI

Kunio Owaki has been a full-time stock photographer for more than 20 years. During most of those two decades, he shot with large- and medium-format film cameras. In 2003 he abandoned those trusty cameras and began exclusively shooting digital. Based in Connecticut, Kunio and his wife, Mary Ann Kulla, work as a team and market their work through Corbis, one of the premier stock photo agencies. Their images have been used in numerous national and international advertisements as well as dozens of leading print publications. To view their work, just search for "Owaki" at www.corbis.com.

that file by selecting **File ➢ File Information** (**Alt**+**Ctrl**+**I** PC, **Cmd**+**Option**+**I** Mac) to get a **File Information** dialog box similar to the one shown in Figure 13.5. In this window, you have the choice of all kinds of information including **Image Title**, **Author**, **Description**, **Keywords**, and much more.

■ Click the **Camera Data 1** item and you get the dialog box shown in Figure 13.6 where you can read and edit various kinds of information. Here you see the **EXIF** data for the selected image. Click **Cancel** to close the dialog box.

■ Any time you have an open image, you can click it to make it the active document and then select **File ➢ File Information** (**Alt**+**Ctrl**+**I** PC, **Cmd**+ **Option**+**I** Mac) to get a **File Information** dialog box similar to the one shown in Figure 13.5.

STEP 2: ADD METADATA TO A BATCH OF FILES

If you share your digital photos with others, if you post your images to a Web site, or you simply want to add textual information to your photos, you ought to

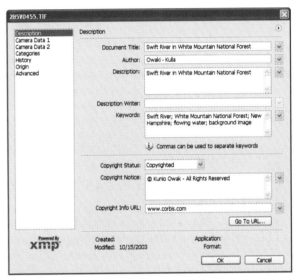

13.5

13.4

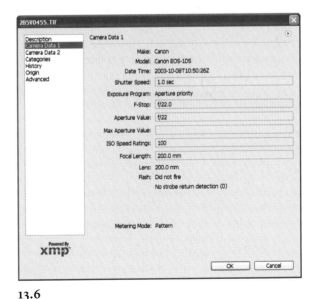

13.6

take a few minutes to learn how to add textual information to a batch of photos. Before you can apply textual information to a batch of photos you must first add the information to a single photo, and then save it as a template. To add the information to a batch of image files you must then apply that template to the batch using the **File Browser**.

- To add metadata to a file select **File ➢ File Info** (**Alt+Ctrl+I** PC, **Cmd+Option+I** Mac) from the **File Browser** menu. Select a category from the list and enter the desired data and click **OK**. Good examples of information that you may want to add to a batch include copyright information, keywords, or a description for the images.
- To save the metadata as a **template**, click the menu icon at the top of the **File Info** dialog box, and choose **Save Metadata Template**. Click **Save** after entering a template name.
- To write the metadata to a batch of files, first select the files using the **File Browser**. Choose **File ➢ File Info** (**Alt+Ctrl+I** PC, **Cmd+Option+I** Mac) from the **File Browser** menu and click the menu icon at the top of the **File Info** dialog box and choose the template from the pop-up box. The metadata will then replace the current metadata in all of the selected files. To append the current metadata instead, hold down **Ctrl** (PC) or **Cmd** (Mac) when you choose the template name.

STEP 3: SAVE AND VIEW EDIT HISTORY

After you begin editing digital photos, it won't take you very long to wish there was a way for Adobe Photoshop CS to document each edit step that you take. Sure, you can use the **History** palette to see what you've done as long as you have a document open;

but, you are in trouble if you need the edit history once you close a file. Now, Adobe Photoshop CS has a feature to document your edit steps. To use it, you just have to turn it on.

- To have Adobe Photoshop CS automatically document your edit steps, you must first turn the **History Log** on. To do so, select **Edit ➢ Preferences ➢ General** on the PC (**Ctrl+K**) or **Photoshop ➢ Preferences ➢ General** (**Cmd+K**) on the Mac to get the **General Preferences** dialog box shown in Figure 13.7.
- Click in the box next to **History Log** to turn the **History Log** on. You have a choice of logging the edit steps to the image files you edit, to a separate text file, or to both. If you want to write the edit steps to a separate text file, you will need to click **Choose** and choose a folder where you want the text file to be saved.
- Click in the **Edit Log Items** box and choose from **Sessions Only**, **Concise**, or **Detailed** logs. Once you've made your choices, click **OK** to apply the settings.

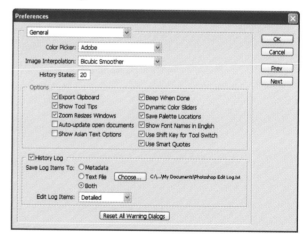

13.7

■ Once you have opened an image and have performed one or more edit steps, you can read a list of the steps by selecting **File ➢ File Information** (**Alt**+**Ctrl**+**I** PC, **Cmd**+**Option**+**I** Mac) to get a **File Information** dialog box. Click **History** to get a dialog box similar to the one shown in Figure 13.8. Or, if you chose to write the edit steps to a text file, you can open up the text file in a text editor to view the steps and specific settings. The **History**

WARNING

Remember to turn off the History Log when you no longer want to use it. Adding edit steps to an image file can increase the size of the file. You may also not want people such as clients to get your digital files with a History Log of the steps that you performed. It is best to keep History Log off, unless you know that you may need it.

Log is a wonderful feature if you want to edit artistically and without taking the time to make notes of your steps, but you on occasion need to have a detailed log of them.

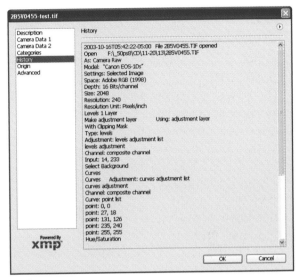

13.8

CHAPTER **3**

WORKING IN BLACK AND WHITE

If you shoot with a digital camera, you can make awesome black and white photographs. You have far more control over your black and white images when shooting in color and using an image editor to convert them into black and white images than you do shooting with film and using colored filters. Plus, fantastic new monochrome ink sets and revolutionary new inkjet printers are becoming available that produce excellent black and white prints with archival qualities and print characteristics that rival or exceed those of traditional chemical-based photographic prints. If you enjoy black and white photography, you'll enjoy this chapter.

The first technique gives you a good overview of several ways you can convert color images into black and white images with more control than was ever possible with all the clever "in-darkroom" techniques and different grades of paper that were used in the traditional darkroom. The next three techniques demonstrate how master photographer and printer Phil Bard produces his wonderful black and white prints. The technique that follows shows how Scott

Dingman tones photographs for his portfolio. The last technique provides a few tips you can use to add "punch" to your black and white photographs.

CONVERTING A COLOR PHOTO TO BLACK AND WHITE

14.1

14.2

Purple Iris Canon EOS D30 mounted on a tripod, 100mm macro f/2.8, ISO 100, RAW setting, $1/4$ @ f/14, 2,160 x 1,440 pixels, edited and converted to 8.9MB .tif

I f you shoot black and white film, you have a black and white photo. If you shoot with color film, or use a digital camera and shoot in color mode, you can have either color or excellent black and white images! In fact, you have so much more control over how your black and white images turn out when converting digitally with Adobe Photoshop CS that you may decide it is not worth shooting black and white film ever again.

There are at least seven basic approaches and many variations to convert a color image into a black and white image using Adobe Photoshop CS. They are as follows:

1. Convert image to black and white by converting image to a grayscale image by using **Image ➢ Mode ➢ Grayscale**. This is the easy way, but it usually produces the least desirable results.

2. Desaturate by using **Image ➢ Adjustments ➢ Desaturate (Shift+Ctrl+U PC, Shift+Cmd+U** Mac). Alternatively, you can use **Image ➢ Adjustments ➢ Hue/Saturation (Ctrl+U PC, Cmd+U** Mac) and slide the **Saturation** slider all the way to the left to a value of **0**. This approach is similar to the first approach in terms of control and results.

3. Use **Image ➢ Mode ➢ Lab Color** and use the **Lightness** channel as the black and white image. This approach is easy, straightforward and can produce excellent results depending on the colors and tones of the original image. We'll use this approach on an iris image a little later in this technique.

4. Choose one of the three channels (**Red**, **Green**, or **Blue**) to use as the black and white image. Often, one of these three channels will be just what you want. At other times, you'll want parts of each of the three channels — mixed. This approach is similar to shooting on black and white film through a color filter and it can lead to some unexpected and yet pleasing results.

5. Use **Image ➢ Adjustments ➢ Channel Mixer** and create your own mix of two or more of the channels. This approach gives you the most control and we'll look at it in detail later in this technique.

6. Select two or more channels; then combine them using **Image ➢ Calculations** by choosing a percentage of each of the three channels to be output to a gray channel.

7. Use a third-party Photoshop–compatible plug-in, such as The Image Factory's Convert to B&W Pro (www.theimagingfactory.com), which has been designed specifically to convert color images into black and white images. Whenever I convert color images to black and white, I almost always use Convert to B&W Pro as it gives you so much control over how the image looks. You will learn more about this plug-in in Technique 37.

CONVERTING COLOR TO BLACK AND WHITE USING LAB COLOR MODE AND THE LIGHTNESS CHANNEL

In this technique, you first use **Lab Color** mode and the **Lightness** channel to create a black and white image; then, you use the **Channel Mixer** and learn how to get even more control during the conversion process. Both of these approaches are well worth learning.

STEP 1: OPEN FILE

■ Choose **File ➢ Open (Ctrl+O PC, Cmd+O** Mac) to display the **Open** dialog box. Double-click the **\14** folder to open it and then click the **iris-before.tif** file to select it. Click **Open** to open the file.

STEP 2: CONVERT TO LAB COLOR

■ Choose **Image** ➢ **Mode** ➢ **Lab Color** to convert from **RGB** to **Lab Color** mode. **Lab Mode** is constructed according to how color actually exists and how our eyes perceive it — a magenta-green relationship, a yellow-blue relationship, and a lightness (or black-white) relationship.

■ Open the **Channels** palette if it is not already open by choosing **Window** ➢ **Channels**. The **Channels** palette should now look like the one shown in Figure 14.3. Notice that there is a **Lightness** channel — this channel represents how bright a color is and so it is an ideal channel to use alone for a black and white image.

14.3

STEP 3: CONVERT TO GRAYSCALE

■ Choose **Image** ➢ **Mode** ➢ **Grayscale**. If the warning box **Discard color information?** appears, click **OK** to convert the image to a grayscale by using the **Lightness** channel. Your image should now look like the one shown in Figure 14.2.

■ If you need an RGB image, convert it back to RGB by choosing **Image** ➢ **Mode** ➢ **RGB Color** — you will then have a black and white image in RGB mode.

CONVERTING COLOR TO BLACK AND WHITE USING CHANNEL MIXER

Now let's try another approach. This time you use the **Channel Mixer** to create a custom mix by choosing from each of the three channels to convert the color image into a black and white image. While this approach offers much more control than using the **Lightness** channel in **Lab Mode**, it can be time-consuming to try various combinations and permutations. If you frequently convert color images to black and white, you will likely want to use the **Lab Mode**, **Channel Mixer**, or the Convert to B&W Pro plug-in, which is covered in Technique 37.

STEP 1: OPEN FILE

■ Choose **File** ➢ **Open** (**Ctrl+O** PC, **Cmd+O** Mac) to display the **Open** dialog box. Double-click the **\14** folder to open it and then click the **iris-before.tif** file to select it. Click **Open** to open the file.

STEP 2: EXAMINE EACH CHANNEL

■ Choose **Window** ➤ **Channels** to display the **Channels** palette if it is not already displayed. The **Channels** palette should look like the one shown in Figure 14.4. Click the **Red** channel (**Ctrl+1** PC, **Cmd+1** Mac) in the **Channels** palette to view the red channel. Click the **Green** channel (**Ctrl+2** PC, **Cmd+2** Mac) and then the **Blue** channel (**Ctrl+3** PC, **Cmd+3** Mac) to view them. Figures 14.5 through 14.7 show each of these three channels. Note that you can tell what channel or channels are being viewed at any time by looking at the document title bar. The title bar also indicates whether the image is an 8- or 16-bit image.

Each of these three different channels shows an entirely different black and white version of the colored iris. Looking at these, you can now begin to understand how much control you have over how your final image looks — that is, if you learn how to mix the channels properly.

Incidentally, I should point out that if you like one of these versions, you are already done. Just click and drag the two channels that you don't want to use onto the trash icon at the bottom of the **Channels** palette. You are then left with a grayscale image.

14.4

14.5

You need an **RGB** image, convert it back to **RGB** by selecting **Image ➢ Mode ➢ Grayscale** and then **Image ➢ Mode ➢ RGB** Color. You will then have a black and white image in RGB mode.

STEP 3: USE CHANNEL MIXER TO MIX CHANNELS

I like the image found in the blue channel; it is a good high-contrast image that shows the detail in all parts of the flower. However, I like parts of the green channel as it shows some of the background. So for simplicity's sake and to match my preferences (yours will undoubtedly be different), combine just the blue and green channels and do not use any of the red channel.

- Click the **RGB** channel in the **Channels** palette to highlight all channels.
- Choose **Image ➢ Adjustments ➢ Channel Mixer** to get the **Channel Mixer** dialog box

14.6

14.7

shown in Figure 14.8. Click in the box next to
Preview (if it is not already checked) to turn
Preview on. Click in the box next to
Monochrome.

■ We don't want to use any of the **Red** channel, so
type **0** in the **%** box in the **Channel Mixer** dialog
box. Because the **Blue** channel offered provides
most of the desired details, slide the **Blue** slider to
70%. To avoid some strange effects, all three channels ought to total **100%**. Therefore, slide the
Green channel slider until it reads **30%**. If you
don't like these results, press **Alt** (**Option** on the
Mac) and the **Cancel** button will change to a **Reset**
button; click **Reset** and try again until you get
your desired results. Click **OK** and your image
should look like the one shown in Figure 14.9.

The differences between this mixed-channel version
and just the blue channel version are subtle, but we
have accomplished what we wanted. The **Channel
Mixer** offers incredible control over your image—
more than you would ever have in the darkroom or
when shooting black and white film and using
assorted color filters. The problem with using the
Channel Mixer is that it is difficult to compare various
mixes. If you are serious about black and white photography, I suggest that you consider using the Convert
to B&W Pro plug-in, covered in Technique 37.

14.8

14.9

BURNING AND DODGING WITH MASKS

15.1 © 2002 Phil Bard

15.2 © 2002 Phil Bard

I n the darkroom, black and white printers alter contrast and dodge and burn (lighten and darken) to improve the looks of their prints. Adobe Photoshop CS's **Adjustment Layers** and **Layer Masks** now make these techniques possible digitally with much more precision, control, and the flexibility to go back and make changes. Rather than making a permanent change to the image's pixel information, **Adjustment Layers** and **Layer Masks** are modifiable at any time after they are created. In this technique, you discover how Phil Bard, a master photographer and printer, uses **Adjustment Layers** and **Layer Masks** to enhance his photo of Kangtega in Nepal.

STEP 1: OPEN FILE

■ Choose **File ➢ Open** (**Ctrl+O** PC, **Cmd+O** Mac) to display the **Open** dialog box. Double-click the **\15** folder to open it and then click the **kangtega-before.tif** file to select it. Click **Open** to open the file.

The image file **kangtega-before.tif** is a low-resolution version of the 100MB grayscale file that Phil uses to print this image. Using a 4×5 camera and a high-quality scanner, he generally works with images around 8,000 x 10,000 pixels or larger. You might be wondering what kind of a computer he uses to work on images this large. In the next technique, you learn his trick for editing large images quickly.

STEP 2: DUPLICATE LAYER

Working on a duplicate layer and keeping the background in its original state makes it possible to quickly compare the differences between the original with the edited image by simply turning layers on and off in **Layers** palette.

■ Choose **Layer ➢ Duplicate Layer** to get the **Duplicate Layer** dialog box; click **OK** to create a **Background copy** layer.

STEP 3: ADJUST SHADOWED FOREGROUND

In this and the next two steps, we selectively apply different adjustments to the shadowed foreground, sky, and snowy peaks.

■ To select the shadowed foreground areas, click the **Lasso** tool (**L**) in the **Toolbox**.
■ Using the **Lasso** tool, click the mountains and drag around them to create a selection like the one shown in Figure 15.3. Selecting the shadowed

15.3

PHIL BARD

Phil Bard is a master black and white photographer and printer with over 30 years of darkroom experience. While he still shoots mostly with large format film cameras and black and white film, he is a leader in developing and using a digital workflow. His work includes some of the most outstanding black and white digital prints that can be found anywhere. His silver gelatin and digital fine prints are collected in both private and corporate collections internationally. His Web site, www.philbard.com, offers portfolios of his images, lots of useful links, techniques, and information about his workshops, which are well-worth attending. Besides having a client list full of prestigious accounts, he has also been published in dozens of magazines including *Life, Time, Newsweek,* and *People.* In 1987, Phil was presented with

foreground precisely is not critical, as we will later soften the selection and make adjustments to the selection where they are needed.

■ Choose **Select ➢ Feather** (**Alt+Ctrl+D** PC, **Opt+Cmd+D** Mac) to get the **Feather Selection** dialog box shown in Figure 15.4. Type **2** in the **Feather Radius** box and click **OK**.

To save this selection, select **Select ➢ Save Selection** to get the **Save Selection** dialog box. Type **shadowed foreground** in the **Name** box and click **OK**.

■ To view the actual feathered selection, click the **Quick Mask** mode (**Q**) button at the bottom of the **Toolbox**. You can make any necessary adjustments to the selected area by using the **Brush** tool (**B**). Again, don't worry about the selection line

between the two mountain ranges; just fix the shadowed foreground area if it is needed. Click the **Standard Mask** mode (**Q**) button at the bottom of the **Toolbox** to turn off the mask.

■ Choose **Layer ➢ New Adjustment Layer ➢ Levels** to get the **New Layer** dialog box shown in Figure 15.5. Type **shadowed foreground** in the **Name** box and click **OK** to get the **Levels** dialog box shown in Figure 15.6.

Set the **Input Levels** boxes to **0**, **.83**, and **105**. Click **OK** to both lighten and add some highlights to the foreground. Because you had an active selection when you chose **New Adjustment Layer**, the selection was automatically used to create the mask for the **Adjustment Layer** to determine which parts of the image the layer affects.

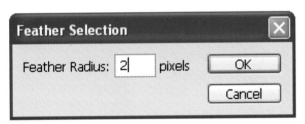

15.4

The "Leica Medal of Excellence," given "In Recognition of Outstanding Photographic Work and Achievement." He resides in Portland, Oregon where he teaches digital imaging at the Pacific Northwest College of Art and runs a digital printing business, Cirrus Digital Images, which specializes in output to the fine art community. Its website is www.cirrus-digital.com.

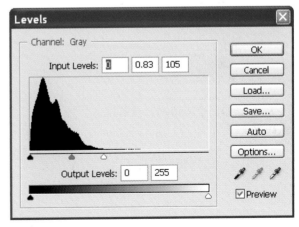

15.5

15.6

■ Your **Layers** palette should now look like the one shown in Figure 15.7.

The feathered selection that was used to create the **Layer Mask** causes a slight "glowing" effect just above the foreground range, and it needs to be removed. The great news is that removing the glow is easy to do because a **Layer Mask** was used.

■ Click the **Brush** tool (**B**) in the **Toolbox**. Click the **Brush Preset Picker** in the **Options** bar to get the **Brush** palette shown in Figure 15.8. Click the **Soft Round 65 Pixels** brush. If the **Brush** palette does not look like the one in Figure 15.8, click the menu button in the upper-right corner of the **Brush** palette to get a pop-up menu. Choose **Reset Brushes**; then click **OK**. You may also need to change the display format of the palette by once again clicking on the menu button in the upper-right corner of the **Brush** palette and choosing **Small Thumbnail**.

In the **Options** bar, set **Mode** to **Normal**, **Opacity** to **20%**, and **Flow** to **100%**.

Set **Foreground** color to **Black** by typing **D**.

You can now carefully brush over the white halo above the lower mountain range to remove the halo effect caused by the feathered selection. You may notice that your painting darkens the image. This is because you are now painting on the mask, affecting the area it covers and, correspondingly, the area that the **Adjustment Layer** influences in the image below. If you overdo the painting, select **White** as the **Foreground** color, and paint with the **Brush** tool to re-paint the mask. Should you want to change the **Levels** settings that were used, simply click the **Levels** adjustment layer in the **Layers** palette and change settings.

■ Now let's add some contrast control to the same foreground area. Click on the **Background copy** layer in the **Layers** palette to make it the active layer.

■ Choose **Select** ➤ **Load Selection** to get the **Load Selection** dialog box. Click in the **Channel** box and select **shadowed foreground**; click **OK** to reload the previous selection. The selection marquee now reappears indicating that the unmasked area is once again selected.

■ Choose **Layer** ➤ **New Adjustment Layer** ➤ **Curves** and click **OK** to get the **Curves** dialog box.

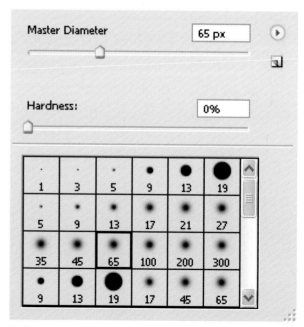

15.7

15.8

Set points on the **Curve**, as shown in Figure 15.9. To display a ten by ten grid instead of the normal four by four grid, press **Alt** (**Option** on the Mac) while clicking in the curved dialog box. You can now set each of the points by clicking the curve and dragging them to where they should be. Or, you can click to set a point and type in the **Input** and **Output** values for each of the three points, which are: **32** and **22**, **56** and **55**, and **80** and **86**. Click **OK** to apply the settings.

With this curve, you are expanding the midtone contrast while slightly compressing the highlights and shadows. As before, the effect is governed by a **Layer Mask**, which is resident to the layer and was created from the loaded selection of the previous layer. You now have separate **Levels** and **Curves** controls for the same foreground region, allowing you to do extremely precise fine-tuning at any time.

■ To darken the thin strip of light-toned gravel on the left hillside, use the **Brush** tool set to **Black** to add mask density to the **Curves 1** layer, which flattens out the gravel tonalities nicely.

STEP 4: ADJUST SNOWY PEAKS AND SKY

Now you are ready to work on the remaining portions of the image: the snowy peaks and the sky. Because you want to work in the areas not governed by the first two **Adjustment Layers**, you load the original selection first and invert it.

■ With the **Background copy** layer in the **Layers** palette highlighted, choose **Select** ➢ **Load Selection** to get the **Load Selection** dialog box. Click in the **Channel** box and select **shadowed foreground**. Make sure to check the **Invert** box and then click **OK**.

A marquee appears around the peaks and sky, and if you retouched the light gravel area, you notice it is selected as well. Deselect the gravel area if you retouched it by selecting the **Lasso** tool (**L**). Press **Alt** (**Option** on the Mac) and draw a marquee around the selected gravel area.

■ Choose **Layer** ➢ **New Adjustment Layer** ➢ **Levels** to get the **New Layer** dialog box. Click **OK** to get the **Levels** dialog box. Set the **Input Levels** to **4**, **1.14**, and **240**. The **Levels** dialog box should now look like the one shown in Figure 15.10. Click **OK** to apply the settings. This produces better contrast and lightens the area a little.

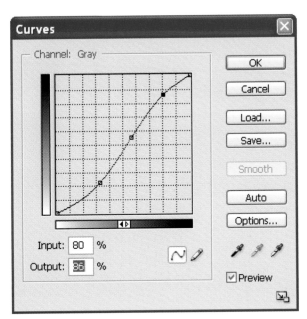

15.9

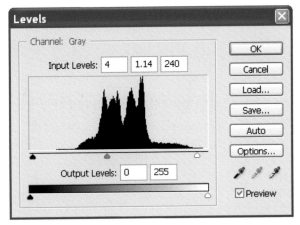

15.10

- Choose **Select** ➢ **Reselect** (**Shift+Ctrl+D** PC, **Shift+Cmd+D** Mac) to reselect the peaks and the sky.
- Choose **Layer** ➢ **New Adjustment Layer** ➢ **Curves** and click **OK** to get the **Curves** dialog box. Set three points on the curve, as shown in Figure 15.11. If you find it easier to type the values in, the three points are: **22** and **15**, **46** and **51**, and **65** and **84**.
- Click **OK** and take a look at your work so far. If the last **Layer Mask** is causing the tops of the foreground hills to look too dark, add some mask density there with the **Brush** tool (**B**). Also feel free to make changes to the other **Adjustment Layers** or **Layer Masks** you have created so far.

STEP 5: DARKEN SKY

- To darken the sky slightly, click the **Curves 2** layer in the **Layers** palette to make it the active layer. Using the **Lasso** tool (**L**), carefully draw a selection marquee, as shown in Figure 15.12. On the left side of the image, drop down into the cloud a small amount. Make sure you select the entire sky, extending all the way to the top of the image.
- Choose **Select** ➢ **Feather** (**Alt+Ctrl+D** PC, **Opt+Cmd+D** Mac) to get the **Feather** dialog box. In the **Feather Radius** box, type **10**, and then click **OK**.
- Choose **Layer** ➢ **New Adjustment Layer** ➢ **Levels** to get the **New Layer** dialog box. Click **OK** to get the **Levels** dialog box. Set **Input Levels** to **0**, **.73**, and **255**. The sky now darkens slightly adding drama to the peaks, which is balanced to the rest of the image.

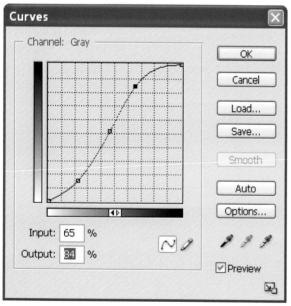

15.11

15.12

One further refinement you can make is a **Levels Adjustment Layer** for the stream in the foreground. In order to place this layer just above the **Levels 1** and **Curves 1** layer, highlight the **Curves 1** layer, and then draw a marquee around the stream and create the new **Adjustment Layer**. The only **Levels** change needed is to drag the middle-tone pointer to the left a bit, thereby lightening the water. Remember that you may go back and make changes to any of these layers at any time, or you can turn any or all of them off if so desired.

When employing this technique on your own images, keep in mind that the layers add together from the bottom up to create changes in the rendering of the tonal range. For the best efficiency, try to avoid overlapping layers of the same type. This is especially true if one layer darkens image pixels and the other lightens. Also, when working with lower resolution scans that have areas of even gradations (open skies, smooth surfaces) avoid making radical changes with the **Levels** or **Curves** tool sthat affect these areas or posterization of the values may result. This technique is applicable to color images as well, and with a little practice you will quickly be achieving professional results in all of your photographs.

USING SCALING MASKS TO SPEED UP EDITS

16.1   © 2002 Phil Bard

16.2   © 2002 Phil Bard

ABOUT THE IMAGE

Birches Along the Kevo River KB Canham 4×5 field camera mounted on tripod, 120mm lens with red filter, Kodak TMax 100, ¹/₂ @ f/22, scanned (wet) on a ScanView drum scanner yielding 100MB grayscale file, down-sampled to 2,400 x 1,920 pixel 4.4MB grayscale .tif

Large image files, multiple layers, slow computer processors, minimal RAM, or extensive edits can all make the editing process painfully slow and time-consuming. If you employ the use of **Adjustment Layers** for making changes (as in Technique 15), this technique by Phil Bard can be an incredible timesaver. This is especially true if you work on files that start off as 100MB or larger files and grow to 300MB or more after six or eight layers are added, as is the norm for Phil.

In this technique, you use a relatively low-resolution image of one of Phil's photographs that he took of birch trees along the Kevo River in Lapland, Finland. Even though this small 4.4MB grayscale file is not likely to test your patience or stress your computer, it will illustrate the technique, which can be used with any size of image.

STEP 1: OPEN FILE

■ Choose **File** ➢ **Open** (**Ctrl+O** PC, **Cmd+O** Mac) to display the **Open** dialog box. Double-click the **\16** folder to open it and then click the **birches-before.tif** file to select it. Click **Open** to open the file.

STEP 2: REDUCE IMAGE SIZE AND SAVE FILE

■ Choose **Image** ➢ **Image Size** to get the **Image Size** dialog box shown in Figure 16.3. Make sure that **Constrain Proportions** and **Resample Image** are both checked and that **Resample Image** is set to **Bicubic Sharper**. In the **Pixel Dimensions** area, change **Width** from **2400** to **500**. Notice that the image size went down from **4.39MB** to **195K**. Click **OK** to resize the image.

An important step at this point is to save the file. If you do not save the file, you won't be able to scale it and apply the masks to the original image after editing is complete.

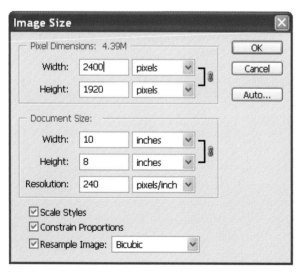

16.3

■ Choose **File** ➢ **Save As** (**Shift+Ctrl+S** PC, **Opt+Cmd+S** Mac) to get the **Save As** dialog box. Type **small-birch** in the **File Name** box. Click in the **Format** box and select **Photoshop (.psd)** as the **Format** type. Then click **Save** to save the file.

STEP 3: INCREASE CONTRAST IN THE WATER PART OF THE IMAGE

■ To select the area containing water, click the **Lasso** tool (**L**) in the **Toolbox**. Click in the image and drag the selection marquee around the water, as shown in Figure 16.4.
■ To feather the selection, choose **Select** ➢ **Feather** (**Alt+Ctrl+D** PC, **Opt+Cmd+D** Mac) to get the **Feather** dialog box. Type **20** into the **Feather Radius** box and click **OK**.
■ Next you must create an **Adjustment Layer** for this selection only. To do so, choose **Layer** ➢ **New Adjustment Layer** ➢ **Curves** to get the **New Layer** dialog box. Click **OK** to get the **Curves** dialog box.
■ Click the bottom part of the line in the **Curves** dialog box to set a point. Type **27** and **18** in the

16.4

Input and Output boxes respectively to adjust the point. Click the upper part of the line to set a second point and then type **75** and **82** in the **Input** and **Output** boxes respectively. The **Curves** dialog box should now look like the one shown in Figure 16.5. Click **OK** to apply the settings and increase contrast in the river area.

STEP 4: INCREASE CONTRAST IN TREE AREA

■ To select the part of the image that was not previously selected, choose **Select** ➢ **Load Selection** to get the **Load Selection** dialog box shown in Figure 16.6. Click in the box next to **Invert** to place a checkmark and to invert the previous selection. Click **OK**. As the previous selection was feathered, there is no reason to feather it now.

■ Choose **Layer** ➢ **New Adjustment Layer** ➢ **Curves** to get the **New Layer** dialog box. Click **OK** to get the **Curves** dialog box.

Once again the slope needs to be increased, but it needs more slope than last time so set two points on the curve at **31**, **18** and **72**, **81**. Click **OK** to apply the settings.

STEP 5: LIGHTEN THE BIRCH TREES

To lighten the birch trees, first select them and then make one last **Adjustment Layer**.

■ Using the **Lasso** tool (**L**), click in the image and select the birch trees only, as shown in Figure 16.7.

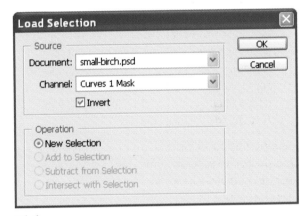

16.6

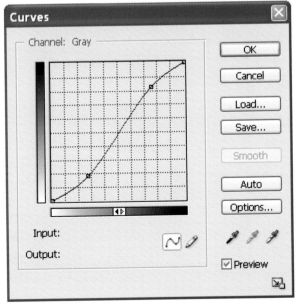

16.5

16.7

■ To feather the selection, choose **Select** ➢ **Feather** (**Alt+Ctrl+D** PC, **Opt+Cmd+D** Mac) to get the **Feather** dialog box. Type **30** into the **Feather Radius** box and click **OK**.

■ Choose **Layer** ➢ **New Adjustment Layer** ➢ **Levels** to get the **New Layer** dialog box. Click **OK** to get the **Levels** dialog box. Drag the **Highlight** slider (the far-right slider) toward the left until it just begins to touch the points on the histogram (about 225), as shown in Figure 16.8. If you were to move the slider any further you would burn out the highlights in the trees. Click **OK** to apply the settings and create a new layer.

STEP 6: INCREASE IMAGE SIZE AND APPLY MASKS TO ORIGINAL IMAGE

In the last step, you finished all of the edits that are to be done to the smaller image. Now, the objective is to scale the masks back up to the size of the original image, and then transfer them to the original image along with the edits. In doing this, you only have to wait one time to have all the edits applied at once to the larger image.

■ Make the **Layers** palette big enough so that you can see all of the layers.

■ Click the topmost layer to highlight it if it is not already highlighted. Then click the **Link** box next to each of the two next layers below the top layer. The **Layers** palette should now look like the one shown in Figure 16.9. Do not link the background!

■ Click the **Menu** button in the upper-corner of the **Layers** palette to get a pop-up menu. Choose **New Set From Linked** to get the **New Set From Linked** dialog box. Type **masks** in the **Name** box and then click **OK**. If you click the small triangle to the left of the **masks** folder icon that you just created in the **Layers** palette, the folder will open to show all of the **Adjustment Layers** you just created. The **Layers** palette should now look like the one shown in Figure 16.10.

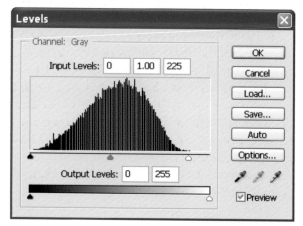

16.8

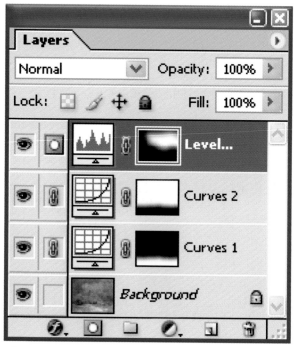

16.9

■ Now reopen the original **birch-before.tif** image. Choose **Image** ➢ **Size** to get the exact pixel dimensions if you forgot them. You find that it shows a **Width** of **2400** pixels and a **Height** of **1920** pixels. Click **Cancel** to close the dialog box.

■ Click the **small-birch.psd** image to make it the active image. Choose **Image** ➢ **Size** to get the **Image Size** dialog box. Type **2400** in the **Width** box and if the **Constrain Proportions** box is checked, Adobe Photoshop CS will automatically place **1920** in the **Height** box in the **Pixel Dimensions** area. Click **OK**. Adobe Photoshop CS now increases the image size but, more importantly, it also increases the size of the masks to be the exact same size as the original image.

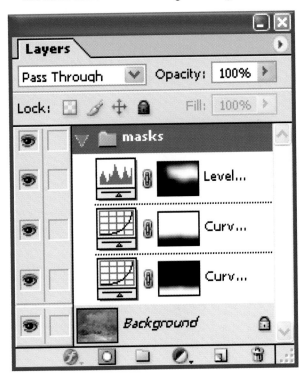

16.10

■ Rearrange and size both images so that you can see both of them in your workspace. Then, click the **small-birch.psd** image to make sure it is the active image.

■ While holding the **Shift** key, drag the **masks** folder icon from the **Layers** palette onto the original **birch-before.tif** image. You must press and hold **Shift** while dragging the **masks** folder to perfectly align the masks from the small **small-birch.psd** image to the large **birch-before.tif** image.

You have now applied the masks from the smaller image to the larger original image. All your edits should now be present in the **birch-before.tif** image and it should now look like the image shown in Figure 16.2. You can continue to work in the large scale image if it needs further editing. Or, you can once again scale it down and transfer it up again; however, be careful not to duplicate layers if you do this.

While this small sample image probably has not pushed the limits of your hardware or your patience, you may find you have to edit a large image, and for that this technique is a real timesaver. You should avoid downsizing your working image too far, however, as there is a point at which the masks will show some loss of shape, particularly if you have one that closely follows a shape and it is not feathered. Dropping to half or one-third of the pixel dimensions is usually safe enough. You could always use this method for the simple "area" masks first, and then create any precision masks in the full size image after the other ones are transferred to it, thereby still saving you considerable time.

To learn more about Phil Bard and his work, read his profile in Technique 15.

ISOLATING AND EXTRACTING DETAIL USING VALUES

17.1   © 2002 Phil Bard

17.2   © 2002 Phil Bard

Cottonwood on the Merced River in Spring Linhof Monorail camera mounted on a tripod, 210mm lens with yellow filter, Kodak PlusX, 10 seconds at f/16, scanned (wet) on a ScanView drum scanner yielding 100MB file, downsampled to 2,400 x 1,920 pixels, 4.4MB grayscale .tif

Phil Bard shot the photo shown in Figure 17.1 in 1986 in Yosemite Valley, California. This image is the result of several contrast manipulations of the original scan, and is basically "finished" except for the fact that, to Phil, the foreground tree details lack sufficient brightness. He wanted them to stand out a little more from their darker background. Selecting the general area of the tree and performing a **Levels** or **Curves** adjustment would be one way to achieve this, but that would also lighten the midtone areas of the background somewhat as well. Instead, he chose a more surgical approach, one that affects only the tree. In this technique, you discover how Phil was able to "extract" the tree based on its "value." In other words, a specific range of tones is selected based on their location in the histogram.

Adobe Photoshop CS **Layer Masks** and **Adjustment Layers** have many applications, one of the less obvious being the ability to extract image information with respect to value. This is a useful technique for mimicking a darkroom technique called "bleaching," in which highlights are lightened without significant effect to the midtones and shadows.

STEP 1: OPEN FILE

- Choose **File ➢ Open** (**Ctrl+O** PC, **Cmd+O** Mac) to display the **Open** dialog box. Double-click the **\17** folder to open it and then click the **cottonwood-before.tif** file to select it. Click **Open** to open the file.

STEP 2: SELECT LIGHTEST PARTS OF THE IMAGE BY VALUE

- If the **Channels** palette is not visible, choose **Window ➢ Channels**. In the **Channels** palette, click the **Load Channel as Selection** button (the left-most button), located at the bottom of the **Channels** palette. This creates a graduated selection of the entire image based on value, with the lightest details being most selected (least masked) and the darkest, least selected (most masked).

If you want to use this technique on RGB or CMYK images, you will need to select the channel or channels you want to load as the selection. The image used in this technique is a grayscale image and there is only a single channel to load.

- Click the **Quick Mask Mode** button (**Q**) in the **Toolbox**, which will create a mask from the selection. Your image should now look like the one shown in Figure 17.3.

- Hide the **Gray** channel by clicking the eye icon (to switch it off) in the **Gray** layer in the **Channels** palette so that you can better view the mask. Notice that the mask is now thinnest (lightest) over the highlight areas. Remember that you are looking at a black and white mask, not the black and white image.

To get an even clearer view of the mask's gradation, increase the image to **100%** by choosing **View ➢ Actual Pixels** (**Ctrl+Alt+0** PC, **Opt+Cmd+0** Mac). Choose **View ➢ Fit on Screen** (**Ctrl+0** PC, **Cmd+0** Mac) to fit the image on the screen.

17.3

STEP 3: REDUCE SELECTION TO JUST THE COTTONWOOD TREE

■ Because we want to further reduce the selection so that we can make changes only to the Cottonwood tree, edit the mask further. Click the **Quick Mask** channel in the **Channels** palette to select it if it is not already highlighted.

■ Choose **Image ➢ Adjustments ➢ Curves** (**Ctrl+M** PC, **Cmd+M** Mac) to get the **Curves** dialog box.

■ In the **Curves** dialog box, drag the curve into the shape illustrated in Figure 17.4.

To make the **Curves** dialog box show a 10 x 10 grid instead of a 4 x 4 grid, press **Alt** (**Opt** on the Mac) while clicking inside the curve box.

Set the lower end-point so that the **Input** and **Output** values are **50%** and **0%** respectively.

Set the upper end-point so that the **Input** and **Output** values are **75%** and **100%** respectively.

Click **OK** to apply the settings.

This **Curves** adjustment increases the density of the mask in the highlight areas, while eliminating the shadow and some of the midtones, which helps to isolate the tree itself. This is a crucial adjustment that must be done to make this technique work.

■ Click the **Lasso** tool to draw a selection around the Cottonwood tree on the left of the image as carefully as you can, excluding the water and rocks where possible. Absolute precision is not necessary, but make sure you include all of the tree branches.

■ Choose **Select ➢ Inverse** (**Shift+Ctrl+I** PC, **Shift+Cmd+I** Mac). Make sure that the background color is set to **Black**. This is very important! Press the **Delete** key. This eliminates the non-tree areas from the mask. Your image should now look similar to the one shown in Figure 17.5.

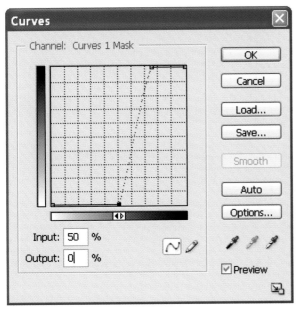

17.4

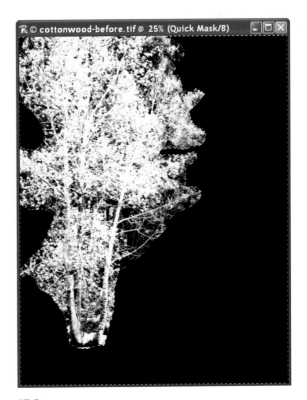

17.5

■ Choose **Select ➢ Deselect** (**Ctrl+D** PC, **Cmd+D** Mac) to remove the selection marquee.

■ Click the **Eraser** tool (**E**) in the **Tool** palette. In the **Options** bar, set **Mode** to **Brush**, **Opacity** to **100%**, and **Flow** to **100%**. Using the **Eraser** tool, erase any of the detail you want, while leaving only the tree. This means that you should be erasing areas where there are large amounts of black. Be careful not to use too large a **Brush** and erase important detail. To do this, you may want to vary the size of the **Eraser** tool from **35** pixels to **100** pixels by clicking the **Brush Preset Picker** on the **Options** bar.

■ Now we are ready to apply the mask. In the **Channels** palette, click the **Gray** layer and then click the **Standard Mode** button in the **Toolbox**. Notice that a marquee appears indicating that the mask has now become a selection.

■ Choose **Layer ➢ New Adjustment Layer ➢ Curves** to get the **New Layer** dialog box. Click **OK** to get the **Curves** dialog box. Click the curve in the **Curves** dialog box to set a point at **34** and **24**. Click the curve again to set a second point at **80** and **85**. The **Curves** dialog box should now look like the one shown in Figure 17.6.

■ Click **OK** to apply the settings. This curve increases the contrast of the layer, which makes the Cottonwood tree stand out from the other trees, as shown in Figure 17.2.

If you uncheck and recheck the eye icon in the **Curves 1** layer in the **Layers** palette, you can view the results of this new **Adjustment Layer**. Of importance is the fact that any changes made to this curve apply only to the tree, which has been "extracted," so to speak. Remember that, because this is an **Adjustment Layer**, you can always go back and edit its effect. And

because the **Layer Mask** you just made resides in this layer, you are able to load it as a selection and add more **Adjustment Layers** if you want.

This useful technique is applicable in many ways beyond what we have explored here. By inverting the color of the mask (during editing in **Quick Mask** mode), it can be used to select shadow areas and therefore increase or decrease their local contrast. Another approach you may want to try to get a similar effect is to duplicate the **Background** layer, and then set the **Blend** mode of the new layer to a lightening mode and use the **Blend If** sliders. This would create the same results; however, it would not be limited to just a masked area.

To learn more about Phil Bard and his work, read his profile at the end of Technique 15.

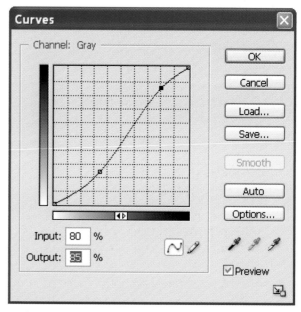

17.6

CREATING A TONED IMAGE

18.1

18.2

Boys Playing Leapfrog
Contax 645 AS, 120mm Macro f/4.0, Kodak Plus-X, four different images have been digitally combined, film was scanned with an Isomet 455 scanner, image reduced to 1,920 x 2,400 pixels, 13.2MB .tif

An example of Scott Dingman's photography, which has been digitally altered with Photoshop by Tammy Kennedy, a digital imaging freelancer, is shown in Figure 18.2. This image showing two boys playing leapfrog was made from four separate images: one of the boys, one for the sky, and one for each of the trees or bushes on either side of the image.

When viewing this image and other images in Scott's portfolio, you become aware of a very distinct and captivating style. He is excellent at capturing his subject's personality and presenting it in a photograph. Most of his images have been shot or digitally edited to draw the viewer in toward the subject. To create consistency between many of his black and white photos in his portfolio, he tones them with his own customized duotone. In this technique, you read how Scott tones many of his black and white portfolio images.

STEP 1: OPEN FILE

■ Choose **File ➤ Open** (**Ctrl+O** PC, **Cmd+O** Mac) to display the **Open** dialog box. Double-click the **\18** folder to open it and then click **leapfrog-before.tif** to select it. Click **Open** to open the file.

STEP 2: CONVERT TO DUOTONE

■ As you cannot directly convert an **RGB** image into a **Duotone** directly, choose **Image ➤ Mode ➤ Grayscale** to first change the image to grayscale. Click **OK** if you get a dialog box asking, "**Discard Color Information?**" Then choose **Image ➤ Mode ➤ Duotone** to get the **Duotone Options** dialog box, which should look similar to the one shown in Figure 18.3. Click in the **Type** box and select **Duotone**.

■ To select the first color, click the color sample box for **Ink 1** to get the **Color Picker** dialog box shown in Figure 18.4. To set **black** as the first color, type **0** in the boxes next to **R, G,** and **B**;

alternatively, you can click in the **Color Picker** box and drag the selection marker all the way to the extreme bottom-right or bottom-left — then the

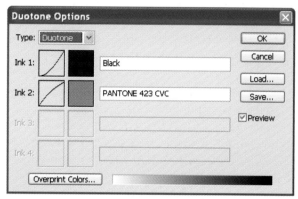

18.3

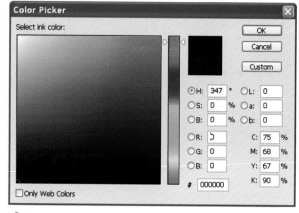

18.4

SCOTT DINGMAN

Scott Dingman is an advertising photographer who specializes in photographing people both on location and in the studio. A graduate of Rochester Institute of Technology, Scott has a BFA in commercial photographic illustration and an exceptional talent for discovering the personality of his subjects and portraying it in unique ways in a photograph. He has a growing list of prestigious clients that include Blue Cross-Blue Shield, Fast Company, Progress Energy, Duke University, Eastman-Kodak, Ericsson, Interpath Communication, Nortel, Siemens, Sprint, and Vector Group. Scott's Web page is www.scottdingman.com.

values of **R**, **G**, and **B** are all set to **0**. Click **OK** to set the color and return to the **Duotone Options** dialog box.

■ Click in the **Color Sample** box for **Ink 2** to get the **Custom Colors** dialog box. If you get the **Color Picker** dialog box instead, click the **Custom** button to get the **Custom Colors** dialog box shown in Figure 18.5.

Now select the **Pantone** color Scott has chosen for his portfolio prints. First, make sure that the **Pantone solid coated** color book is open. If another book is showing, click in the **Book** field and select **Pantone solid coated**. The color you want is **Pantone 728 C**, so click one of the horizontal colors on the left side of the dialog box and type **7** to view the colors starting with a **7**. Scroll down by clicking the down arrow at the bottom of the color spectrum in the middle of the dialog box until you see **Pantone 728 C**; click it to select it. Click **OK** to select the color and return to the **Duotone Options** dialog box.

■ To create more contrast and darker brown colors, Scott modified the **Duotone Curve** for both of the selected colors. Click in the **Curves** box for **Ink 1** to get the **Duotone Curve** dialog box shown in Figure 18.6. Type **50** in the **30** box and then click **OK** to return to the **Duotone Options** dialog box.

Do the same for the **Pantone 728 C** color; click in the **Curves** box for **Ink 2** to once again get the **Duotone Curve** dialog box. Type **70** in the **50** box and click **OK** to return to the **Duotone Options** dialog box.

■ Click **OK** to apply the **Duotone**.

■ To convert the image back to an RGB file, choose **Image** ➢ **Mode** ➢ **RGB Color**. The image now looks like the one shown in Figure 18.2.

You have many issues to consider when using duotones, especially when manually adjusting duotone inks, which is a complex science. That is one of the reasons that Adobe provides so many preset curves for duotones, tritones, and quadtones settings. If you want to learn more about creating and using duotones, I highly recommend *Professional Photoshop — The Classic Guide to Color Correction*, by Dan Margulis.

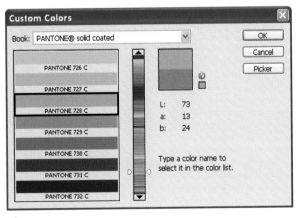

18.5

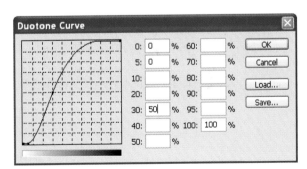

18.6

TAMMY KENNEDY

Tammy Kennedy, The Retouching Fairy Godmother, is a freelance graphic artist who specializes in photo editing. Besides working directly for clients, she has become the photo-retouching expert of choice for many photographers who need some editing magic performed on their images. As she is a highly organized expert in working with layers, her work may be easily adjusted at any time throughout the design process. Tammy uses a dual processor Mac G4 with a 21" monitor and a pen tablet. Tammy may be contacted by e-mail at photogodmom@ nc.rr.com or by telephone at (919) 662-9387.

ADDING "PUNCH" TO A BLACK AND WHITE PHOTO

19.1

19.2

ABOUT THE IMAGE

1949 Chevy Pickup Canon EOS 1D mounted on a tripod, 16-35mm f/2.8 @ 16mm, 200 ISO, f/14 @ 1/236, 1,656 x 2,448 pixels, 4.1MB RAW file, original RGB file was converted to a 24.7MB .tif image with Capture One DSLR and then converted to black and white using The Imaging Factory's Convert to B&W Pro plug-in, all in 16-bit mode

Driving in a rural area of Maryland I noticed two old trucks behind a barn. I liked the colors of the trucks and the contrast of the white puffy clouds against a relatively blue sky so I stopped to ask if I could shoot a few photos. From when I first saw the trucks, my plan was to make a good black and white print. After choosing a wide-angle lens to add some distortion to the nose of the Chevy truck and to help fill the frame with just one truck and the sky, I shot the photo shown in Figure 19.1.

If you shoot with a digital camera and you enjoy making black and white prints; you may already know that you have tremendous control over how colors are converted to shades of gray when using one or more digital imaging tools such as Adobe Photoshop CS or The Imaging Factory's Convert to B&W Pro plug-in (see Technique 37). While the original photo is a pretty good conversion from the original color image, it lacks the "punch" that it could have with a bit more editing, as shown in Figure 19.2.

137

STEP 1: OPEN FILE

- Choose **File** ➤ **Open** (**Ctrl+O** PC, **Cmd+O** Mac) to display the **Open** dialog box. Double-click the **\19** folder to open it and then click the **49chevy-before.tif** file to select it. Click **Open** to open the file.

If you select **Image** ➤ **Mode**, you'll find a checkmark next to **16 Bits/Channel**. This means that this image is a 16-bit image and we'll edit in 16-bit mode in such a way that we can go back at any time in the edit process and fine-tune the edits. You can also tell that the image is a 16-bit image by looking at the document title bar where it shows (RGB/16). To give us the flexibility of making changes to any of our settings at any time during the editing process, we'll use **Adjustment Layers** and **Layer Masks** to prevent the loss of any picture information. To learn more about non-destructive image editing, see Technique 9.

STEP 2: MAKE AN EDITING PLAN

Once again, I'll make the important point: Before you begin editing this or any other photo, it is always wise to spend some time deciding what needs to be improved in the image. Not only will a good understanding of what you want to do help you get better results, but it will also help you to perform the needed edits in the most efficient manner.

The clouds in the original image were well-exposed. Important cloud details are visible and there are no blown-out highlights. However, the image would look better if there were more pronounced details in the clouds and more contrast between the clouds and the sky. Finally, an increase in contrast in the truck and the foreground area would be good as well and even better if we could use image contrast to put more focus on

the truck in the foreground. So, with that plan in mind, let's edit in a non-destructive manner so that we can go back and fine-tune any editing steps we make at any time to get the exact results we want. We'll also be working in 16-bit mode to get the best possible results.

STEP 3: DARKEN AND IMPROVE CONTRAST IN THE SKY

To darken and improve contrast in the clouds, we will use the **Multiply** blend mode, which darkens an image by multiplying the pixel values of the two layers that are blended—making everything darker and, most importantly, making the details in the clouds more visible without tossing out picture information that could occur if you used **Levels** or **Curves**.

Before you begin editing, you should open up the new **Histogram** palette to give you a view of each edit step you take. Keeping your eye on the **Histogram** helps you avoid posterizing the image by making too severe of a change to the image. What you generally want to avoid is having an image with a **Histogram** that has gaps that look like the teeth in a comb. The **Histogram** also gives you a graphical representation of tonal range and helps you to decide if you have lost details in shadows and highlights. To learn more about this new and improved **Histogram**, read **Photoshop Help** (**F1**).

- If the **Histogram** palette is not visible, select **Window** ➤ **Histogram**. If the **Histogram** does not look like the one shown in Figure 19.3, click the palette menu button and select **Compact View** from the pop-up menu.
- Select **Layer** ➤ **Duplicate Layer** to get the **Duplicate Layer** dialog box. Click in the **As:** box and type **Clouds** to name the new layer. Click **OK** to create the new layer.

Next, we want to apply the **Blend** mode. Because our intent is to make it easy to go back at any point during the editing or printing process and change edit settings we will use the **Apply Image** feature to apply the **Blend** mode instead of creating an extra layer and blending it with the layer below. This makes the steps clearer and it reduces the number of layers by one, which has the added benefit of requiring less RAM.

- Select **Image** ➤ **Apply Image** to get the **Apply Image** dialog box shown in Figure 19.4.
- Click in the **Blending** box and select the **Multiply** blend mode. Click in the **Opacity** box and slide the slider to around **70%** to lighten the image. Click **OK** to apply the settings.

The clouds now have an improved tonal range with darker tones, which reveals more detail in them. However, this adjustment darkened the truck and the foreground too much. To limit this adjustment just to the clouds and the sky, we'll now create a layer mask to avoid applying this edit to the areas where it makes the image too dark.

- Select **Layer** ➤ **Add Layer Mask** ➤ **Hide All** and the image will look as it did before we applied the **Multiply** blend mode. The **Layers** palette should now look like the one shown in Figure 19.5.

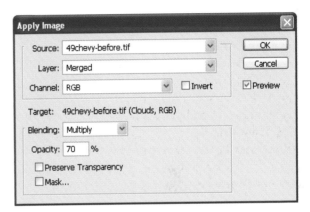

19.4

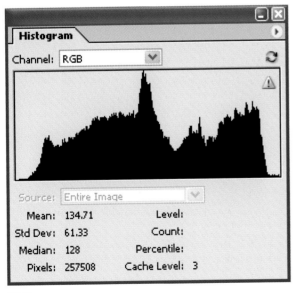

19.3

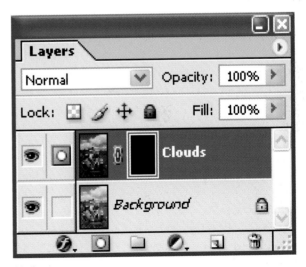

19.5

■ We now need to paint the mask to reveal the darkened clouds and sky. Click the **Brush** tool (**B**). Click in the **Options** bar to get the **Brush** palette shown in Figure 19.6. If your **Brush** palette looks different, click the palette menu button and select **Reset Brushes**. Click once more on the palette menu button and select **Small Thumbnail**.

■ Select the **Soft Round 300 Pixels** brush in the **Brush** palette. Make sure the **Options** bar shows **Mode** set to **Normal**, **Opacity** to **100%**, and **Flow** to **100%**, as shown in Figure 19.7.

■ Set the **Foreground** color to **White** by typing **D** or by clicking the **Default Foreground and Background Colors** icon at the bottom of the **Toolbox**.

■ Begin painting from the top of the image down to the bottom of the background trees on the horizon. As you paint, you will see the darker sky and clouds create with the **Blend** moderevealed from the layer beneath the **Layer Mask**. Once you completed the painting of the mask your image should now look like the one shown in Figure 19.8. You don't have to be too careful when painting as the **Soft Round 300 Pixels** brush has soft edges and the edge you are painting into on the horizon is a dark line of trees. If you over-painted an area, type **X** to switch to **Black** and you can paint the mask back in. You can also change brush sizes and add or remove the mask with more precision.

19.8

19.6

Brush: 65   Mode: Normal   Opacity: 100%   Flow: 100%

19.7

STEP 4: IMPROVE THE CONTRAST OF THE TRUCK AND THE FOREGROUND AREA

Before making any final adjustments on the sky, let's see what we can do with the truck and foreground area. The image can be improved by increasing contrast while taking the necessary steps to avoid pushing too much of the shadow area into black where detail will be lost. To do this, we will once again want to use a layer mask and do some selective lightening of the image.

- Click **Background** in the **Layers** palette to make it the active layer.
- Select **Layer ➢ New Adjustment Layer ➢ Curves** to get the **New Layer** dialog box shown in Figure 19.9. Type **Foreground** in the **Name** box. Make sure you click in the box next to **Use Previous Layer to Create Clipping Mask**! This ensures that the **Curves** edits will only be applied to the **Background** layer. Click **OK** to get the **Curves** dialog box.
- When working with the **Curves** tool, contrast is increased as slope increases. For this image, let's increase the slope by setting one point at **32** and **24** and a second point at **147** and **166** to get a curve like the one shown in Figure 19.10. Click **OK** to apply the settings.

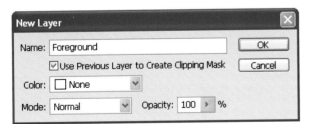

19.9

STEP 5: FOCUS ATTENTION ON THE TRUCK

The image continues to look better with each step. Let's see if we can darken the image around the truck in the foreground so that attention is focused on the lighter-toned truck. To do that we will use a **Levels Adjustment Layer** and as you might have expected: one more **Layer Mask**.

- Click the **Background** layer in the **Layers** palette. Select **Layer ➢ New Adjustment Layer ➢ Levels** to get the **New Layer** dialog box. Type **Around Truck** in the **Name** box to note that this adjustment layer is for darkening the area around the truck. Make sure you click in the box next to **Use Previous Layer** to **Create Clipping Mask**. Click **OK** to get the **Levels** dialog box. Set **Input Levels** to **12**, **0.79**, and **250** and click **OK** to apply the settings.

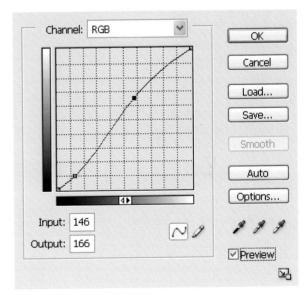

19.10

- Click **OK** to apply the settings.
- I agree with you if you are thinking the foreground is too dark, but wait and see what we do next. Whenever you create an **Adjustment Layer**, you also automatically create a **Layer Mask**, too, so there is no need to create a new **Layer Mask**. Click the **Layer Mask** thumbnail, which is the thumbnail image just to the right of the **Levels** thumbnail image in the **Around Truck** layer.
- Select the **Brush** tool (**B**) and choose the **Soft Round 300 Pixels** brush we used before. Set **Opacity** in the **Options** bar to **34%**. When **Opacity** is set to **34%**, you will have to paint over an area three times to get 100% of the mask painted. Using this lower value for **Opacity** gives you more control as you can build the mask up with multiple strokes rather than attempting to make perfect strokes the first time.
- After setting the **Foreground** color to **black**, begin painting on the truck to lighten it. The more you paint on the mask, the more the image will lighten. Be careful not to paint on the truck's windows as you may lighten it more than you want. Change brush size if you need to and change to **White** to paint the mask back when needed. When you are finished the image will draw the viewer toward the truck — that was our initial goal.

STEP 6: FINE-TUNE ADJUSTMENTS

With the image just about complete, take a close look to see if there is anything else that you can do to make it better. Now that the truck and foreground area are complete, we can possibly make a final adjustment to the sky area.

- Click the **Clouds** layer in the **Layers** palette. Let's use **Levels** to increase the contrast in the sky so that it looks better with the now complete foreground. Select **Layer ➤ New Adjustment Layer ➤ Levels** to get the **New Layer** dialog box. Click inside the box next to **Use Previous Layer to Create Clipping Mask** to limit the **Levels** edit to the sky area — this is very important! Click **OK** to get the **Levels** dialog box. Drag the sliders to set **Input Levels** to **25**, **0.81**, and **232** to get wonderful clouds that work well with the high-contrast foreground. Click **OK** to apply the settings. Your image should now look like the one shown in Figure 19.11.

I grant you that we may have worked a little harder to get the results we got with all the **Adjustment Layers** and **Layer Masks**, but you can now click on any one of the **Layer Masks** or **Adjustment Layers** and make changes to the masks or the settings — a huge advantage if you really care about your work!

The **Layers** palette should now look like the one shown in Figure 19.12. To try this out, double-click the **Levels 1** layer in the **Layers** palette to get the **Levels** dialog box. Now slide the sliders to set the **Input levels** at **50**, **0.70**, and **232**. Click **OK** to apply the new settings. Instantly, you have a significantly different image without having to go back and do all the steps again. More importantly, you never toss out picture information by applying destructive commands. No picture information is lost forever until you flatten the image. You should also be aware that if you save this image as a .psd file you can even open it up at a later time and make any necessary changes to suit your new view on how the image should look or to get a better print.

That concludes this chapter. Next up is a chapter on editing portraits.

19.11

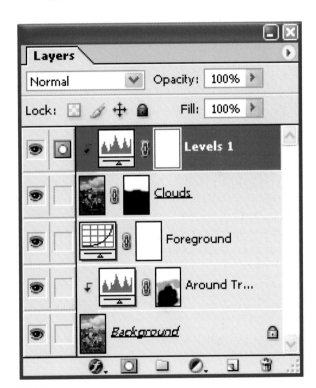

19.12

4

ENHANCING PORTRAITS

I f you take photos of people, then this chapter will be a fun one for you. If you have an old photo to restore, the first technique shows you how to use many of the powerful "retouching" tools that can be found in Adobe Photoshop CS. In the next technique you learn how to retouch a portrait to raise an eyebrow, diminish age lines, and more. Making a coloredized black and white image is the next topic. You also learn how to make your own toning "style." The next technique shows how to create a traditional darkroom texture effect, and in the final technique you learn how to efficiently use the Automate and Camera RAW features to batch process proofs to save you lots of time.

RESTORING AN OLD PORTRAIT

20.1

20.2

ABOUT THE IMAGE

Grandfather Abraham Old photo scanned with HP DeskScan 3c 1,591 x 2,400 pixels, 10.9MB .tif

Sometimes, the goal is not to fix a digital image taken with a digital camera or from a scanned slide or negative, but to restore an old damaged photographic print. Besides usually being faded, many old prints can have tears, crinkles, or even missing parts. They can be discolored or have stains, blotches, spots, chunks, and many other undesirables.

When looking for a challenging photo for this technique, a friend gladly provided me with one with *all* the previously mentioned undesirables. But, that is okay as Photoshop has always been the tool of choice for restoring images such as this one. With Adobe Photoshop CS's specialized tools for photographic restoration, you'll learn that restoring this image is simply a piece of the proverbial cake. This is a fun image to work on and it is old — so old in fact, that the photo was taken way back when they believed that you should not smile when having your portrait made!

147

STEP 1: OPEN FILE

■ Choose **File** ➢ **Open** (**Ctrl+O** PC, **Cmd+O** Mac) to display the **Open** dialog box. Double-click the **\20** folder to open it and then click the **grandfather-before.tif** file to select it. Click **Open** to open the file.

STEP 2: STRAIGHTEN AND CROP IMAGE

This photo has been mounted onto a piece of thin leather. So, the first challenge is straighten the image and to crop the image to just the photo.

■ To straighten the image, click and hold the **Eyedropper** tool icon in the **Toolbox** to get a pop-up menu; select the **Measure** tool. Click the image in the upper-left corner of the photo and drag a line down to the bottom-left corner of the photo while keeping the line parallel to the edge of the photo.
■ Choose **Image** ➢ **Rotate Canvas** ➢ **Arbitrary** to get the **Rotate Canvas** dialog box. You will notice that there is a value in the **Angle** box. This is the amount of rotation that Adobe Photoshop CS has determined is needed to straighten the image. Click **OK** and the image will be straightened.
■ Now click the **Crop** tool (**C**) in the **Toolbox**. If there are values in the **Width**, **Height**, or **Resolution** boxes in the **Options** bar, click **Clear**. Click just inside the upper-left corner of the edge of the photo and drag the marquee down and to the right to the corner of the photo to select the entire photo. To save time editing the edges of the photo, click a selection handle to move the selection marquee if needed to avoid selecting any dark edge or part of the leather the photo has been mounted on. Press **Enter** (**Return** on the Mac) to crop the image. Your image should now look like the one shown in Figure 20.3.

STEP 3: REPAIR LONG VERTICAL FOLD LINE

The upper-right corner needs to be created so you'll have to create more paper to fill in the missing parts! Before we begin that task, however, it is best to first fix the areas around the missing corner so that we can clone in the missing corner.

20.3

■ One tool that you can use to fix the vertical fold line is the new **Patch** tool, which you can select by clicking on and holding the **Healing Brush** tool in the **Toolbox**. After getting a pop-up menu, choose the **Patch** tool.

■ Make sure **Source** is checked in the **Options** bar. Click and drag a selection marquee around part of the fold line, as shown in Figure 20.4. Click inside the selection marquee and carefully drag it to the left where there is a very similar part of paper. When you let go of the mouse button, the fold will be gone! Do this several more times until you have fixed most of the line down to the man's shoulder.

20.4

■ There is one more tiny fold line that runs horizontally just under the missing corner. Use the **Patch** tool to fix it, too. When you have finished, remove any selection marquee by choosing **Select** ➢ **Deselect** (**Ctrl+D** PC, **Cmd+D** Mac).

STEP 4: REPLACE THE TORN CORNER

■ Now that we have some reasonably good paper near the missing corner, we can use it as a clone source to fill in the missing corner. Click the **Clone Stamp** tool (**S**) in the **Toolbox**. Click in the **Brush Preset Picker** box in the **Options** bar to get the **Brush** palette shown in Figure 20.5. If the palette looks different, click the menu button in the upper-right corner of the **Brush** palette to get a pop-up menu; choose **Reset Brushes**. Click the **Soft Round 100 Pixels** brush.

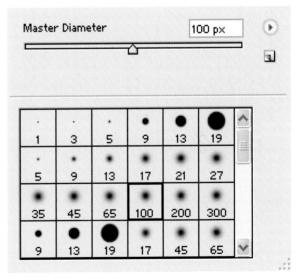

20.5

■ Before you can begin cloning in the missing corner you must first set the clone source by pressing **Alt** (**Option** on the Mac) and then clicking once in the image where you want to set the source image. I suggest that you click to the left of the missing corner and then click the same distance down from the top to begin cloning. Click often and reset your clone source so that you don't end up with two parts of the paper that have exactly the same stain!

STEP 5: USE CLONE STAMP TOOL TO FIX BEARD AND THE FOLD IN COAT

Using the **Clone Stamp** tool (**S**) and a smaller brush size, clone the beard without ink over the beard where there are ink lines until all of the ink lines are gone. To easily change brush sizes press [to reduce brush size and] to increase brush size. While you have the **Clone Stamp** tool (**S**) selected, carefully select your clone source and clone out the rest of the vertical fold in the right shoulder. If you set your clone source carefully, you can perfectly match the shadow lines caused by the fold in the man's coat. You will get the best results by clicking often and rarely dragging the **Clone Stamp** tool (**S**).

STEP 6: REMOVE RED INK SPOTS

Use the **Clone Stamp** tool (**S**) to remove the red ink spots next to the left edge of the photo and on the white shirt next to his tie.

STEP 7: REMOVE ALL THE SPOTS AND PERFORATIONS ON THE IMAGE

Now is the time to gather all of your patience and remove the spots and perforations on the image with the wonderful Adobe Photoshop CS **Healing Brush** tool! This useful tool automatically "heals" an area by matching the lighting and shading of the "to be healed area" to the texture of the source pixels — a far better approach than using the **Clone Stamp** tool.

■ Click the **Healing Brush** tool (**J**) in the **Toolbox**. Using a variety of **Brush** sizes, you can select different source points and click to "heal" all the spots on the image. Because the **Healing Brush** tool does not match the source lighting, you can select the best part of the image to use as the source texture, and then heal other areas and not have the healed areas look lighter or darker than they should!

STEP 8: MINIMIZE STAINING

The bottom part of the man has obviously been vignetted during the exposure process; however, I think that part of that same area has either been stained or lightened more than when it was first printed. We also need to fix the lighter areas that have been stained or faded in the rest of the image as well.

■ To darken the light areas, you need to selectively increase image density. To do that, duplicate the layer by choosing **Layer** ➢ **Duplicate Layer**; click **OK** to duplicate the layer.

■ Click in the **Blend Mode** box in the **Layers** palette and select **Multiply**. The idea is to set **Opacity** at a level that creates the darkest background color that is needed to cover the stain. Set **Opacity** in the **Layers** dialog box to **65%**.

■ Choose **Layer** ➢ **Add Layer Mask** ➢ **Hide All** to hide the entire dark layer. You can now paint on the **Layer** mask and gently build up the density level wherever it is needed.

■ Select the **Brush** tool (**B**) by clicking it in the **Toolbox**. Click on the **Brush Picker** in the **Options** bar and select the **Soft Round 200 Pixels** brush. Set **Opacity** in the **Options** bar to **10%**. Make sure that the foreground color is **White**.

■ You can now begin painting on the image to darken the lighter stained areas. If you paint too much and part of the image gets too dark, you can switch to **Black** (**X**) and paint the mask so that you lighten the image again. Click often and gradually build up the color. It is best to work in **Full Screen** mode by pressing **F**, **F**, and then **Tab.** Remember you can move the image around with the **Hand** tool (**H**) by pressing and holding the **Spacebar** to get the **Hand** tool (**H**).

■ Notice that it is also possible to paint some of the image density back into the bottom part of the coat. Once you have completed painting the mask, you may find that you will need to use the **Healing Brush** (**J**) to fix any spots that have now become more pronounced.

■ When you are happy with the results, choose **Layer** ➤ **Flatten Image**.

STEP 9: MAKE FINAL TONAL ADJUSTMENTS

Using **Levels** or **Curves** you can make minor adjustments to the tonal range to get an image that looks similar to the one shown in Figure 20.6.

When faced with a restoration job like this one, the more time and patience you have, the better job you can do. Adobe Photoshop CS offers so many wonderfully useful tools, you can just about fix any image! Try these tools on one of your old images or restore one for a client or friend. They'll believe that you can perform magic.

Admittedly, this one technique shows only a small part of what you can do to restore an old image—there is so much that can be done that people have written entire books on how to use Photoshop just to restore images. If you plan on doing lots of restoration work, I highly recommend that you purchase Katrin Eismann's *Photoshop Restoration & Retouching, Second Edition* book to get a whole book full of restoration and retouching tips and techniques.

20.6

RETOUCHING PORTRAITS

21.1

21.2

ABOUT THE IMAGE

Business Portrait FujiFilm FinePix S2 Pro, 28-105mm f/3.5-5.6 with studio lights, ISO 200, .jpg image setting, f/11.0 @ 1/125, 3.5MB 2,016 x 3,024 pixel .jpg file

One of the truly magical aspects of a powerful image editor such as Adobe Photoshop CS is how it can be used to significantly enhance a portrait. If you have ever had an opportunity to see many of Hollywood's finest movie stars up close, you were more than likely shocked to see what they looked like compared to all the heavily "Photoshopped" glamour portraits that get printed in newspapers, magazines, calendars, and posters.

The goal of this technique is to show you some of the tricks that you can use to enhance a portrait while also cautioning you to use Adobe Photoshop CS's features in moderation to leave important character in a person's face when retouching. We'll be using a photograph taken by Lance Richardson in his studio for this project.

Before beginning the editing process, you should have a clear idea of what the completed photo should look like and what steps you must take to achieve those results. With the many powerful image editing tools that can be found in Adobe Photoshop CS, you can do everything from remove imperfections, reduce or entirely remove age lines, and even create soft beautiful new skin. Some people are pleased to have a photo that "glamorizes" them to look like a Hollywood movie star, whereas others are more comfortable with facial features that are part of their personality and leaving them without having to offer an "explanation" when they are face-to-face with their photo.

STEP 1: OPEN "BEFORE" AND "AFTER" FILES

- Choose **File** ➢ **Open** (**Ctrl+O** PC, **Cmd+O** Mac) to display the **Open** dialog box. Double-click the **\21** folder to open it and then press **Ctrl** on the PC (**Cmd** on the Mac) while clicking the **portrait-before.jpg** file and the **portrait-after.jpg** file to select them both. Click **Open** to open the files.

- Click the **portrait-after.jpg** file to make it the active file. Click the **Move** tool (**V**) and press **Shift** while you click and drag the **portrait-after.jpg** image onto the **portrait-before.jpg** image. Pressing and holding **Shift** will cause the images to be perfectly aligned. You can now close the **portrait-after.jpg** image as it will no longer be needed.
- The **Layers** palette will now show two layers. Double-click the **Background** layer in the **Layers** palette to get the **New Layer** dialog box. Type **original** in the **Name** box and click **OK** to name the layer. Double-click in the **Layer 1** text to highlight the text; then type in **after**.

The reason we added one image to the other is that it makes it easy to compare the original image with the "after" one done by the author — and once we add a new layer for your work, you, too, can easily compare your work. Once you begin editing, you will learn how useful it is to be able to turn on, or turn off, a layer to compare images to see how well you are doing.

- Click the **original** layer; then, choose **Layer** ➢ **Duplicate Layer** to get the **Duplicate Layer** dialog box. Type **My Retouching** in the **As** box and click **OK**.

LANCE RICHARDSON

Lance Richardson is somewhat of a Renaissance photographer as he first excelled as a photojournalist and fine art photographer before mastering fine art portraiture. During the past 25 years he has moved from exclusively employing traditional photographic techniques to the new digital tools and mixed media output. At the national level, Lance has received two Fuji Masterpiece Awards and one Kodak Gallery Award for outstanding photographic achievement. You may learn more about Lance and his work at: www.lancerichardson.com.

■ Click the **Layer Visibilities** icon to the left of the **after** layer to make the **My Retouching** layer visible. The **Layers** palette should now look like the one shown in Figure 21.3. The **My Retouching** layer should still be highlighted as the active layer — you are now ready to begin editing.

STEP 2: COMPLETE TONE AND COLOR ADJUSTMENTS

There are a number of steps you could take to adjust the tonal range and color of this image, but for this technique we'll just make a few quick adjustments to color.

■ Select **Image** ➢ **Adjustment** ➢ **Hue/Saturation** (**Ctrl+U** PC, **Cmd+U** Mac) and set **Saturation** to +20. Click in the **Edit** box and select **Yellows** (**Ctrl+2** PC, **Cmd+2** Mac). Set **Saturation** to –25 to remove some of the yellow tint. Click **OK** to apply the settings.

STEP 3: REDUCE FACIAL LINES

There are many approaches you can take to remove age lines. Using Adobe Photoshop 6, Lance Richardson has become a master of retouching with the **Clone Stamp** tool (**S**), with the **Blend** mode set to **Lighten** and **Opacity** set anywhere from **3** to **10%**. Carefully and slowly he can remove age lines — from barely visible ones to very pronounced lines. If you have good skin tone and texture near the age lines you want to remove, the **Patch** tool can work wonders, too. Setting the **Dodge** or **Burn** tools to **Lighten** or **Darken** at a very low **Opacity** level is another approach. Or, you can use the **Healing** brush tool as well. Depending on the intended effect, you may even want to use a combination of these tools.

My choice of tools for this project is the **Patch** tool and the **Healing** brush. However, we are going to first use the **Patch** brush exclusively, but we are going to do it on a new layer. The advantage of this is that you can entirely remove all of the facial lines — then by simply adjusting layer **Opacity**, you can "dial" in the amount of lines you want to show from **0** to **100%**. This is a huge advantage if you want to please the person featured in the portrait. They can tell you exactly how glamorized they want to be — or not be.

■ Select **Layer** ➢ **Duplicate Layer** to get the **Duplicate Layer** dialog box. Type **facial lines** in the **As** box; then, click **OK**.
■ Choose **View** ➢ **Actual Pixels** (**Alt+Ctrl+0** PC, **Option+Cmd+0** Mac) to zoom in to **100%**. Press the **Spacebar** to get the **Hand** tool and click and drag the image until you get a good view of the right eye.
■ Click the **Patch** tool in the **Toolbox** (press and hold the **Healing Brush** tool to get a menu, then select **Patch** tool). Click the image and drag the

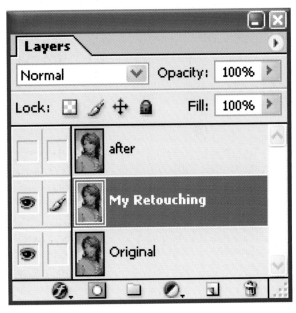

21.3

selection marquee around the image, as shown in Figure 21.4. Click inside the selection marquee and drag the selection straight down until the entire selection has been filled with new skin texture; release the mouse button. Click outside the selection marquee to remove the selection. The eye should now look like the one shown in Figure 21.5. To view how accurately the skin tone was matched, click on, and click off, the **Layer Visibility** icon to the left of the **facial lines** layer in the **Layers** palette to compare "before" and "after" effects. You can also click the **Layer Visibility** icon in the **after** layer to see my results.

■ Make sure that the **after** layer is no longer visible and that the **facial lines** layer is highlighted and visible. You can now adjust **Opacity** in the **Layers** palette from **0** to **100%** to select the amount of the facial lines you want to see! Set **Opacity** back to **100%**.

■ Using the **Patch** tool continue to "patch" all the facial lines you think ought to be removed or toned down. If you keep all these edits on the **facial lines** layer, you will later be able to adjust them all in a relative amount using the **Opacity** slider. If you feel that some need to be reduced more or less than others, you can copy the layer and cut to transparency parts of the layer so that **Opacity** may be set at different values. I liked the results of setting **Opacity** to **70%**, as shown in Figure 21.6. What do you think? It doesn't matter as you can set it to whatever value is needed — that easy!

STEP 4: SMOOTH SKIN TEXTURE

Now let's perform some skin texture smoothing with the **Healing** brush (**J**) tool. In order to do this and to

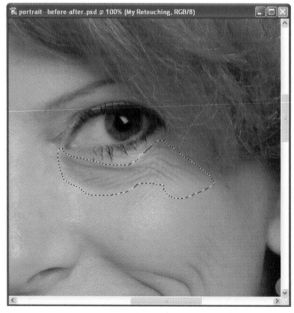

21.4

21.5

keep this project easy to follow we will first merge the **facial lines** layer with the **My Retouching** layer.

- In the **Layers** palette, set **Opacity** for the **facial lines** layer as you want. I liked the results of **70%**. Select **Layer ➤ Merge Down** (**Ctrl+E** PC, **Cmd+E** Mac). You should now have just three layers: **after**, **My Retouching**, and **original**.
- After clicking the **Healing** brush (**J**) tool in the **Toolbox**, press **Alt** (**Option** on the Mac) and click in an area of the skin that has texture that you like to set as the source point. Now you can click and paint over the area you want to add new and improved texture to. You may need to change the size of the brush, which you can easily do by repeatedly pressing the [key to reduce the brush size, or the] key to increase the brush size.
- To remove the overly bright highlight on her lip, use the **Clone Stamp** tool (**S**). In the **Options** bar set **Mode** to **Normal**, and **Opacity** to about **25%** and paint using another part of her lip as the

source. While it is tempting, you do not want to eliminate the highlight as this is a key part of the image — just tone it down a small amount. The image is looking pretty good at this point I think.

STEP 5: SHAPE THE LOWER LIP, THE LEFT SIDE OF THE FACE, AND OPEN THE RIGHT EYE

There are many additional steps you could take to further improve this image. You could, for example, reshape the lower lip, pull the left side of the cheek in a small amount, and slightly open the right eye — all with the **Liquify** tool.

- Click the **Rectangular Marquee** tool (**M**) in the **Toolbox**. Zoom the image in or out as needed so that you can select the entire mouth, as shown in Figure 21.7. Select **Filter ➤ Liquify** (**Shift+Ctrl+ X** PC, **Shift+Cmd+X**) to get the **Liquify** dialog

21.6

21.7

box shown in Figure 21.8. Click the **Forward Warp** tool (**W**). Set **Brush Size** to **150**; then click and carefully pull the lip straight down until it forms a smooth curve that matches the left side of the lower lip. If you make a mistake, click the **Reconstruct** tool (**R**) and paint over the area you edited to restore the original. You can then try again. When the lip looks as you want it to, click **OK** to apply the settings.

■ Now do the same thing to the left side of the face. Zoom in to show that area. Select the area with the **Rectangular Marquee** tool (**M**) and run the **Liquify** filter (**Shift+Ctrl+X** PC, **Shift+Cmd+X**). Making a smooth curve to the left side of the face is more challenging. However, don't fret over it; set **Brush Size** to **300**. Try gently pulling the face in a small amount. If it doesn't look good, reconstruct it with the **Reconstruct** tool (**R**) and try it again until it looks perfect. Once again, I caution you to not overdo it. The human face, like this one, is often quite beautiful with distinguishing characteristics. Very small adjustments can make wonderful improvements. Perfect faces are not realistic and are therefore not as interesting.

■ After dragging the **Rectangular Marquee** (**M**) around both eyes, use the **Liquify** tool to open the right eyelid a small amount. In my opinion, it should be open a bit more, but not so much as to make it the same size as the left eye. This leaves her with both a twinkle and a "wink." Try setting **Brush Size** to 200.

Each time you make an edit, check out the results by carefully comparing them with the original image. Check to make sure that you have not made an edit

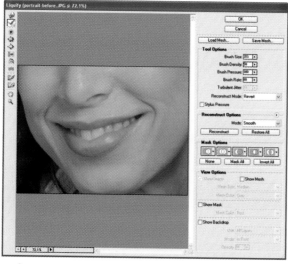

21.8

that changes the shape of the face if that was not the intent. Also, make sure you have not added a texture, color, or tone that does not fit with the surrounding area. The easy way to do this is to turn on, and turn off, one of the layers so that you can switch between your work and the original image. Once you have completed your work, your image should look similar to the one in Figure 21.9. If you were to take a more aggressive approach to editing, you might get a more glamorized image like the one shown in Figure 21.10.

21.9

21.10

ADDING COLOR TO A BLACK AND WHITE PORTRAIT

22.1

22.2

Traditional Indian Dress Canon EOS 1D, 70-200mm f/2.8 @170mm, ISO 200, RAW image setting, f/9.0 @ 1/250, 4.9MB 2,464 x 1,648 pixel .crw

The results of this technique are somewhat similar to what you might get if you hand-painted a black and white photograph — except it is much, much faster to do! If you want this image to look more "hand-painted" then it does, you could take the time to digitally paint it with a pen tablet. Alternatively, you could follow this technique step-by-step; then, add hand-painted steps to add color outside the perfect image created by using the **Color Selection** tool. For this technique, you will be working with another one of Lance Richardson's photos. You can learn more about Lance and his work in the profile found in Technique 21.

STEP 1: OPEN FILE

■ Choose **File ➢ Open** (**Ctrl+O** PC, **Cmd+O** Mac) to display the **Open** dialog box. Double-click the **\22** folder to open it and then click the **preddy-beforeRAW.tif** file to select it. Click **Open** to open the file with **Adobe Camera RAW** as shown in Figure 22.3. If you don't have a RAW conversion tool to convert this image you can use the **preddy-before.jpg** file in the **\22** folder on the companion CD-ROM.

■ Choose **Camera RAW** settings to adjust the image. Let's take advantage of the extra picture information available in the RAW file and convert to **16 bits/channel**. Click **OK** to convert the image and open it in an Adobe Photoshop CS document window.

STEP 2: CROP AND RESIZE IMAGE

■ Click the **Crop** tool (**C**) in the **Toolbox**. In the **Options** bar, set **Width** and **Height** to **5** and **7** respectively; set **Resolution** to **240** to make a 5" x 7" print on a printer such as an Epson 2200. Crop the image as shown in Figure 22.1 by pressing **Enter** on a PC (**Return** on a Mac).

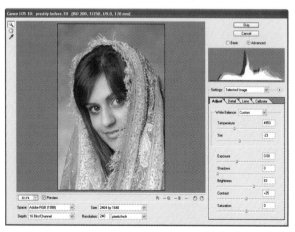

22.3

STEP 3: DUPLICATE LAYER AND CONVERT LAYER TO BLACK AND WHITE

■ Select **Layer ➢ Duplicate Layer** to get the **Duplicate Layer** dialog box. Type **b/w** in the **As** box and click **OK**. The **Layers** palette should now look similar to the one shown in Figure 22.4.

■ You can now use any method that you want to convert this image to a black and white image. To learn more about converting color images to black and white images, read Technique 14 and Technique 37. My preferred method is to use the Convert to B&W Pro plug-in, which is covered in Technique 37 as it is flexible and it works on 16-bit images. If you are using the **Channel Mixer** to convert the image, use mostly the **Red** channel. You should end up with an image that looks similar to the one shown in Figure 22.5.

STEP 4: ADD MAGENTA COLOR TO A NEW LAYER

■ To quickly add color and to make it easy to make any adjustments you may want to make, we

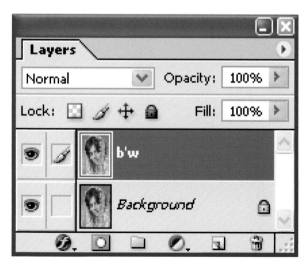

22.4

will add each different color to a separate layer. Click the **b/w** layer in the **Layers** palette to make it the active layer. Select **Layer ➤ New ➤ Layer** (**Shift+Ctrl+N** PC, **Shift+Cmd+N** Mac) to get the **New Layer** dialog box. Type **magenta** in the **Name** box and set **Blend Mode** to **Color**; click **OK** to create the new layer.

■ While we are at it, let's make two more layers. Select **Layer ➤ New Layer** (**Shift+Ctrl+N** PC, **Shift+Cmd+N** Mac) to get the **New Layer** dialog box. Type **gold** in the **Name** box and set **Mode** to **Color**; click **OK** to create the new layer.

■ Select **Layer ➤ New ➤ Layer** (**Shift+Ctrl+N** PC, **Shift+Cmd+N** Mac) to get the **New Layer** dialog box. Type **lips** in the **Name** box and set **Mode** to **Color**; click **OK** to create the new layer. We now have one layer for each of the three colors we will add.

■ Click the **Layer Visibility** icon to the left of the **b/w** layer in the **Layers** palette to turn visibility off. You should now see the color image from the **Background** layer.

■ Select **Select ➤ Color Range** to get the **Color Range** dialog box shown in Figure 22.6. Set **Fuzziness** to around **125** and click in a part of the image (not the preview image in the **Color Range** dialog box) that shows a dark **magenta** while viewing the colors that are being selected in the **Color Range** preview window. The goal is to choose a **Fuzziness** setting and to click the right magenta color to get a good selection that will not require much erasing. Once you are happy with the selection, click **OK** to complete the selection.

■ Click the **Eyedropper tool** (**I**) in the **Toolbox**. Click on the **Background** layer in the **Layers** palette to make it the active layer. Set **Sample Size**

22.5

22.6

in the **Options** bar to **3 x 3 Average**. To select a color from the original image, click in the image to select a dark magenta color. As you click and drag the cursor, you can see the selected color in the **Foreground color** box in the **Toolbox**.

■ Click the **magenta** layer in the **Layers** palette to make it the active layer. Fill the selection marquee with the selected magenta color by selecting **Edit ➤ Fill** (**Shift+F5**) to get the **Fill** dialog box. Set **Use** to **Foreground Color**; click **OK**.

■ Click the **Layer Visibility** icon to the left of the **Background** in the **Layers** palette to turn off visibility. Select **Select ➤ Deselect** (**Ctrl+D** PC, **Cmd+D** Mac). The image should now look similar to the one shown in Figure 22.7.

22.7

■ Click the **Eraser** tool (**E**) in the **Toolbox** and erase all the soft colors leaving only the dark magenta where it shows in the clothing. Click the **Layer Visibility** icon to the left of the **b/w** layer in the **Layers** palette to get a better idea of where you might need to erase the magenta color. For now, don't worry if the color is not as you'd like it — we can change both hue and saturation later.

■ You can now repeat this process for the color **gold**. First, set **Layer Visibility** to off for the **b/w** layer. Select **Select ➤ Deselect** (**Ctrl+D** PC, **Cmd+D** Mac). Make sure to click the **Background** layer in the **Layers** palette to make it active. Then, select the **gold** color using **Select ➤ Color Range**. Try varying the **Fuzziness** setting to minimize the erasing you will have to do. Use the **Eyedropper tool** to choose a good gold color. Then, select the **gold** layer in the **Layers** palette and fill the selection marquee with the gold color. Once again, you will need to use the **Eraser** tool (**E**) to clean up the image.

■ The last color we need to add is for the lips. Click the **Background** layer once more. Click the **Eyedropper tool** (**I**). Click the lightest **magenta** color you can find to use as the color of the lips. As you drag your cursor, remember that you can view the selected color in the **Foreground** box at the bottom of the **Toolbox**.

■ Once you have a good color for the lips, click the **lips** layer to make it the active layer. Select **View ➤ Actual Pixels** (**Alt+Ctrl+0** PC, **Option+Cmd+0** Mac) to get a close-up view of the lips. You may have to press the **Spacebar** to get the **Hand** tool; click and drag the image until the lips are visible.

■ This time we will hand-paint the color on the image. Click the **Brush** tool (**B**) in the **Toolbox**. Click the **Brush Preset Picker** button on the **Options** bar to get the **Brush** palette. Click the **Soft Round 21 Pixels** brush. Make sure **Opacity** is set to **100%**. You can now carefully paint the magenta color on the lips. If you over-paint, simply use the **Eraser** tool (**E**) and paint again. Once you have painted the lips, you may want to change the **Opacity** for the **lips** layer in the **Layers** palette to around **30%**.

■ To view your work, select **View** ➢ **Fit on Screen** (**Ctrl+0** PC, **Cmd+0** Mac). Your image should look similar to the one in Figure 22.2.

■ At this point, the **Layers** palette should look like the one shown in Figure 22.8. To modify the colors on any layer, you can add an **Adjustment Layer** such as **Hue/Saturation**. This allows you to change the bold colors that we currently have to much more pale colors that would be more like what you would have if you used a traditional photographic paint.

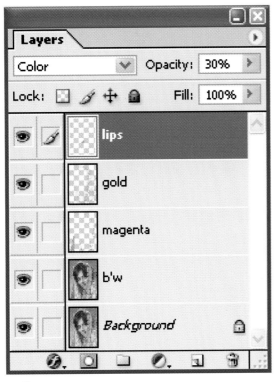

22.8

STEP 5: TONE BLACK AND WHITE BACKGROUND LAYER

After a good examination of our work so far, I think that the black and white layer could be warmed up a bit to improve the overall image — what do you think?

■ Click the **b/w** layer in the **Layers** palette. As this is an important change that we may want to alter later, let's make the change with an adjustment layer.

■ Select **Layer** ➢ **New Adjustment Layer** ➢ **Photo Filter** to get the **New Layer** dialog box. Type **background tone** in the **Name** box and click **OK** to get the **Photo Filter** dialog box shown in Figure 22.9.

■ Click in the **Filter** box and select the **Warming Filter (81)**. Slide the **Density** slider down to about **15%**, or even less. **10%** is even better as all we want to do is ever so slightly warm up the black and white image. Click **OK** to apply the filter. If you don't like this effect, you can at any time go back and change settings or turn off the **background tone** layer completely. Ah — the magic of adjustment layers! What did we do before we had them? That is it. You are now finished with this technique.

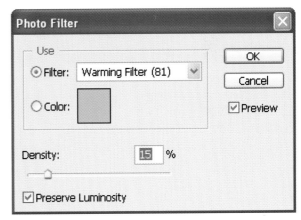

22.9

CREATING YOUR OWN TONING STYLE

23.1

23.2

ABOUT THE IMAGE

Preddy in Business Attire
Canon EOS 1D, 70-200mm
f/2.8 @ 95mm with studio
flash, ISO 200, RAW image
setting, f/9 @ 1/250, 3.1MB
2,464 x 1,648 pixel .crw file

Toning a photograph is the process of changing the color of a black and white photographic print from the typical black to that of another appealing color. Prints have been toned almost as long as photographic prints have been made. In a chemical darkroom, there are dozens of different ways to tone a print. There are other ways to change the color of a print that are not technically toning techniques, but the results are the same — a changed color. Now with the many features in digital image editors such as Adobe Photoshop CS, you can tone images digitally without having to source, mix, and handle all the nasty chemicals you might have to use in a wet darkroom.

In this technique, you will learn how to tone an image in such a way that you can make adjustments to it any time you want. The possibilities for digitally toning an image are endless. If you want to learn more about the

167

traditional toning processes to inspire your digital toning, I highly recommend Tim Rudman's *The Photographer's Toning Book: The Definitive Guide.*

STEP 1: OPEN FILE IN ADOBE CAMERA RAW AND CONVERT IT

Once again, you will be working with one of Lance Richardson's photos. You can learn more about Lance and his work in the profile found in Technique 21.

- Select **File** ➢ **Open** (**Ctrl+O** PC, **Cmd+O** Mac) to display the **Open** dialog box. Double-click the **\23** folder to open it and then click the **preddy-beforeRAW.tif** file to select it. Click **Open** to open the file in Adobe Camera RAW. If you don't have a RAW image file converter but would like to complete this technique, a converted 16-bit file can be found in the **\23** folder. It is named **preddy-before.tif.**
- Set **Temperature** to **4000**, **Tint** to **–28**, **Exposure** to **+0.40**, **Shadow** to **0**, **Brightness** to **56**, **Contrast** to **0**, and **Saturation** to **0**. Because we have 16 bits of picture information when working with a RAW file, let's take advantage of it and set **Depth** to **16 Bits/Channel**. Set **Size** to **2464 by 1648** and set **Resolution** to **240 pixels/inch**. Click on **Rotate Image 90° Counter Clockwise (L)**. Click **OK** to convert the image and open it in Adobe Photoshop CS.

STEP 2: CROP AND SIZE IMAGE

- Now let's crop the image and resize it to make a 5" x 7" print at 240 dpi. Click the **Crop** tool (**C**) in the **Toolbox**. Type **5 in** in the **Width** box, **7 in** in the **Height** box, and **240** in the **Resolution** box.

- Type **F** to change to **Full Screen** mode. Click once outside the image and then drag the selection marquee to crop the image as shown in Figure 23.2. Press **Enter** on the PC, or **Return** on the Mac to commit the crop. The image is now 5" × 7" at 240 dpi.

STEP 3: CONVERT IMAGE TO BLACK AND WHITE

- You can now use any method that you want to convert this image to a black and white image. To learn more about converting color images to black and white images, read Technique 14 and Technique 37. My preferred method is to use the **Convert to B&W Pro** plug-in, which is covered in Technique 37. It is very flexible and it works with 16-bit images. If you are using the **Channel Mixer** to convert the image you should use about **80%** or more of the **Red** channel. You should end up with an image that looks similar to the one shown in Figure 23.3.

STEP 4: CREATE TONE LAYER

- To tone this image we will use a layer filled with a solid color and with the blend mode set to **Color**. Select **Layer** ➢ **New Layer** (**Shift+Ctrl+N** PC, **Shift+Cmd+N** Mac) to get the **New Layer** dialog box shown in Figure 23.4. Type **Color tone** in the **Name** box and click **OK**.
- To choose a color, click the **Foreground Color** box in the **Toolbox** to get the **Color Picker** dialog box shown in Figure 23.5. Type **210** in the **R** box, **195** in the **G** box, and **147** in the **B** box to get a tan color; click **OK**.

■ Select **Edit** ➢ **Fill** (**Shift**+**F5**) to get the **Fill** dialog box shown in Figure 23.6. Set **Use** to **Foreground Color**, **Mode** to **Normal**, and **Opacity** to **100%**. Make sure that **Preserve Transparency** is not checked. Click **OK** to fill the **color tone** layer. Click in the **Blend** mode box in the **Layers** palette and select the **Color** blend mode. The image should now have a rich brown tone with too much of a yellow cast — but, that is okay as we can fix it.

■ To fine-tune the color and the richness of the tone, click in the **Opacity** box in the **Layers** palette and adjust the slider to get the results you want. For this image try setting **Opacity** at **45%** or less. The image should look even better now as the rich brown tone has been reduced by about half and the yellow cast is mostly gone.

23.3

23.4

23.5

23.6

STEP 5: FINE-TUNE TONE COLOR

■ If you are not happy with the tone you have, you can fill the color tone layer with a different color, or you can make adjustments to the current layer. To allow unlimited adjustments to the color, click the **color tone** layer in the **Layers** palette to make it the active layer. Select **Layer ➤ New Adjustment Layer ➤ Hue/Saturation** to get the **New Layer** dialog box. Click **OK** to get the **Hue/Saturation** dialog box shown in Figure 23.7. If you set **Hue** to –5 and **Saturation** to +14, you

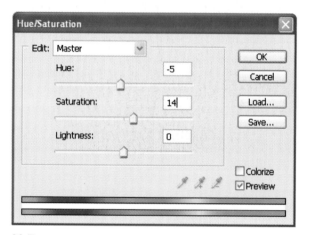

23.7

will get a slightly richer and warmer brown tone. Click **OK** to apply the changes or try any that you want to try. The **Layers** palette should now look like the one shown in Figure 23.8.

■ After carefully examining the image, or after making a print, you can easily make further

> **TIP**
>
> Once you find one or more tones that you like to use, you can create an Action to apply them. Applying a single tone to multiple images is a wonderful way to add continuity between a set of images. Spend some time finding a few different tones that you like and add the colors to the Swatches palette for easy access. Make sure to create some that are warm (a tone in the red color family) and some that are cold (a tone in the blue color family). For most photos, you are usually better off using a light color rather than a dark color as dark colors can cause posterization. Also, try using the Overlay or Pin Light blend modes. If you do, you may need to also change the Opacity. The more you experiment, the better results you will get.

changes to the tone. To do so, simply double-click the **Hue/Saturation Layer** in the **Layers** palette to once again get the **Hue/Saturation** dialog box. Make any adjustment you want and then click **OK** to apply them. My final settings for the image shown in Figure 23.9 are: **Hue** set to **–5%**, **Saturation** set to **+20%**, and **Lightness** set to **0**. This image makes a wonderful print on a fine art paper using an inkjet printer such as the Epson 1280 or Epson 2200.

23.9

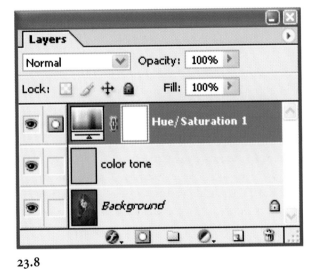

23.8

ADDING A TRADITIONAL DARKROOM TEXTURE SCREEN EFFECT

24.1

24.2

ABOUT THE IMAGE

Lady in Light Nikon 8008s film camera mounted on a tripod, 105mm f/2.8, Fuji Sensia-RH slide film, ISO 400, image taken from Kodak Photo-CD, 2,048 x 3,077 pixels reduced to 1,920 x 2,400 pixels, 13.8MB .tif

I learned about the wonderful photography and unique techniques of William Mortensen from Alan Scharf's postings to an e-mail group that we both belong to. As a long-time photographer and darkroom printer, as well as one who is interested in the history of photography, Alan has created his own *digital* Steeline texture screens to get results similar to those of William Mortensen and his texture screens, which Mortensen used extensively in the 1920s and 30s.

A texture screen is a film that is used in the darkroom. The screen has a texture printed on it and it is placed over the photographic paper or sandwiched with the negative during exposure. The use of these texture screens enables photographs to take on the characteristics of an etching, canvas, charcoal, pastel, or fresco.

173

As there is limited space in this book to cover the techniques or the work of William Mortensen, I highly recommend that you search the Internet for Web pages about him or that you attempt to find one of his long out-of-print books. One of Mortensen's students is still creating texture screens as he created them. You can learn more about these screens and purchase one if you'd like from the Web site `www.texturefects.com`.

STEP 1: OPEN FILE

As William Mortensen's photographs frequently featured women (often nude) in rich brown tones with lots of grain, we use a wonderful photograph taken by photographer Peter Balazsy to try out the Steeline texture contributed by Alan Scharf.

- Choose **File** ➢ **Open** (**Ctrl+O** PC, **Cmd+O** Mac) to display the **Open** dialog box. Double-click the **\24** folder to open it and then click the **lady-before.tif** file (shown in Figure 24.3) to select it. Click **Open** to open the file.

STEP 2: CREATE DIGITAL TEXTURE SCREEN

Digital texture screens can be created by photographing appropriate textures, manually creating them on paper and then scanning them, or creating them digitally. Alan Scharf found that Andromeda's EtchTone Filter (`www.andromeda.com`), a Photoshop plug-in, works beautifully for creating certain types of screens. After some experimentation, he found that different images require different screen line frequency (spacing) and line thickness. Using the EtchTone Filter, he created the sample screen found on the companion CD-ROM, which you use in this technique.

- Choose **File** ➢ **Open** (**Ctrl+O** PC, **Cmd+O** Mac) to display the **Open** dialog box. Double-click the **\24** folder to open it. Click the **scharf-steeline1.tif** image to select it. Click **Open**.

STEP 3: APPLY DIGITAL SCREEN TEXTURE EFFECT

Using this screen full-size is important. After the screen is applied to an image, the image should not

PETER BALAZSY

Peter Balazsy is recognized as one of the most accomplished photographers in the art of the Polaroid photo-image transfer technique. Peter currently divides his professional life, working as both a portrait photographer and artist, as well as heading up a small computer consulting company where digital-image manipulation provides yet another creative outlet for his artistry. Increasingly, Peter is working with new digital tools, including Photoshop, to create exciting new photographic art. About half of Peter's work consists of female nudes and portraits while the other half consists of cityscapes and still lifes that present his unique artistic-style. You can read more about Peter and his work on his Web site at `www.pbpix.com`.

be resized or saved as a JPEG as it causes deterioration of the screen effect.

- To apply Scharf's texture effect, click on the **Move** tool (**V**) and then click the **scharf-steeline1.tif** image to make it the active image; then press **Shift** and click the thumbnail image in the **Background** layer in the **Layers** palette; then drag and drop the image onto the **lady-before.tif** image.
- To blend the screen with the image, click in the **Blend** mode box in the **Layers** palette and select **Multiply**. You can try other **Blend** modes as well. In particular, the **Darken** mode can work well. Additionally, you can reduce the **Opacity** level in the **Layers** palette. For this image, I used **Multiply** as the **Blend** mode and set **Opacity** to **40%**, as shown in the **Layers** palette in Figure 24.4.

STEP 4: FINE-TUNE EFFECT

This technique has many variations. Besides reducing **Opacity**, you can create a **Layer Mask** and mask out parts of the screens where there are either important details (for example, eyes) or where highlights occur, such as those on the back of the lady in the photo used for this technique. Figure 24.2 shows the results of carefully painting with a **300-pixel** brush at **10% Opacity** to remove the texture screen effects on the lady's back and in the brightest part of the light.

After you try this technique, consider creating your own screens textures and experiment with them on black and white photos as well as color photos. Thanks to Alan Scharf, this technique is a great start to what may well become a widely practiced technique for those working in the new digital darkroom—thanks, Alan. Also, thanks to Peter Balazsy for his perfect photograph for this technique! If you would like to contact Alan Scharf, he can be reached via e-mail at `ascharf@sk.sympatico.ca`. If you are interested in getting a set of his Steeline texture filters, send him an e-mail and ask him about them—he is continually experimenting and is creating a nice collection of them.

24.3

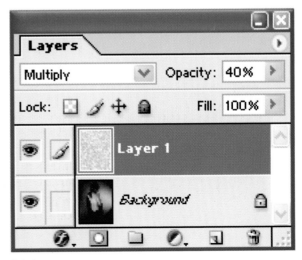

24.4

25

CREATING PROOFS IN A BATCH WHEN SHOOTING IN RAW FORMAT

25.1

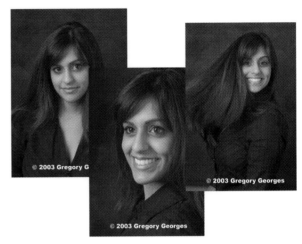

25.2

ABOUT THE IMAGE

Low-key Portrait Shoot FujiFilm FinePix S2 Pro, 28-105mm f/3.5-5. mounted on a tripod, 160 ISO, RAW file setting, f/8.0 @ 1/125, 3,024 x 2,024 pixels, 13MB .RAF

There are so very many benefits of shooting using RAW file format. The one big downside is that RAW files can take considerable time to convert, edit, and save. Fortunately, if you plan your portrait shoots and you use some of the timesaving features found in Adobe Photoshop CS, the creation of proofs can take place while you take a break or even shoot more photos. In this technique, you learn how to batch process selected files in a folder that you want to print as proofs. Let's assume that we want to print 5" x 7" proofs on an inkjet printer such as the Epson 2200P, which means that we will want to create images with 240 dpi and 5x7 proportions.

One last time you get to work with a few more photographs of Preddy that were taken by Lance Richardson. You can learn more about Lance and his work in the profile found at the end of Technique 21.

STEP 1: CHOOSE IMAGE TO USE
TO CREATE SETTINGS

When taking portraits in a studio, you typically shoot in sets. Each set usually has a similar background, similar lighting, and can generally be edited in a similar manner. This technique shows you how you can quickly edit and make proofs from one or more different sets in a single batch.

■ You will need to choose one photo from each set to use to determine the **Camera RAW** settings for that specific set. An easy way to do this is to use the **File Browser**. The **File Browser** in Figure 25.3 shows two different sets. The first set is of a model in a black dress against a dark background and the other set is of the same model dressed in traditional Indian clothing. Double-click the image you want to use to determine the RAW file conversion settings for the first set. In this case, double-click the file named **DSCF0951.RAF** that can be found in the **25** folder to open it in Adobe Camera RAW.

■ Using **Camera RAW**, you can now make the adjustments you want for the photo shown in the viewer. For this photo, **temperature** was set to **4500** and **Tint** to **–43**. **Exposure** was left at **0**, **Brightness** was bumped to **60**, **Contrast** was left

at **0**, and **Saturation** was pushed to **+5**. We don't need 16-bit images, so set **Depth** to **8 Bits/Channel**. You can save additional time and memory by changing **Size** to **2128 by 1424** and setting **Resolution** to **240 pixels/inch**. The **Camera RAW** dialog box should now look similar to the one shown in Figure 25.4.

To adjust image sharpness, click the **Detail** tab and set **Sharpness** to **65**, and leave the other two settings set to their default values. Generally, you want to sharpen an image just before you print it. Here we will sharpen the image as it is a good "quick and dirty" way to get pretty good results for a batch of proofs without having to later apply sharpening.

■ To save these settings, click the menu icon to the right of the **Settings** box to get a pop-up menu. Choose **Save Settings** to get the **Save Raw Conversion Settings** dialog box. Type **Preddy-Set-1** in the **File name** box and click **Save**. You now have an .XMP file that contains all the settings for this set, which can be used later for making the same changes to other photos in the set.

■ As we now need to make an **Action**, click **OK** to convert this file and load it into Adobe Photoshop CS.

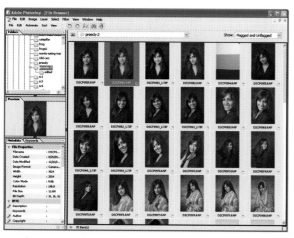

25.3

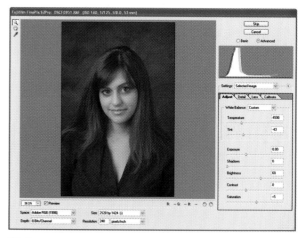

25.4

STEP 2: CREATE ACTION TO CROP AND PRINT IMAGE

- In the **Actions** palette, click the menu button and select **New Set** and type in **Preddy** in the **Name box** in the **New Set** dialog box; click **OK** to create a new set. Click the menu button again and select **New Action** to get the **New Action** dialog box shown in Figure 25.5. Type **Preddy 5x7 Proofs** in the **Name** box and click **Record** to begin recording the **Action**.
- Click the **Crop** tool (**C**) in the **Toolbox**. In the **Options** bar type **5 in**, **7 in**, and **240** in the **Width**, **Height**, and **Resolution** boxes respectively. Select **View** ➢ **Fit on Screen** (**Ctrl + 0** PC, **Cmd+0** Mac). Using the **Crop** tool, click the image and drag the selection marquee to crop the photo as you desire. Press **Enter** (**Return** on the Mac) or click the **Commit Crop Operation** icon on the **Options** bar to crop the image.
- If you want to add any copyright text to the images, now is the time to do so. Simply click the **Horizontal Type** tool in the **Toolbox** and click in the image where you want to set the text. For images in this set, choose **Arial Black** as the text style, set **Font Size** to **18 pt**, and choose **White** as the **color**.

  Press **ALT+0169** to create a copyright © symbol (press **Option+G** on the Mac); then type in the year and your name. Click the **Move** tool (**V**) in the **Toolbox** and click inside the text and drag it to where you want it.
- If you want to add any other edits to the **Action**, this is the time to do it.

- Select **Layer** ➢ **Flatten Image**.
- Select **File** ➢ **Save As** (**Shift + Ctrl + S** PC, **Shift + Cmd + S** Mac) to save the file. Make sure to choose a new folder.
- Select **File** ➢ **Close** (**Ctrl+W** PC, **Cmd+W** Mac).
- Click the **Stop Recording** button at the bottom of the **Actions** palette. The **Actions** palette should now look similar to the one shown in Figure 25.6.
- If you want to be able to manually choose where to crop the image when batch processing, click in the **Toggle Dialog On/Off** box just to the left of the **Crop** step in the **Actions** palette. Checking here will make the **Action** stop to allow you to manually select the part of the image you want cropped.

STEP 3: APPLY CAMERA RAW SETTINGS TO OTHER IMAGES IN THE SET

- Open the **File Browser** and while pressing **Ctrl** on the **PC** (**Option** on the Mac), click each image that you want to print as a proof.

25.5

25.6

■ In the menu in the **File Browser**, select **Automate** ➤ **Apply Camera RAW Settings** to get the **Apply Camera RAW Settings** dialog box shown in Figure 25.7. Click in the **Apply Settings From** box and choose **Preddy-Set-1**. This is the .xmp file that we created in Step 2 that contains the **Camera RAW** settings.

If you want to have more flexibility over which **Camera RAW** settings get applied to each of the selected images, click in the **Advanced** box to get the advanced **Apply Camera RAW Settings** box shown in Figure 25.8. Not only can you change the settings from those in the .xmp file, but you can also selectively choose which settings to apply or not apply.

■ Click **Update** to apply the settings to the image files.

STEP 4: PROCESS BATCH

At this point, you have chosen settings for one specific set of images. If you have more than one set, you can select a single image from each set and then create and save the settings. You would then apply them to each of the photos you want to print as proofs as we did in the prior step. This allows you to run an entire batch of photos, which could include more than one set of **Camera RAW** settings, and then batch process them all at once.

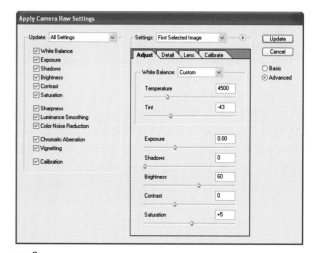

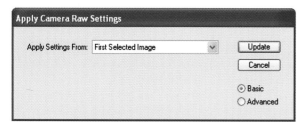

25.7

25.8

■ You are now ready to process the batch. Assuming you still have the images selected in the **File Browser** that you want to process, select **Automate** ➤ **Batch** in the **File Browser Menu** to get the **Batch** dialog box shown in Figure 25.9. Use the same settings that are shown in the figure. In the **Destination** box select **Folder** and then click the **Choose** button to select a folder to use to save the processed file. Click **OK** to begin processing them.

Remember that if you used different **Camera RAW** settings for different "sets" of portraits, you can still apply them with the **File Browser** — then run one **Action** against all the sets in one batch and get the results you want. This is a wonderful time-saving **Action** that you can use when shooting photos of all subjects, not just portraits.

The end of this technique is also the end of this chapter on portraits. In the next chapter, we investigate some techniques that will help you to make montages, collages, and image composites.

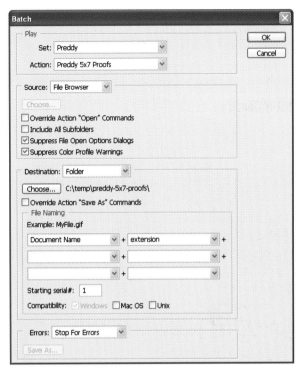

25.9

CHAPTER 5

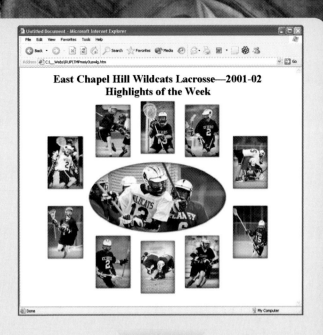

COMBINING PHOTOS IN MONTAGES, COLLAGES, AND COMPOSITES

In this chapter, you will learn how to combine images. First, we look at how to use the Adobe Photoshop CS Extract feature to remove an object from a background image. Next is a fun technique that shows several different approaches to creating a photomontage. The end result of these techniques is a cool-looking building comprised of many parts of many old buildings. It is not a very inviting place, but it surely is amusing to look at. Then, we cover one of the most useful techniques in the entire book — a way to combine two bracketed photos into a single image with dynamic range that is much wider than can be captured with a digital or film camera. The last technique demonstrates a collage mask and a technique that can be used to create a traditional photo collage. This photo collage is especially useful for displaying photos on Web pages.

LIBRA

CREATING PHOTO OBJECTS

26.1

26.2

California Brown Pelican
Canon EOS D30 digital camera mounted on a tripod, 300mm f/2.8 IS, ISO 100, Fine image setting, f/4.5 @ 1/500, original .jpg file has been cropped and edited, 1,095 x 1,665 pixels, 5.5MB .tif file

Removing an element from one image and using it in another image is one of the more exciting things you can do when using an image editor such as Adobe Photoshop CS. You can easily create photo objects (an element taken from an image) with one or more Adobe Photoshop CS tools, such as the Rectangular Marquee, Lasso, or Magnetic Lasso tool, Color Range, and so on, and you can improve the results of these tools by using them on layers or even channels. However, in this technique, we focus only on how to use the powerful Adobe Photoshop CS Extract tool, a tool made especially for creating photo objects.

The objective of this technique is to remove the California brown pelican from his seaside view on top of a rocky overlook so that he may be placed in another image of your choice. You will create a transparent layer containing only the pelican, which may be dragged and dropped onto another image.

STEP 1: OPEN FILE

■ Choose **File ➤ Open** (**Ctrl+O** PC, **Cmd+O** Mac) to display the **Open** dialog box. Double-click the **\26** folder to open it and then click the **pelican-before.tif** file to select it. Click **Open** to open the file.

STEP 2: DUPLICATE LAYER

Before beginning the extract process, it is wise to first duplicate the layer so that you have the option of correcting parts of the image and so that you can easily compare your extracted image with the original.

■ Choose **Layer ➤ Duplicate Layer** to get the **Duplicate Layer** dialog box; click **OK**.

STEP 3: SELECT EXTRACT TOOL

■ Choose **Filter ➤ Extract** (**Alt+Ctrl+X** PC, **Option+Cmd+X** Mac) to get the **Extract** dialog box shown in Figure 26.3.

STEP 4: DRAW AROUND PELICAN

The **Extract** tool is simple to use; you draw around the edge of the object that you want to remove, and then fill the interior of the object with paint and the **Extract** tool removes all the background leaving just the object.

■ Click the **Edge Highlighter** tool (**B**).
■ In the **Tool Options** box on the right side of the **Extract** dialog box, you find a box next to **Smart Highlighting**; click in it to turn on **Smart Highlighting**, which helps you find strong edges.

■ Carefully trace around the pelican with the **Edge Highlighter** tool (**B**). When needed, you can click the **Zoom** tool (**Z**) to increase the size of the image. To reduce the image size, press **Alt** (**Option** on the Mac) while clicking the image with the **Zoom** tool (**Z**).
■ To move around the image, you can also press the **Spacebar** to get the **Hand** tool (**H**), which allows you to click on the image and drag it to see the part of the image you want. When you release the **Spacebar**, the **Hand** tool (**H**) returns to the previous tool. Alternatively, you can click the **Hand** tool (**H**) to select it.
■ If the **Edge Highlighter** tool's paint color blends in with the image, select another color by clicking the box next to **Highlight** in the **Tool Options** area and select a color that offers more contrast with the background.
■ When using the **Edge Highlighter** tool (**B**) you can change the size of the brush by typing a new size in the **Brush Size** box or by clicking in the **Brush Size** box and dragging the slider to choose a new brush size. As you are using the **Edge Highlighter** tool (**B**) to straddle the edge of the targeted elements, you may sometimes find that a larger brush makes this task easier. Use a small brush for hard edges and a large brush for softer edges.

26.3

■ If you make a mistake while painting with the **Edge Highlighter** tool (**B**), click the **Eraser** tool (**E**) and erase the misplaced highlighting.

■ When the entire pelican has been selected, click the **Fill** tool (**G**) and click inside the pelican. The image should now look like the one shown in Figure 26.4.

■ If you decide that you want to start over, press **Alt** (**Option** on the Mac) and the **Cancel** button will turn into a **Reset** button; click the **Reset** button and you will be back where you started.

STEP 5: VIEW PREVIEW

■ To view the extracted pelican, click **Preview** and the **Extract** dialog box now looks similar to the one shown in Figure 26.5. If you want to see the pelican against a different background, click **Display** in the **Preview** area and select your choice of matte colors. Try **White Matte** for this image.

■ If you need to make corrections to the extraction, you can now use the **Cleanup** tool (**C**) or the **Edge Touchup** tool (**T**). Drag the appropriate tool to erase or to make pixels visible.

■ When the extraction appears as you want it to, click **OK** and the extraction is placed on the top layer in the Adobe Photoshop CS workspace.

■ Key features of the pelican are the soft, light-colored feathers on the head. If you click the **Layer Visibility** icon on the **Background** layer on and off, you can see that some of those all-important feathers have been clipped! To put them back on, you can very carefully paint them back by using the **Clone Stamp** tool set to the **Background** layer and by painting on the extracted layer.

You now have an extracted pelican; or in the graphic arts field, you might say a pelican "photo object." To place the pelican in another image, simply drag and drop the extracted layer onto another image. You can then position it, size it, and edit as you like. If you want to save the pelican for later use, you can delete the background layer and just save the extracted pelican layer as a .PSD file.

Just for fun, Figure 26.2 shows the pelican placed on a swing in the woods — it was a simple drag and drop task. A small part of the nearest rope had to be cut and pasted as a new layer so that it could be put in front of the pelican, but that was easily done by using the **Magnetic Lasso** tool. Where do you want to put the pelican today? If you'd like to put it on the swing, the original swing image is in the **\26** folder on the companion CD-ROM named **swing-before.jpg**.

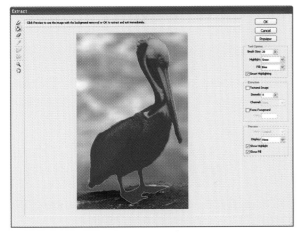

26.4

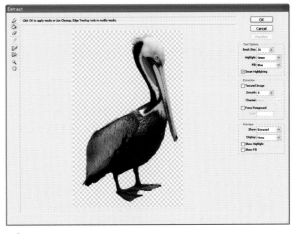

26.5

MAKING A PHOTOMONTAGE

27.1

27.2

ABOUT THE IMAGE

A Home Fit for a Gargoyle
Seventeen digital photos
taken with a Canon D30 digital camera and a variety of
lenses. Images are all 1,440 x
2,160 pixel .jpg images. No
editing has been done to the
images.

As the title of the image suggests — we are going to create an image of a home fit for a gargoyle by combining up to 17 different images of parts of old buildings. To do this, we use an underlying layer with some color and texture and the **Luminosity** blend mode to get a unifying effect that will help us avoid some heavy-duty color adjustments. We then look at a few ways to "merge" the images. From there, you are on your own. If you create an award-winning home that looks like it would suit an upscale gargoyle, please create a small .jpg file (one that fits in a 640 x 640 area) and e-mail it to me at ggeorges@reallyusefulpage.com. Good submissions will be put on display on this book's companion Web page at www.reallyusefulpage.com\pscs\gargoyle-home.htm. You'll get credit for the creation and who knows — you may even get an offer or two to buy the home!

STEP 1: OPEN AND SCALE BACKGROUND IMAGE

■ Choose **File ➤ Open** (**Ctrl+O** PC, **Cmd+O** Mac) to display the **Open** dialog box. Double-click the **\27** folder to open it and then click the **background.jpg** file to select it. Click **Open** to open the file.

If you have a relatively fast computer and 256MB or more of RAM, I suggest that you double the size of the background image and use each of the other files at full-size. Otherwise, you may want to keep the background image at its original size and reduce each of the image files that you use by 50 percent by using **Image ➤ Image Size** after opening each image.

STEP 2: ADD IMAGE

■ Choose **File ➤ Open** (**Ctrl+O** PC, **Cmd+O** Mac) to display the **Open** dialog box. Double-click the **\27** folder to open it and then click **image02.jpg** (a door image) to select it. Click **Open** to open the file.

■ Arrange your workspace so that you can view the background image, plus **image02.jpg** or whatever image you have just opened. Click the **Move** tool (**V**) in the **Toolbox**. Click the **image02.jpg** image and then drag and drop it onto the background image to make it a new layer in the **background.jpg** image file. Alternatively, you can click the **Background** layer in the **Layers** palette while the **image02.jpg** is the active image and drag and drop it onto the **background.jpg** image to create a new layer.

■ After an image has been loaded as a layer on the **background.jpg** image, you can close it to conserve memory. Make sure you do not close the **background.jpg** image.

STEP 3: USE BLEND MODE TO UNIFY COLOR AND TEXTURE

If you look at the 17 images that are available in folder **\27**, you will find that they are quite different in terms of color, focus, texture, and tonal range. To avoid having to make a multitude of adjustments to each image so that they can all be combined to look like they are part of the same building, a blend mode will be used to pick up color and texture from the **background.jpg** image.

■ To blend **image02.jpg** with the **background.jpg** image so that it picks up the color of the **background.jpg** image, click in the **Blend** mode box in the **Layers** palette to get a pop-up menu; choose **Luminosity** as the blend mode.

Using the **Move** tool (**V**), you can click the **image02.jpg** layer and drag it around on the background image. Notice how it picks up the underlying color and textures. Place **image02.jpg** where you want it before going on to the next step.

STEP 4: POSITION AND SIZE IMAGE

One of the challenges in creating a successful image from the 17 images is to position, size, and "blend" each of the images into a building that looks, well, like a building and not 17 images pasted together in a haphazard fashion.

■ To position each image, use the **Move** tool (**V**)
■ To size an image, choose **Edit ➤ Transform ➤ Scale**, or **Edit ➤ Free Transform** (**Ctrl+T** PC, **Cmd+T** Mac); then, click one of the handles found on the selection marquee and drag the image to size or scale it as you desire. If you want to keep the width to height proportions the same, press **Shift** before dragging the selection marquee. On the **Edit ➤ Transform** menu, you find other useful transformation options, such as **Scale, Rotate, Skew, Distort, Perspective,** and so on.

Each time you have an image placed where you think you want it, go back to Step 2 and add another image until you have added them all, or as many as you want to complete your image. After the images are approximately sized and placed where you want them, you can begin "blending" them.

STEP 5: USE "BLEND" TECHNIQUE

Because the goal of this technique is to create a photomontage by combining digital photos into a single image, some parts of the images either have to be cut out (using **Edit ➢ Cut**) or hidden from view, by using a mask. While **Cut** can be used to selectively remove (permanently) parts of an image, it is a destructive command. That is, it tosses out or destroys the part of the image that is cut and you cannot get it back later if you want it. For this reason, I suggest that you create a **Layer Mask** for each of the images that you bring in as a layer. **Layer Masks** allow you to mask off parts of an image and then later unmask them should you change your mind about what parts of an image should be visible.

■ To create a **Layer Mask**, click the chosen layer in the **Layers** palette to make it the active layer. Choose **Layer ➢ Add Layer Mask ➢ Reveal All**. This creates a **Layer Mask** icon on the layer in the **Layers** palette. Figure 27.3 shows the **Layers** palette after a **Layer Mask** was added to the first layer; it is the white rectangle just to the right of the thumbnail.

After you create a **Layer Mask**, you can click it to make it active; then paint on it with the **Brush** tool (**B**) by using **Black** to hide parts of the image. If you want to add back part of the image, just paint it back by using the **Brush** tool (**B**) with color set to **White**.

When painting a **Layer Mask**, you can vary the **Opacity** level in the **Options** bar to get fine control over smooth blends, as shown in Figure 27.4.

Notice how the door has been blended into the underlying rusty metal — you no longer realize that it was previously a square image. Later if you need to paint back some of the door image, just change the **Foreground Color** to **White** and paint the mask back to once again reveal the image. If you had used **Cut**, the portion of the image that you cut would be gone for good. As you begin adding more images, you will learn how invaluable the **Layer Masks** can be.

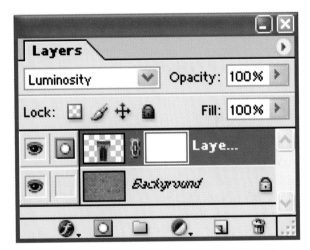

27.3

27.4

■ To make one layer lie on top of another layer, click a layer in the **Layers** palette and drag and drop the layer where you want it. To avoid having to select each layer by clicking it in the **Layers** palette, click in the box next to **Auto Select Layer** in the **Options** bar when the **Move** tool (**V**) has been selected. This enables the **Move** tool to select a layer based upon the image that you click.

Figure 27.5 shows the results and the **Layers** palette after two images were added to the **Background** layer and a **Layer Mask** was created to blend each of the layers. With a little more painting on the **Layer Mask**, the two images will look like they were taken as a single photo.

■ Another way to blend two or more images is to use the **Clone Stamp** tool (**S**). After selecting the **Clone Stamp** tool, click a layer to set the source image; then click a layer and a place where you want to paint the source image and begin painting. You can change the **Clone Stamp** tool (**S**) brush size to suit the cloning requirements. Notice that **Layer 2** has been turned off, and that **Layer 3** also has a **Layer Mask** to use for fine-tuning of the image.

When experimenting with the **Clone Stamp** tool (**S**), try creating a new blank layer by selecting **Layer ➢ New Layer** (**Shift+Ctrl+N** PC, **Shift+Cmd+N** Mac); then, clone onto that new layer part of another layer with the **Clone Stamp** tool (**S**). Just click the layer you want to use as the source image to select it. With the **Clone Stamp** tool (**S**) selected, press **Alt** (**Option** on a Mac) and click the layer where you want to set the clone source. Then, click the new blank layer to make it the active layer and paint with the **Clone Stamp** tool (**S**). Remember, that once you have painted a new layer, you can also move it to position it as you want and even create a **Layer Mask** if one is needed to hide or reveal parts of the image. Figure 27.6 shows the results of using the **Clone Stamp** tool (**S**) tool to paint the image on the right across the door image.

To summarize: You can "blend" images by adjusting the layer order, by painting on a **Layer Mask** to hide part of an image, or by using the **Clone Stamp** tool (**S**) to paint part of one layer onto another part of the image. When you vary **Opacity** as you paint on a **Layer Mask** or with the **Clone Stamp** tool (**S**), you can get even smoother "blends" of images than if you keep **Opacity** set to **100%**.

STEP 6: MAKE ADJUSTMENTS TO LAYERS

After all the images are added, sized, positioned, and "blended," you may find that one or two of the images looks too dark or too light. As you might suspect, I recommend that you create **Adjustment Layers** to make necessary changes. This allows you to

27.5

27.6

go back at any time to fine-tune the settings with tools like **Levels** or **Curves.** Figure 27.7 shows the **Layers** palette after 11 images were added, plus one **Adjustment Levels** layer for **Layer 2.**

STEP 7: FLATTEN IMAGE AND MAKE A FEW FINAL ADJUSTMENTS

■ When you are happy with the image, save it as a **.psd** file with the **Layers** box checked so that you can go back and make further changes to the layers if you choose. Then, choose **Layer ➢ Flatten** image.

■ You can now treat this newly created image as an original photo. Create **Adjustment Layers** for

Levels, Curves, and **Hue/Saturation.** Use the **Unsharp Mask** to sharpen the image or make changes to the color by using one of the many Adobe Photoshop CS color adjustment tools.

Figure 27.2 shows the results of increasing contrast and slightly adjusting colors by using **Hue/Saturation.** I confess that I got a carried away with this image and did about a half-dozen different prints. Try making a few of your own and make some to experiment with a **Hue/Saturation Adjustment Layer** as the **Blend** modes as they can produce some really cool effects when the images are composed with the rusty background layer.

Don't let this funky image of a home fit for gargoyles make you think this technique is not particularly useful — as it is. You can use this same approach to create a photomontage of sporting events, family events, or just about any combination of images that you want to add to one image. It does take some patience and time — making a flawless montage is not easy, but the technique is!

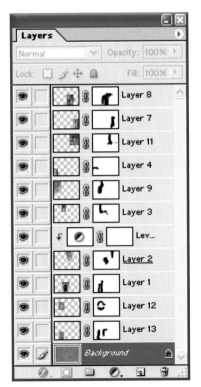

27.7

> **TIP**
>
> Adobe Photoshop CS's new **Replace Color** feature is an excellent tool to use to replace the greens and purples in the finished gargoyle image created in this technique. Select **Image ➢ Adjustments ➢ Replace Color** to get the **Replace Color** dialog box. Click the color you want to change in the image and then adjust the **Hue, Saturation,** and **Lightness** sliders to get the color you want. You can change one or more colors with **Replace Color** and it can be applied as an **Adjustment Layer,** which allows you to go back at a later time and make further adjustments to your original settings.

USING A MASK TO CREATE A COLLAGE

28.1

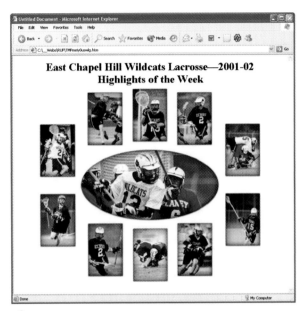

28.2

Many art stores, frame shops, and photo stores offer pre-cut collage matte boards, which make it easy to display multiple photos on a single matte board. This technique shows you how to create a similar collage digitally using a collage mask. The advantage to this approach is that you can create a collage mask once, and then use it each time you need to display new photos.

Figure 28.2 shows the results of using a collage mask to display 11 lacrosse "action photos of the week" on a Web page. The predefined collage mask used for this image may be found on the companion CD-ROM. If you need a collage mask for print purposes, you will need to create a higher resolution mask yourself. To learn how to make a higher resolution version, or to make one of your own design, follow the instructions in Step 1. Otherwise, skip to Step 2 and use the predefined mask.

STEP 1: CREATE COLLAGE MASK

Figure 28.3 shows the layout of the collage found on the companion CD-ROM. It was easily created in just minutes by using Adobe Photoshop CS **Rulers** and **Guidelines**. Technique 1, Step 5 shows how to set up the **Rulers** and how to use **Guidelines** to create layouts such as this one.

The steps for creating the collage mask are as follows:

1. Create a new image. As this particular collage mask was created for a Web page, it was sized at 800 x 600 pixels and **Background Contents** was set to **White**.
2. Select **Layer ➢ Duplicate Layer** so that digital photos can slide beneath the collage mask layer (top layer) and above the **Background** layer.
3. Set **Rulers** to **Pixels** by using **Edit ➢ Preferences ➢ Units & Rulers**, as discussed in Technique 1.
4. Drag **Guidelines** from the **Rulers** and drop them where **Guidelines** are needed for locating the masks. To learn more about using **Guidelines**, see Technique 1.
5. Using the **Rectangular Marquee** and **Elliptical Marquee** tools, select each area to be masked (on the top layer) and fill them with **Black** by using **Edit ➢ Fill** after having set **Foreground** color to **black** in the **Toolbox**.

6. After all the "openings" have been filled with **Black**, select them all with **Select ➢ Color Range** or with the **Magic Wand** tool. To cut them out, load the **Frames.atn** actions into the **Actions** palette and then run the **Cutout** (selection) **Action**. To learn how to use **Actions**, see Technique 6.

That's it — your collage mask is now ready for photos to be placed beneath each opening.

STEP 2: INSERT DIGITAL PHOTOS

■ If you did not create your own collage mask in Step 1, choose **File ➢ Open** (**Ctrl+O** PC, **Cmd+O** Mac) to display the **Open** dialog box. Double-click the **\28** folder to open it and then click the **collage-mask.psd** file to select it. Click **Open** to open the file. You should now have an image that looks like the one shown in Figure 28.4 and the **Layers** palette should look like the one shown in Figure 28.5 only with guidelines showing. To turn off the guidelines, select **View ➢ Show Guides** (**Ctrl+ ;** PC, **Cmd+ ;** Mac).

Eleven lacrosse images can be found in the **\28** folder. The original full-size digital action photos were cropped, edited, resized, and then sharpened so that they would fit inside the masked openings. They

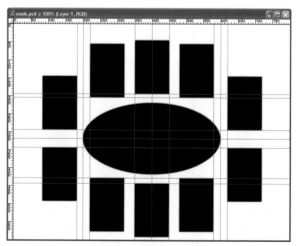

28.3

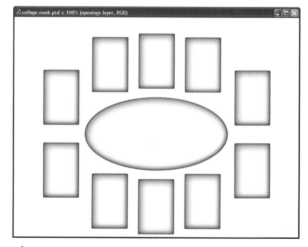

28.4

were then saved as .jpg files by using the Adobe PhotoshopCS **Save for Web** feature.

■ To open all 11 images at once, choose **File ➤ Open** (**Ctrl+O** PC, **Cmd+O** Mac) to display the **Open** dialog box. Double-click the **\28** folder to open it. Press and hold **Ctrl** (**Cmd** on the Mac); then click each file named **image01.jpg** through **image11.jpg** to select them all. Alternatively, while pressing **Shift**, you can select them all by clicking on the first image and on the last image. Click **Open** to open all the files into the Adobe Photoshop CS workspace.

■ Click on the **collage-mask.psd** image to make it the active image.

■ Click **Background** layer in the **Layers** palette to make it the active layer and to make sure that you do not add the action photo images above the collage mask

■ Click the **Move** tool (**V**) in the **Toolbox**.

■ To insert the first photo, click **image01.jpg** to make it the active image and drag it onto the **collage-mask.psd** image. Using the **Move** tool, click and drag the image so that it shows through the center elliptical opening.

■ Using the **Move** tool, continue clicking each image and dragging it onto the **collage-mask.psd**

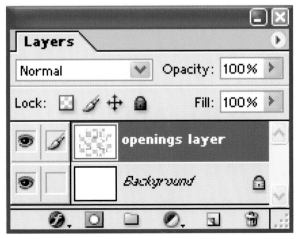

28.5

image until all images have been correctly positioned. After you place all of the images, the **Layers** palette shows the **Background** layer, the **openings layer**, and 11 image layers.

Depending on how you select and position the images, you may find that one or more images overlap another image. If this occurs, make sure **Auto Select Layer** is turned on by clicking in the box next to it in the **Options** bar. Then, click the overlapping image by using the **Move** tool (**V**) to select it. Click the **Lasso** tool (**L**); then click and draw a selection marquee around the part of the image that you want to remove. Choose **Edit ➤ Cut** (**Ctrl+X** PC, **Cmd+X** Mac) to cut the overlapping part of the image. Alternatively, you can create a **Layer Mask** and paint out the part of the image that you do not want to show. Or, you can drag and drop layers in the **Layers** palette so that the order of the images eliminates the overlapped image problem.

STEP 3: FLATTEN IMAGE AND SAVE AS A NEW FILE

■ Choose **Layer ➤ Flatten Image**.

■ To minimize image size, click the **Rectangular Marquee** tool (**M**) and drag a selection marquee around all the images. Choose **Image ➤ Crop** to crop the image.

■ To save as an optimized **.jpg** file to be used on a Web page, choose **File ➤ Save For Web** (**Alt+Shift+Ctrl+S** PC, **Option+Shift+Cmd+S** Mac) to get the **Save For Web** dialog box. Select the **JPEG Medium** setting and click **Save**. Name the file and save it in an appropriate folder.

The image is now a mere 52K and is ready to be placed on a Web page. Figure 28.2 shows how the image looks in an Internet browser after an HTML editor has been used to add a title. If you had to create such an image each week for weekly action photos, you would simply need to open the collage mask and drag and drop images — it is that easy.

COMBINING BRACKETED PHOTOS

29.1

29.2

Shenandoah National Forest After Sunset Canon EOS D30 digital camera, 28-70mm f/2.8 at 34mm, ISO 100, RAW image quality, f/2.8 @ 1/10 and f/4.0 @ 1/10, 2,160 x 1,440 pixels. Images have been converted from 16-bit RAW to 8-bit .tif.

J ust looking at these photos makes me cold. When getting out of the car to take them, I seriously questioned whether I *really* wanted to take photos that much. The temperature dropped about 30 degrees in an hour — it was around 18 degrees Fahrenheit with a 40-mph wind blowing the light rain up the side of the mountain directly into my face and the camera lens. By the time I got the camera set up on a tripod and took two shots, my face and hands were numb. A quick look at the images shown in Figure 29.1 gives you an idea of the challenge — to blend the best parts of the bracketed images together to give good detail in the light areas and good detail in the shadows.

Admittedly, I did not take the best possible photos in this case. Given a more relaxed shooting environment, I would have used the camera's spot-metering capability and metered the sky and then the foreground, while taking a photo in each case. Instead, I set up the camera very quickly — took one shot — changed from f/2.8 to f/4.0, took a second shot, and jumped back into the car!

After you complete this technique, my bet is you'll find that shooting bracketed photos and combining them by using this technique will yield better results than if you were to take the time to use a graduated neutral density filter. As you will see, this technique does not force you into positioning a perfectly graduated filter over an image of a scene where life is not so perfect, and, where the dynamic range of the subject exceeds the dynamic range of your digital camera's imaging chip. Try this technique on the images supplied on the companion CD-ROM. Then, try it on some of your own.

STEP 1: OPEN FILES

- Choose **File ➤ Open** (**Ctrl+O** PC, **Cmd+O** Mac) to display the **Open** dialog box. Double-click the **\29** folder to open it. Press **Ctrl** (or **Cmd** on Mac) and click **sunset-before1.tif** and **sunset-before2.tif** to highlight both files; then, click **Open** to open both files.

STEP 2: COMBINE BOTH FILES INTO ONE IMAGE

- To place the lighter of the two images on top of the darker image, click once in the **sunset-before1. tif** image to make it the active image. Click on the **Move** tool (**V**) in the **Toolbox**. Press the **Shift** key

while clicking the **Background** layer in the **Layers** palette; then, drag and drop the layer onto the top of the **sunset.before2.tif** image. The **Layers** palette should now show a **Background** layer and a **Layer 1**.

- You no longer need the **sunset-before1.tif** image, so you can close it.
- Choose **View ➤ Fit on Screen** (**Ctrl+0** PC; **F**, then **Cmd+0** Mac) to maximize the image.

STEP 3: CREATE LAYER MASK

Next you combine the two images by using a **Layer Mask**.

- Click **Layer 1** in the **Layers** palette if it is not already highlighted.
- Choose **Layer ➤ Add Layer Mask ➤ Reveal All**. Looking at the **Layers** palette now, you notice that there is a **Layer Mask** just to the right of the **Layer 1** thumbnail (see Figure 29.3); click it to make it active.

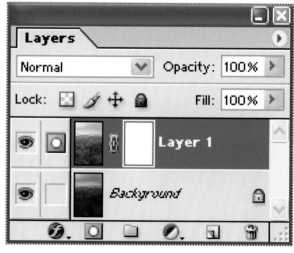

29.3

■ To set **Black** as the **Foreground** click the **Default Foreground and Background colors (D)** icon at the bottom of the **Toolbox**; then, click on **Switch Foreground and Background Colors (X)**

■ Click the **Brush** tool (**B**) in the **Toolbox**. Click the **Brush Preset Picker** in the **Options** bar to get the **Brush** palette shown in Figure 29.4. If you get a different palette, click the menu button at the upper-right corner of the **Brush Preset Picker** palette and choose **Reset Brushes** from the pop-up menu. Select the **Soft Round 200 Pixels** brush.

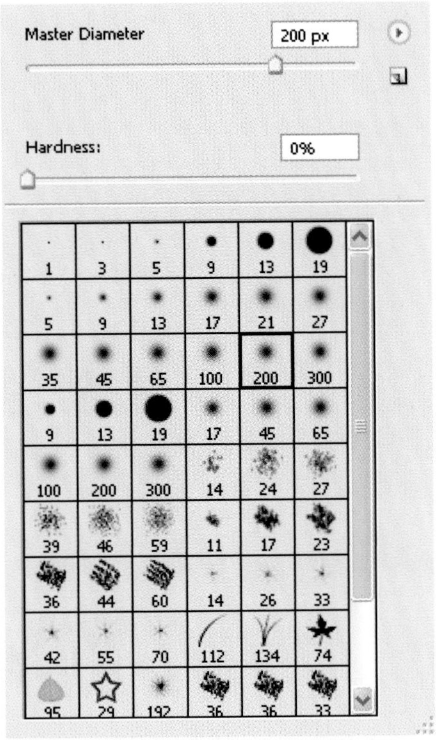

29.4

■ Click in the **Opacity** box in the **Options** bar to get a slider; set **Opacity** to **10%**. Make sure **Mode** is set to **Normal** and **Flow** to **100%**.

STEP 4: PAINT ON THE LAYER MASK TO REVEAL THE LOWER LAYER

In the prior step, a **Layer Mask** was created, the Brush tool (**B**) was set to **Black**, and **Opacity** was set to **10%**. As the **Layer Mask** is painted with **Black**, it allows the **Background** layer to show through. If you paint with **White**, it will once again hide the **Background** layer. To get the best results, try painting with **Opacity** set to **10%**, which is a 10% gray. This means that you will have to paint over the image 10 times to build up to a pure black enabling the entire layer below to show through. Using a low **Opacity** setting such as **10%**, allows you to more carefully build up the mask to show precisely what you want. Each time you click, you increase the buildup of the mask by 10 percent. Painting an image like this one is vastly easier, more fun, and more accurate than if you have a pen tablet like one of the Wacom pen tablets (www.wacom.com).

■ Begin carefully painting the sky with the **Brush** tool (**B**) until you have increased the image density to match the foreground. I suggest that you vary the size of the **Brush** and that you increase the image to **100%** when painting the edges between the sky and the distant mountain range, especially when painting the edge between the middle mountain range and the foreground trees. Later, when you make further adjustments to the image, your careful painting eliminates the need to go back and try again. Yes, there is a corollary to this — don't paint carefully and you'll have to paint again! After some painting, your image should look similar to the one shown in Figure 29.5.

If you change your **Brush** to a **Soft Round 65** or **Soft Round 100 Pixel** brush, you can increase contrast in the mountains in the middle of the image by painting only on the denser green areas. You could never do this with a split neutral density filter!

■ Once you are happy with the image, select **Layer ➢ Flatten Image**. By flattening the image you are able to apply **Adjustment Layers** to the foreground and background equally. If you didn't flatten the image, you would run the risk of getting a miss-match between the foreground layer and the background layer.

29.5

STEP 5: CREATE ADJUSTMENT LAYERS AND MAKE FINAL ADJUSTMENTS TO THE IMAGE

After you blend and flatten the image, you can begin making the same kinds of image adjustments that were covered in Chapter 2. Make sure that you use **Adjustment Layers** for each of the adjustments. Using **Adjustment Layer**s allows you to go back and modify the settings.

■ Choose **Layer ➢ New Adjustment Layer ➢ Levels** to get the **New Layer** dialog box; click **OK** to get the **Levels** dialog box. Click **Use Previous Layer to Create Clipping Mask.** Using the **RGB** channel, slide the left slider toward the right until **Input Levels** shows **10**, **1.20**, and **255**, as shown in Figure 29.6. Click **OK** to apply the settings.

■ Click on the **Background** layer.

■ Choose **Layer ➢ New Adjustment Layer ➢ Curves** to get the **New Layer** dialog box; click **OK** to get the **Curves** dialog box. Click in the image in the foreground and drag around the foreground while watching where the point moves up and down the curve in the **Curves** dialog box. This indicates the part of the curve where the slope must be increased to increase contrast in the rich-colored foreground trees.

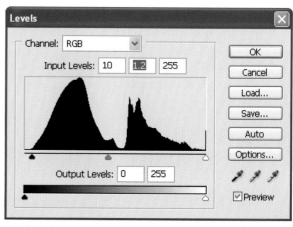

29.6

- Try setting one point at **60** and **58**, and a second point at **103** and **112**. Setting these two points greatly improves the foreground tree area.
- If you want to perform a similar adjustment to the sky to increase the contrast of the sky, once again drag your cursor over the sky to see what area of the curve needs to have the slope increased, which increases contrast. I liked the results of setting two points at **185** and **182** and another one at **227** and **222**. The curve in the **Curves** dialog box should now look like the one shown in Figure 29.7.
- Click **OK** to apply the settings.

Even though the image now shows some rich fall colors, they looked much richer and brighter before the wind and rain began. So, just because we can, let's increase color saturation a tiny bit more to make those orange colors pop off the screen and later off a printed photograph.

- Click on the **Background** layer. Choose **Layer ➤ New Adjustment Layer ➤ Hue/Saturation** to get the **New Layer** dialog box; click **OK** to get the

Hue/Saturation dialog box shown in Figure 29.8. Using the **Master** channel in the **Edit** box, slide the **Saturation** slider to **+12**. As you move the slider, watch carefully to see how the red and orange trees begin to glow — stop before you overdo it. Click **OK** to apply the settings. Your image now looks like the one shown in Figure 29.2.

At this point, the **Layers** palette should look like the one shown in Figure 29.9. The significant point here:

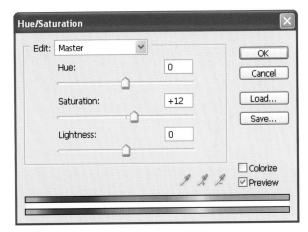

29.8

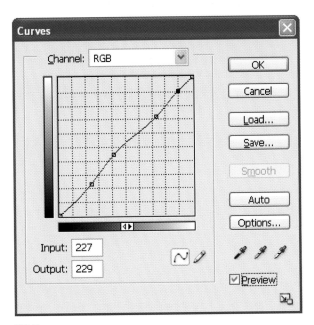

29.7

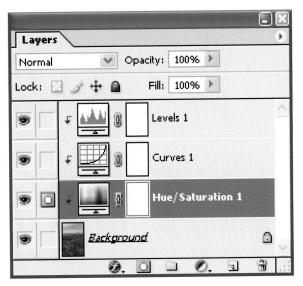

29.9

By clicking on any one of the **Adjustment Layers**, you can go back and change any of the settings you want.

As these few steps fully illustrate this approach to capturing the full dynamic range found in real life settings, we end this technique here. However, be aware that many other changes can still be applied to this image. Some of the other techniques in this book can be used on this image to further improve it, such as sharpening.

SHOOTING IN A RAW FORMAT

One of the greatest challenges in photography is to capture the full dynamic range in a scene with a digital camera image sensor. This is a particularly common challenge when shooting landscapes like the one of the Smokey Mountains shown earlier in this technique. If you expose to capture the detail in the sky, you lose detail in the foreground trees as they are covered in shadow. Likewise, if you expose for the shadows to show detail in the foreground trees, then the sky is overly bright and you lose detail in the clouds.

One solution to this problem is to shoot two photos and use Technique 29 to combine them. Another solution is to shoot one photo with a camera that offers a RAW image format. If you expose the photo so that you do not have blown-out highlights, you can use Adobe Photoshop CS's Camera RAW plug-in to create two different images (with different exposures) from the same file. First, choose settings to expose for the highlights and convert the file. Rename the converted file. Then, convert the same RAW file a second time, but this time use settings to show details in the shadows. Once you have converted two separate images, you can use Technique 29 to combine them into one well-exposed image. With this approach you can even capture full dynamic range in images where there is a moving subject and you can only shoot once, such as an ocean view with large moving waves, or even a bird in flight.

In order to be able to get two well-bracketed images from a single RAW file, you must take care when shooting not to overexpose the highlights. You can generally bring back detail in shadow area, but blown-out highlights will never show detail. So, expose to avoid blown-out highlights and you are usually able to get two good exposures that will allow you to create a single image that covers the full dynamic range of the original scene. If you want to try this approach, an original RAW file for the Smokey Mountain photo is in the \29 folder. It is named CRW_2438.CRW.

Technique 8 shows how you can convert a RAW image file with exposure settings of −2 to +4. In Technique 36 you learn to convert images with the Phase One DSLR RAW file converter to get similar results. Shooting with the RAW file format gives you one more major advantage of shooting digital over film.

CHAPTER 6

FINE ART TECHNIQUES

This chapter is for photographers who either have always wanted to be a painter or who have painted and now want to learn how to use Photoshop to transform digital photographs into graphic art or fine art prints. This chapter is also for graphic and fine artists who want to effectively use their traditional media skills in the new digital paint studio. Of all the chapters in this book, this is the chapter that shows off the awesome power Adobe Photoshop CS has for transforming digital photographs into art of an entirely different type.

The techniques in this chapter cover how to create line drawings, rough marker sketches, pen and ink sketches with a watercolor wash, fine art images using filters, and more—all with Adobe Photoshop CS. While one technique is for those with traditional painting skills, the others may be used by just about anyone with a few digital photos. While I would consider this to be a fun chapter, some of the techniques are rather long and they can be time-consuming.

TOTAL COLOR TRANSFORMATION

30.1

30.2

A digital photo that was created by digitally stitching together five photos that were taken with a digital camera on a tripod is shown in Figure 30.1. Each photo was overlapped about one-third and then combined into a single image by using Enroute PowerStitch software, which is no longer available. You can achieve the same digital stitching effect by using the Photomerge feature found in Adobe Photoshop CS. The photo was shot in the early afternoon, and the bright blue color of the sky dominates the image. Our objective for this image is not insignificant — to turn the image into an after-dusk image with a rich orange sunset color and a magical tree just to add a bit of intrigue.

STEP 1: OPEN FILE

■ Choose **File ➢ Open** (**Ctrl+O** PC, **Cmd+O** Mac) to display the **Open** dialog box. Double-click the **\30** folder to open it and then click the **farm-before.tif** file to select it. Click **Open** to open the file.

STEP 2: CREATE MIRRORED TREE

The objective of this step is to select a portion of the image between the middle of two trees, copy it, and paste it back into the image. Then, flip it horizontally and slide it to the right so that part of the image is mirrored.

■ Click the **Rectangular Marquee** tool (**M**) in the **Toolbox**. In the **Options** bar, set **Feather** to **0 px** and **Style** to **Normal**.

■ Double-click the document window title bar to maximize it on the PC (on the Mac type **F** or select **View ➢ Screen Mode ➢ Full Screen Mode With Menu Bar**). Using a maximized window makes it much easier to select an image all the way to the edges.

■ Choose **View ➢ Fit on Screen** (**Ctrl+0** PC, **Cmd+0** Mac) to make the image as large as it can be and yet have all of it be visible.

■ Click on the **Rectangular Marquee** tool (**M**) in the **Toolbox** and then click just below the image and in line with the middle of the largest tree; drag the marquee up toward the left until the left side of the marquee is in the middle of another tree, as shown in Figure 30.3.

■ Choose **Layer ➢ New ➢ Layer via Copy** (**Ctrl+J** PC, **Cmd+J** Mac) to copy the selection and paste it back into the image as a layer.

■ Choose **Edit ➢ Transform ➢ Flip Horizontal** to flip the pasted layer horizontally.

■ Click the **Move** tool (**V**) in the **Toolbox**. Press **Shift** and click inside the pasted portion of the image and move it toward the right until the two middles of the big tree mirror each other, as shown in Figure 30.4. Pressing **Shift** will help you to keep the image aligned vertically with the **Background**.

30.3

30.4

■ To make final adjustments to the location of the pasted layer, click the **Zoom** tool (**Z**). Click once and drag the **Zoom** selection marquee around the largest tree so that it fills up the desktop.

■ Once again, click the **Move** tool (**V**) in the **Toolbox**. Now press the **Right Arrow** or **Left Arrow** keys to move the pasted layer 1 pixel at a time. If you press **Shift** and one of the arrow keys, the layer will move 10 pixels at a time. Keep making adjustments until the tree is perfectly symmetrical.

■ After **Layer 1** is accurately positioned, choose **Layer** ➤ **Flatten Image** to flatten the layer.

STEP 3: CROP IMAGE

If you look toward the right side of the image, you will find a part of the image that no longer fits with the rest of the image. The break occurs where there is a break in the white fence. The image to the right of the break in the fence needs to be cropped out.

■ Click the **Crop** tool (**C**) in the **Toolbox**. In the **Options** bar, delete any values in the **Width** and **Height** boxes by clicking **Clear** in the **Options** bar.

■ Double-click the document window title bar to maximize it if it is not already maximized (press **F** if you are using a Mac).

■ Choose **View** ➤ **Fit on Screen** (**Ctrl+0** PC, **Cmd+0** Mac) to make the image as large as it can be while still allowing you to see the entire image.

■ Using the **Crop** tool, click just outside the upper-left side of the image. Then, drag the marquee down and to the right until you have all of the image selected up to the end of the white fence on the right side.

■ Click the **Commit Current Crop Operation** button on the **Options** bar, or choose **Image** ➤ **Crop**, or press **Enter** on the PC or **Return** on the Mac to crop the image

You should now create a snapshot, as this is a key state in this technique. You can create a snapshot by clicking the menu button in the **History** palette to get a pop-up menu. Choose **New Snapshot** to get the **New Snapshot** dialog box. If you want to name the snapshot, type **mirrored tree** in the **Name** box and then click **OK**. You also can click the **Create New Snapshot** icon at the bottom of the **History** palette, but creating a new snapshot this way does not allow you to name the snapshot while creating it. Another alternative is to press **Alt** (**Option** on the Mac) while clicking the **New Snapshot** button and you will be prompted for a name. Pressing **Alt** (**Option** on the Mac) when choosing a command or clicking a button usually means "show a dialog box if you normally wouldn't" or "don't show a dialog box if you normally would."

STEP 4: REDUCE THE APPEARANCE OF SYMMETRY

While I like the magical-looking tree, I do not like the fact that everything around the tree also looks "mirrored." So let's mess up the symmetry a bit so that only the tree appears to have been touched by magic when it was a mere seed in the woods.

■ Click the **Clone Stamp** tool (**S**) in the **Toolbox**.

■ In the **Clone Stamp** tool **Options** box, make sure **Mode** is set to **Normal**, **Opacity** to **100%**, and **Flow** to **100%**.

■ Click the **Brush Preset Picker** icon, which is the second icon from the left on the **Options** bar to get the **Brush Preset Picker** palette shown in Figure 30.5.

■ If the **Brush Preset Picker** does not look the same as the one in Figure 30.5, you may need to either reset the brushes or change the layout. To reset the picker, click the menu button in the upper-right corner of the **Brush Preset Picker** palette to get a pop-menu. Choose **Reset Brushes** and click **OK** when asked: **Replace current brushes with the default brushes?**

■ To change the layout of the **Brush Preset Picker**, click the menu button and choose **Small Thumbnail** from the pop-up menu.

■ Click the **Soft Round 65 Pixels** brush to select it.

■ To help make your cloning work as easy and accurate as possible, choose **View ➢ Actual Pixels** (**Alt+Ctrl+0** PC, **Opt+Cmd+0** Mac), and then press **F**, **F**, and **Tab**. You now have an uncluttered screen full of the image at 100 percent.

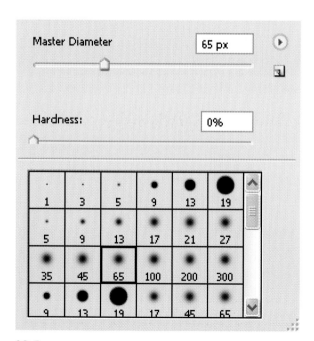

30.5

■ Press the **Spacebar** to get the **Hand** tool. Then, drag the image so that the largest tree and the two silos are in the middle of your screen. You are now ready to begin painting with the **Clone Stamp** tool.

■ First paint the white fence all the way across the gap beneath the large symmetrical tree. When you press **Alt** (**Opt** on the Mac), you get a new cursor, which allows you to set the source of the clone brush. With this cursor, click once on the bottom rung of the fence on the second fence post to the right of the two silos — this sets the clone source to that point.

■ To begin cloning, press the left mouse button after aligning the center of the **Clone Stamp** tool cursor on the bottom rung at a post where you want to begin cloning. Drag the cursor to paint in the fence.

When needed, reset the clone source by pressing **Alt** (**Opt** on the Mac) and then paint in more of the fence until the entire fence looks correct.

■ The brown silo on the right really ought to go as well. Once again, find some good source branches and clone them until the silo is no longer there. I suggest that you also get rid of one of the little outbuildings on either side of the symmetrical tree. As you eliminate the symmetry in everything around the single large symmetrical tree, your image begins to look more realistic (with the exception of the single magical tree) and that is just what we want.

As you paint with the **Clone Stamp** tool, you may want to select a different brush size or maybe even one with a hard edge. To do so, simply click the **Brush Preset Picker** icon in the **Option** bar and select a new brush. There is some art to cloning. Carefully consider where and how often you set your source. When painting, click often and change to an appropriate brush to get the best results. Using many short strokes instead of a few long ones also helps to cover your tracks as well.

■ Press **Tab** and **F** to return to normal view again. Double-click the document window to maximize it; then choose **View** ➤ **Fit on Screen** (**Ctrl+0** PC, **Cmd+0** Mac).

Now is a good time to once again take a **snapshot**. Alternatively, you can save your file as a temporary file with a filename, such as "**farm-mirrored**."

Before you begin changing the colors in the image, create a duplicate layer, as it may be needed later. How do I know this? Well I do, because I have experimented enough to know that some really cool things can happen when you use some of the blend modes to darken images. After you complete this technique, you'll find yourself keeping a few extra layers around just in case, too!

■ Choose **Layer** ➤ **Duplicate Layer** to get the **Duplicate Layer** dialog box. Click **OK** to create a duplicate layer that automatically gets named **Background copy** in the **Layers** palette.

STEP 5: CHANGE BLUE SKY TO A DARK ORANGE SUNSET COLOR

The process of changing colors as much as we are attempting is fraught with difficulties. As you go on, you see that you will have some strange colorcasts to remove.

■ Choose **Image** ➤ **Apply Image** to get the **Apply Image** dialog box shown in Figure 30.6. Click in the **Blending** box to get a pop-up menu; choose **Multiply**. Type **65** in the **Opacity** box and then click **OK** to blend the layer with itself. The colors will now be much more saturated.
■ Choose **Image** ➤ **Adjustments** ➤ **Hue/Saturation** (**Ctrl+U** PC, **Cmd+U** Mac) to get the **Hue/Saturation** dialog box shown in Figure 30.7.
■ Set **Hue** to **+165**, **Saturation** to **+30**, and **Lightness** to **0**. Click **OK** to apply the settings.

Now the challenge is to remove the green, cyan, and blue hues that are in the field and trees.

■ Choose **Image** ➤ **Adjustments** ➤ **Hue/Saturation** (**Ctrl+U** PC, **Cmd+U** Mac) to get the **Hue/Saturation** dialog box.
■ Click in the **Edit** box to get a pop-up menu. Choose **Greens** (**Ctrl+3** PC, **Cmd+3** Mac).
■ Set **Hue** to **0**, **Saturation** to **–100**, and leave **Lightness** set to **0**.
■ Click in the **Edit** box to get a pop-up menu. Choose **Cyans** (**Ctrl+4** PC, **Cmd+4** Mac).
■ Set **Hue** to **0**, **Saturation** to **–100**, and leave **Lightness** set to **0**.

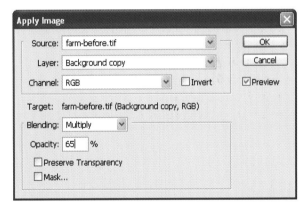

30.6

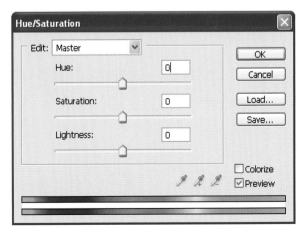

30.7

■ Click in the **Edit** box to get a pop-up menu. Choose **Blues** (**Ctrl+5** PC, **Cmd+5** Mac).
■ Set **Hue** to **0**, **Saturation** to **–60**, and leave **Lightness** set to **0**.
■ Click **OK** to apply the settings.

The objective now is to darken the image and to add some contrast to the sky so that it looks like there is an orange glow caused by the sun setting below the far off horizon. To do this, we use the **Soft Light** blend mode, which compares two images and selects values from both images based upon the lightest values.

■ Make sure that the **Background copy** layer (not the **Background** layer) is highlighted in the **Layers** palette by clicking on it to make it the active layer.
■ Choose **Image** ➤ **Apply Image** to get the **Apply Image** dialog box shown in Figure 30.8.

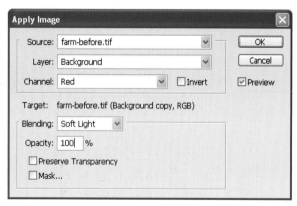

30.8

■ Click in the **Layer** box and choose **Background** from the pop-up menu.
■ Click in the **Channel** box to get a pop-up menu. Choose **Red**.
■ Click in the **Blending** box to get a pop-up. Choose **Soft Light**.
■ Set **Opacity** to **100%** and click **OK** to apply the blend.

Notice how the **Soft Light** blend mode created a nice glow to the image.

STEP 6: MAKE FINAL COLOR AND TONAL CHANGES

You can improve the image easily by increasing image contrast using **Levels**.

■ Choose **Image** ➤ **Adjustments** ➤ **Levels** (**Ctrl+L** PC, **Cmd+L** Mac) to get the **Levels** dialog box. Set **Input** levels to **20**, **.95**, and **235**. Click **OK** to apply the settings. Your image should now look like the image shown in Figure 30.2.

If the orange color is not exactly as you want it, you can further fine-tune the colors by using the **Hue/Saturation** command once again. As for me, I've done enough to be happy with this image as it is. I should mention that while this heavily saturated red image looks good on a PC screen, it is a true challenge to get it to print correctly on consumer level inkjet printers. It can be done, but you may have to do some tweaking of your printer's controls to get a print as you want it.

USING FILTERS TO CREATE FINE ART PRINTS

31.1

31.2

ABOUT THE IMAGE

Country Farm House Canon D30 mounted on a tripod, 28-70mm f/2.8 @ 58mm, ISO 100, f/7.1 @ 1/8, 2,160 x 1,440 pixels, Fine image quality, 2.3MB .jpg

The photo of the country farmhouse shown in Figure 31.1 was taken in Virginia on a freezing, rainy day. One of the neighbors told me some local folklore about the house. The story is that the house contains some rather significant distillery capabilities. The color of the laundry is a coded message that tells what is brewing and invites friends to drop in for a drink. I don't know if the story is true, but I wouldn't knock on the door to ask!

Anyone that takes photographs knows that you can try as hard as possible to take great photos with each click of the exposure button. Yet, later you find out, that you didn't get the shot you had hoped to have. One of the exciting things about using a digital image editor such as Adobe Photoshop CS is that you can often fix those not "quite right" photos. Or you can apply a half-dozen filters and end up with a good print you are pleased to have made. This technique shows how a few commonly used filters can be combined so that you end up with an image that makes a nice print.

STEP 1: OPEN FILE

■ Choose **File** ➢ **Open** (**Ctrl+O** PC, **Cmd+O** Mac) to display the **Open** dialog box. Double-click the **\31** folder to open it and then click the **cabin-before.jpg** file to select it. Click **Open** to open the file.

One tip for getting better effects when using some of the filters in the **Filter** menu is to use a filter on one layer and blend it with a second layer, which may or may not have been edited. As we intend to do this later in this technique, we need to create a second layer now.

■ Choose **Layer** ➢ **Duplicate Layer** to get the **Duplicate Layer** dialog box. Click **OK** to create a layer we can later use to apply a blend mode to increase density and soften the effects of a couple of filters.

STEP 2: SOFTEN IMAGE

To dramatically change the character of this digital photo, we are going to apply a few filters to soften the edges and add depth to shadows.

■ First it's a good idea to increase the image to 100% before applying filters so that you can clearly see the effects that you will get. You can zoom to **100%** by double-clicking the **Zoom** tool (**Z**) in the **Toolbox,** or you can choose **View** ➢ **Actual Pixels** (**Alt+Ctrl+0** PC, **Opt+Cmd+0** Mac).

■ Press the **Spacebar** to get the **Hand** tool; then click the image and drag it up toward the right until you can see the red shirt on the laundry line. Also, look at the brown grass in the bottom-left corner of the image. As you apply effects to the image, check both of these areas to make sure the effects are what you want.

■ Choose **Filter** ➢ **Blur** ➢ **Smart Blur** to get the **Smart Blur** dialog box shown in Figure 31.3. When you move your cursor over the preview image in the **Smart Blur** dialog box, the cursor changes into the **Grab** tool icon. Click and drag the image around until the red shirt on the laundry line shows in the middle of the preview box.

■ In the **Smart Blur** dialog box, set **Quality** to **High** and **Mode** to **Normal**. Try using a **Threshold** setting of **25.0** and then begin sliding the **Radius** slider until you get the results you like. I found a **Radius** setting of **3.0** to be just about right. Click **OK** to apply the blur.

■ Choose **Filter** ➢ **Artistic** ➢ **Poster Edges** to get the **Poster Edges** filter in Adobe Photoshop CS's

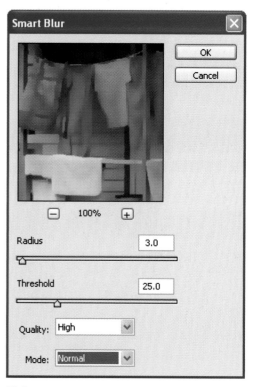

31.3

new **Filter Gallery** dialog box shown in Figure 31.4. To view more of the image, click the **Expand Preview** button just to the left of the **OK** button to close the filter effects window. Once again, click inside the preview box and drag the image around until you can see the red shirt on the laundry line and then look at an area where there are leaves. Experiment with different settings to make sure there are enough dark edges, but not too many. Try setting **Edge Thickness**, **Edge Intensity**, and **Posterization** to **1**, **1**, and **6** respectively. Click **OK** to apply the effect.

STEP 3: DARKEN THE IMAGE

■ To darken the image, you blend the two layers in the **Layers** palette. The **Layers** palette should now look like the one in Figure 31.5. Click the **Blend** mode box to get a pop-up menu. Choose **Multiply** and set **Opacity** to **66%**.
■ Flatten the image by choosing **Layer** ➢ **Flatten Image**.

Another way to darken an image without getting a posterization effect like you can get when using **Levels** is to duplicate a layer and then blend it with itself by using the **Multiply** blend mode. However, rather than taking the effort to duplicate a layer, blend it and then flatten it again — the **Apply Image** command does it all in a single step with less consumption of your time and your PC's memory resources.

STEP 4: MAKE FINAL COLOR AND TONE ADJUSTMENTS

Now increase color saturation and try to add some "punch" to the image to make the cabin stand out from the background.

■ As we are not particularly concerned about posterization in this image (having used the **Poster Edges** effect), choose **Image** ➢ **Adjustments** ➢ **Auto Color** (**Shift+Ctrl+B** PC, **Shift+Cmd+B** Mac) to improve the tonal range of each of the three color channels (red, green, and blue).

31.4

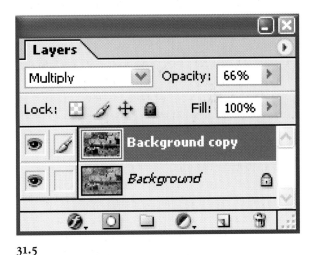

31.5

■ Choose **Image ➢ Adjustments ➢ Hue/ Saturation** (**Ctrl+U** PC, **Cmd+U** Mac) to get the **Hue/Saturation** dialog box shown in Figure 31.6. Set **Hue** to **0**, **Saturation** to **25**, and **Lightness** to **0**. Click **OK** to apply the settings.

■ The image now needs some "punch," so let's increase contrast and brightness. Choose **Image ➢ Adjustments ➢ Curves** (**Ctrl+M** PC, **Cmd+M** Mac) to get the **Curves** dialog box.

■ Click once on the top half of the line to set a point. In the **Input** box, type **158** and in the **Output** box type **168**.

■ Click the bottom half of the line to set a second point. In the **Input** box, type **100** and in the **Output** box, type **83**.

■ The **Curves** dialog box now looks like the one shown in Figure 31.7.

■ Click **OK** to apply the settings.

■ Choose **Layer ➢ Duplicate Layer** to get the **Duplicate Layer** dialog box and then click **OK**.

■ Choose **Filter ➢ Blur ➢ Gaussian Blur** to get the **Gaussian Blur** dialog box. Set **Radius** to **4.0** and click **OK**.

■ Click in the **Blend Mode** box in the **Layers** palette and select **Luminosity** as the blend mode. Set **Opacity** to **40%**.

■ Select **Layer ➢ Flatten Image**.

■ We need to make one last change to lighten the shadow areas. Choose **Image ➢ Adjustments ➢ Curves** (**Ctrl+M** PC, **Cmd+M** Mac) to get the **Curves** dialog box. Click once on the line to set a point. In the **Input** box, type **43** and in the **Output** box type **58**.

That completes this image and this technique — that is unless you are inclined to do some more tweaking. If changing colors is your objective, I suggest you try **Hue/Saturation**. Using the **Hue/ Saturation** command you can make global changes to the colors by using the **Master** channel as we just did, or you can click in the **Edit** box and select **Reds**, **Yellows**, **Greens**, **Cyans**, **Blues**, or **Magentas** to adjust each color independently. If you make a few adjustments and you want to start all over, press **Alt** on the PC (**Option** on the Mac) and the **Cancel** button changes to **Reset**. Click **Reset** to reset all the settings.

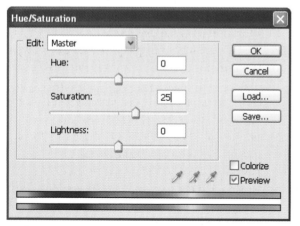

31.6

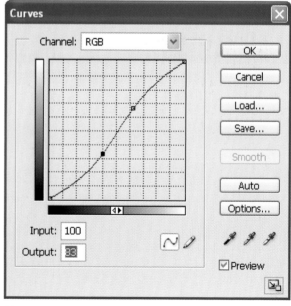

31.7

COLORING A DIGITAL SKETCH

32.1

32.2

Because a line drawing is generally the first of a progression of steps taken to create all artwork, it seems reasonable to spend a few pages of this book on several different techniques for creating line drawings. A line drawing created from a digital photograph can be used for many purposes. As most inkjet printers can print on fine art paper, it is possible to print a line drawing on fine art paper and use it to begin a traditional media painting. Digital photos turned into line drawings can also be used as the starting sketch for a digital painting. Line drawings can also be incorporated into other digital techniques, as shown in Technique 33, where a digital photograph is turned into a very elegant "pen and ink" sketch with a watercolor wash.

Because the line drawing is so important for both traditional media and for digital art, we look at three different approaches to create line drawings. These three approaches not only help ensure that you can get a successful line drawing from most digital photos, but they also allow you to vary the style of the lines in your digital drawings.

While it is possible to make line drawings from a grayscale digital photo by applying a single filter, you may obtain superior results with the five-step process outlined here. This process is the basis for the three line drawing techniques that follow — the only significant difference is that each of the three different techniques uses a different "find edge" filter — either the **Find Edges**, or **Poster Edges**, or **Smart Blur** filters.

1. *Convert image into a grayscale* image by choosing **Image ➢ Mode ➢ Grayscale** or by choosing **Image ➢ Adjustments ➢ Desaturate** (**Shift+Ctrl+U** PC, **Shift+Cmd+U** Mac) and then setting **Saturation** to −100. While these are the easy ways to convert a color image into a grayscale image, you can also perform this conversion by using Technique 14 or 37 to get more control over the shades of gray.

2. *Pre-process the image* to get optimal results from the filter that is to be applied to find edges. As most of the edge-finding filters work on contrast, you can often get much better effects by adjusting contrast either by choosing **Image ➢ Adjustments ➢ Brightness/Contrast**, **Image ➢ Adjustments ➢ Levels**, or **Image ➢ Adjustments ➢ Curves**. Some images will have so much texture that it is difficult to differentiate the texture edges from the important edges. In this case, you may be able to reduce some of the texture by experimenting with either the **Gaussian Blur** or **Median** filters. You may have to experiment with both filters and several different setting until you get the results that you want.

3. *Apply an edge-finding filter* that creates lines. While there are many filters that can find edges, we will use the **Find Edges**, **Smart Blur**, and **Poster Edges** filters. I generally get the best results with the little known **Edges Only** feature in the **Smart Blur** filter. Having said that, you still ought to try the other two filters because they, too, can produce good results and possibly exactly the effects that you want.

4. *Adjust the resulting line drawing* to improve contrast and remove undesirable effects. Depending on the image and the results of the prior three steps, you may have some work to do to clean up your line drawing. The results you want can help you decide what is needed. You may want to use the **Levels** or **Brightness/Contrast** filters to increase the darkness of the lines and remove unwanted artifacts. The **Eraser** tool may be used to remove "spots." Large areas containing spots may be selected by using one of the many selection tools and then deleted all at once.

5. *Apply one or more filters to add character to the lines.* After you have lines where you want them and no additional spots, dots, or other unwanted artifacts — you can use one or more filters to add character to the lines. My favorite character-adding filters are the **Poster Edges** and **Dark Stroke** filters. There are other filters, but these can add lots of character to your lines — try them. If you don't get what you want after applying them once, apply them more than once or use a combination of them.

By now, unless you are like me and you appreciate a quality line drawing made with lines that have lots of character, you're probably thinking that I'm a bit over the top on this one! Nevertheless, read on, as these line creation techniques can be exceedingly useful as they can be the basis for some outstanding work such as you see later in this chapter. We first use the **Find Edges** and **Poster Edges** filters. Then, we use the **Smart Blur** filter and digitally paint the resulting ink sketch.

FIND EDGES FILTER APPROACH TO CREATING A LINE DRAWING

The **Find Edges** filter is possibly the most commonly used filter to create line drawings, but the filter results in lines made with shades of gray. The reason for this is that **Find Edges** makes low-contrast areas white, medium-contrast areas gray, and high-contrast areas black. It also turns hard edges into thin lines and soft edges into fat lines. The result is a line drawing that is very different from the thin lines that we get by using the **Smart Blur** filter. It can, however, transform some digital photos into some pretty cool line drawings.

STEP 1: OPEN FILE AND REMOVE COLOR

- Choose **File** ➢ **Open** (Ctrl+O PC, Cmd+O Mac) to display the **Open** dialog box. Double-click the **\32** folder to open it and then click the **bottles-before.tif** file to select it. Click **Open** to open the file.
- Choose **Image** ➢ **Mode** ➢ **Grayscale.** Click **OK** to remove the color from the image and turn it into a grayscale image where color can no longer be added.

After a quick look at the **Histogram** for this image, I decided not to experiment with the **Brightness/Contrast** and **Levels** filters. Some preprocessing may improve the ability of the **Find Edges** filter to find edges and get your desired effects. We look more carefully at this when we get to the **Smart Blur** technique.

STEP 2: FIND EDGES AND CREATE LINES

- Choose **Filter** ➢ **Stylize** ➢ **Find Edges** to apply the **Find Edges** filter.

After applying the **Find Edges** filter you have a good line drawing, except it has lines that are made of three shades of grays — not just black lines. You can see the results in the drawing shown in Figure 32.3.

STEP 3: REMOVE SOME LINES AND MAKE THE REST BLACK

- Choose **Image** ➢ **Adjustments** ➢ **Threshold** to get the **Threshold** dialog box shown in Figure 32.4. Set the **Threshold Level** to **175** and then click **OK** to apply the setting.

32.3

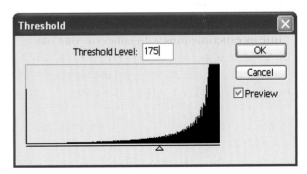

32.4

STEP 4: CLEAN UP THE DRAWING

- Click the **Eraser** tool (**E**) in the **Toolbox** and drag the cursor over the few stray marks that need to be removed.

The final line drawing is shown in Figure 32.5.

POSTER EDGES FILTER APPROACH TO CREATING A LINE DRAWING

The **Poster Edges** filter reduces the number of colors (or shades of gray) in an image according to your chosen settings. Besides drawing lines between contrasting edges, it also shades areas, which means it does not directly create a line drawing. You can use these shaded areas to create solid black areas, which can result in what may look more like a line drawing with black ink shades. This filter does require some experimentation to get good results.

32.5

STEP 1: OPEN FILE AND REMOVE COLOR

- Choose **File ➢ Open** (**Ctrl+O** PC, **Cmd+O** Mac) to display the **Open** dialog box. Double-click the **\32** folder to open it and then click the **bottles-before.tif** file to select it. Click **Open** to open the file.
- Choose **Image ➢ Adjustments ➢ Desaturate** (**Shift+Ctrl+U** PC, **Shift+Cmd+U** Mac) to remove the color from the image.

STEP 2: ADJUST LEVELS

- Choose **Image ➢ Adjustments ➢ Levels** (**Ctrl+L** PC, **Cmd+L** Mac) to get the **Levels** dialog box. Set **Input Levels** to **15**, **1.70**, and **220** and then click **OK** to apply the settings. These settings were used because we wanted to both lighten the image and increase image contrast to make it easier for the **Poster Edges** filter to find edges to be used for creating lines.

STEP 3: FIND EDGES AND CREATE LINES

- Choose **Filter ➢ Artistic ➢ Poster Edges** to get the **Poster Edges** filter in the **Filter Gallery** dialog box shown in Figure 32.6. Set **Edge Thickness**, **Edge Intensity**, and **Posterization** to **1**, **10**, and **6** respectively. Click **OK** to apply the filter.

STEP 4: REDUCE SHADES OF GRAYS AND SOME LINES

After applying the **Poster Edges** filter, you begin to see a semblance of a line drawing! Now we need to remove some of the shades of gray and some lines.

- Choose **Image** ➤ **Adjustments** ➤ **Posterize** to get the **Posterize** filter dialog box shown in Figure 32.7. Set **Levels** to **2** and then click **OK** to apply the filter. These settings result in only black and white with no shades of gray.

STEP 5: REMOVE SOME LINES AND MAKE THE REST BLACK

You are just about done; you need to remove some lines and all the unnecessary background must go.

- Click the **Eraser** tool (**E**) in the **Toolbox** to select the **Eraser** tool. Click in the **Options** box to select the **Hard Round 19 Pixels** brush. Carefully erase a path of the unwanted dots all around the outside edge of the objects.
- Click the **Lasso** tool (**L**) in the **Toolbox** to select the **Lasso** selection tool.
- Click and drag the selection marquee around the objects where you just erased a path.
- After the selection is complete, choose **Select** ➤ **Inverse** (**Shift+Ctrl+I** PC, **Shift+Cmd+I** Mac) to invert the selection.
- Choose **Edit** ➤ **Cut** (**Ctrl+X** PC, **Cmd+X** Mac) to delete all of the remaining unwanted dots in the background.

You can see the results of this technique in Figure 32.8.

SMART BLUR FILTER APPROACH TO CREATING A LINE DRAWING

Due to **Smart Blur's Radius** and **Threshold** settings and its ability to make very fine lines, this filter has become my favorite for creating line drawings. After you have lines where you want them, you can use several other filters to change the character of the lines.

32.6

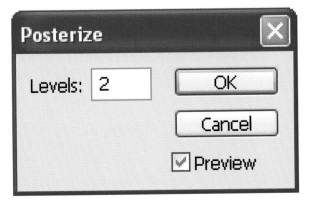

32.7

32.8

STEP 1: OPEN FILE AND REMOVE COLOR

■ Choose **File** ➢ **Open** (**Ctrl+O** PC, **Cmd+O** Mac) to display the **Open** dialog box. Double-click the **\32** folder to open it and then click the **bottles-before.tif** file to select it. Click **Open** to open the file.

■ Choose **Image** ➢ **Adjustments** ➢ **Desaturate** (**Shift+Ctrl+U** PC, **Shift+Cmd+U** Mac) to remove the color from the image.

We can use the **Brightness/Contrast** or **Levels** filters to adjust the contrast in the image; however, use it as it is. This image is an especially good one to use to create a line drawing, as it requires little work to get excellent results.

STEP 2: FIND EDGES AND CREATE LINES

■ Choose **Filter** ➢ **Blur** ➢ **Smart Blur** to get the **Smart Blur** filter dialog box shown in Figure 32.9. Set **Quality** to **High** and **Mode** to **Edge Only**.

■ The preview box in the **Smart Blur** dialog box shows white lines on a black background. Click inside the preview window and drag the preview image around until you see an area on a bottle where you want to make sure you have the right level of detail. Begin sliding the **Radius** and **Threshold** sliders around until you get enough detail in the image — but not too much. After you have a setting that you like, click inside the preview box once again and drag the image around to make sure you have the right level of detail in all parts of the image.

■ Try using a **Radius** setting of **5.0** and a **Threshold** setting of **20.0**. Click **OK** to apply the settings.

Using **5.0** and **20.0** as the settings for **Radius** and **Threshold** produces a line drawing with as few lines as is needed to outline the bottles and some of the ingredients. Increasing the **Threshold** setting increases

the number of lines and adds increasing detail to the drawing. Depending on the desired effects, a higher setting can create an even more visually interesting line drawing — more of a "sketchy sketch" than a mere line drawing.

■ Invert the white lines on a black background image by choosing **Image** ➢ **Adjustments** ➢ **Invert** (**Ctrl+I** PC, **Cmd+I** Mac).

After applying the **Smart Blur** filter, you have an excellent line drawing, as shown in Figure 32.10. This drawing has very fine lines and can be used as a sketch to begin a painting or other kind of artwork.

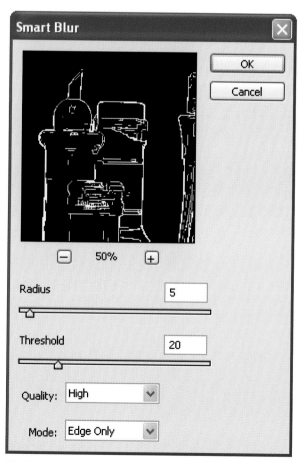

32.9

STEP 3: INCREASE THE WIDTH OF THE LINES

■ To make the lines darker and wider, choose **Filter ➢ Artistic ➢ Poster Edges** to get the **Poster Edges** filter in the **Filter Gallery** dialog box shown in Figure 32.11. Set **Edge Thickness**, **Edge Intensity**, and **Posterization** to **10**, **0**, and **0** and click **OK** to apply the settings.

The results of applying the **Poster Edges** filter are shown in Figure 32.12. If you want even thicker and bolder lines, apply the **Poster Edges** filter once or twice more.

32.10

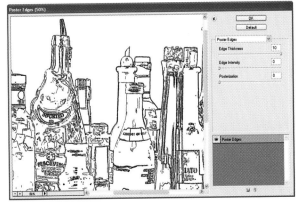

32.11

■ To make the lines even bolder so that they look like they were created with a marker, choose **Filter ➢ Brush Strokes ➢ Dark Strokes** to get the **Dark Strokes** dialog box shown in Figure 32.13.

32.12

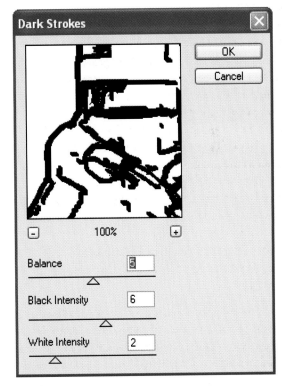

32.13

Try using a setting of **5**, **6**, and **2** for **Balance**, **Black Intensity**, and **White Intensity** respectively, which results in the image shown in Figure 32.14.

One of the new features in Adobe Photoshop CS is the Filter Gallery. It allows you to apply one or more filters to the image at a time and see the results. In Figure 32.15, you can see how the Poster Edges filter was first applied and then how the Dark Strokes filter was applied by looking in the bottom-right corner of the Filter Gallery dialog box. Not only can you add filter effects and stack them, but you can also reorder them and change the settings.

32.14

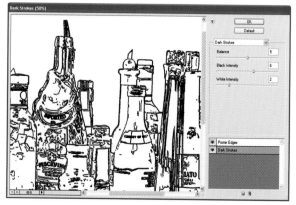

32.15

- Now save your image to your hard drive because you use this drawing a little later in the technique. Save it as **bottles-rough-sketch.tif**.
- Close the file.

If you don't get the results you want from any of these "find edges" filters, I suggest you investigate the possibilities of the **Trace Contour**, **High Pass**, and **Glowing Edges** filters.

Okay, enough of these line drawing techniques. Now we can use the rough sketch that we just created and digitally hand paint it to add some color.

COLORING THE ROUGH MARKER SKETCH

So far in this technique you have looked at three different ways to create black and white line, or ink drawings from photographs. You also looked at a number of ways to modify the character of those lines and have converted one of them into a marker-like sketch. Now you are going to paint in color on the sketch you just created.

While it is not difficult to set up this painting technique, it must be done correctly and you need to have a good understanding of why there are three layers and what some of the more important blend modes can or cannot do. Finally, you need to understand how to paint with brushes and use the **History Brush** tool. After you understand the underlying concept, you should be able to create thousands of different kinds of images. Varying pen strokes, image sources, textures, blend modes, and other variables can allow you to produce effects to meet your most conservative to most wild tastes!

STEP 1: OPEN FILES

- Choose **File ➤ Open** (**Ctrl+O** PC, **Cmd+O** Mac) to display the **Open** dialog box. Double-click the **\32** folder to open it and then click the **bottles-before.tif** file to select it. Click **Open** to open the file.

■ If the **bottles-rough-sketch.tif** file that you just created is not already open, then open it from the folder where you saved it.

STEP 2: CREATE A PAINTING LAYER

■ Click the **bottles-before.tif** image to make it the active document if it isn't already.

■ Choose **Layer ➢ New ➢ Layer** (**Shift+Ctrl+N** PC, **Shift+Cmd+N** Mac) to get the **New Layer** dialog box. Type **Paint Layer** in the **Name** box and click **OK** to create a new transparent layer for painting.

■ To copy the rough sketch into the **bottles-before.tif** document, click the **bottles-rough-sketch.tif** document to make it the active document. Then click in the **Background** layer thumbnail in the **Layers** palette while pressing **Shift** and drag it onto the **bottles-before.tif** document. Pressing the **Shift** key makes the layers align perfectly. The **Layers** palette now looks like the one shown in Figure 32.16.

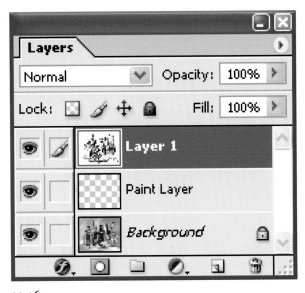

32.16

■ Now close the **bottles-rough-sketch.tif** because it is no longer needed.

■ Click the **Paint Layer** layer in the **Layers** palette to make it the active layer.

■ Choose **Edit ➢ Fill** (**Shift+F5** PC and Mac) to get the **Fill** dialog box shown in Figure 32.17. Click the **Use** box and select **White**. Set **Mode** to **Normal** and set **Opacity** to **100%**. Click **OK** to fill the layer.

■ Now click the **Layer Visiblity** icon in left column of the **Layer 1** layer in the **Layers** palette to hide the rough sketch.

If at any point, you want to paint on the **Paint Layer** layer while being able to view the original image below, first hide the "rough sketch" layer and then click the **Fill** box in the **Layers** palette to get a slider. Slowly slide the slider to the left until you can see the underlying image. At about **80%** you can see the image below well enough to paint directly on this layer to make a painting. However, we won't be painting in this manner in this technique. Instead, we use the **History Brush** tool and paint directly from a snapshot. We also have a sketch to guide our painting so being able to view the underlying image is not a requirement in this case. Make sure to slide the **Fill** slider back to **100%**.

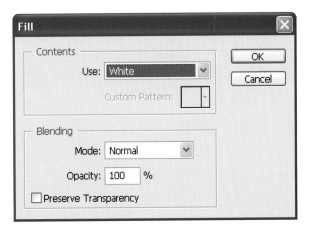

32.17

STEP 3: SET UP HISTORY BRUSH TOOL

Before you can begin painting, you must select the **History Brush** tool, pick an appropriate brush size and style, select a suitable blend mode and opacity level, and set the source history state. After you accomplish this, you can begin painting on the paint layer. As the paint layer is below the sketch layer, the paint won't interfere with the rough sketch.

- Click the **History Brush** tool (**Y**) in the **Toolbox**.
- Click the **Brush Preset Picker** in the **Options** bar, which is the second brush box from the left, as shown in Figure 32.18. Click the menu button to get a pop-up menu. Choose **Reset Brushes** and click **OK** to get the default set of brushes. For this technique I find that the **Small List** view (see Figure 32.19) is a better view than one of the thumbnail views as the full descriptive name is helpful for getting an appropriate brush. To change to the **Small List** view, after clicking the **Brush Preset Picker** box, click the menu button to get a pop-up menu and choose **Small List**.
- If the **History** palette is not already visible, choose **Window ➢ History**. Scroll to the top of the **History** palette and you should see a snapshot named **bottles-before.tif**, as shown in Figure 32.20. As this is the only snapshot, the **History Brush** automatically sets this snapshot to be the source image for painting. If there were more than one snapshot, you would click in the box to the left of the thumbnail image to set this chosen snapshot to be the source for the **History Brush** tool.
- To start painting, use the **Watercolor Loaded Flat Tip** brush. Click the **Brush Preset Picker** in the **Options** bar to get the **Brush Preset Picker**,

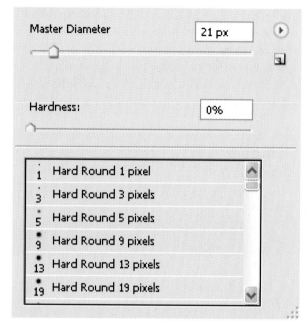

32.19

32.20

32.18

which is shown in Figure 32.21. Scroll toward the bottom of the palette and click the **Watercolor Loaded Wet Flat Tip** brush.

■ Because we are cloning from a photograph and because we want to build up layers, set **Opacity** to **34%** in the **Options** bar. Set **Mode** to **Normal** and set **Flow** to **100%**.

> **NOTE**
>
> The **Watercolor Loaded Wet Flat Tip** brush is an excellent brush to use for this technique as it allows wet-on-wet painting — that is, you can see the paint build up, plus you can see where it overlaps. The looseness of this brush matches the looseness of the rough sketch you created earlier.

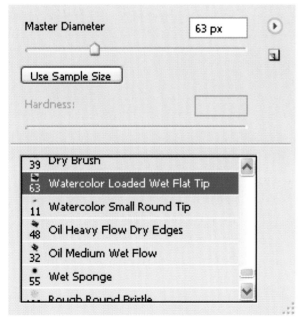

32.21

STEP 4: BEGIN PAINTING

■ You could begin painting now, but you would not be able to see the rough sketch, so you do not know where to paint! To view the sketch, too, click **Layer 1** in the **Layers** palette to make it the active layer. Click in the **Mode** box and choose **Multiply** from the pop-up menu.

■ You must now click the **Paint Layer** layer in the **Layers** box to reset it as the active layer. If you do not, you will paint over the rough sketch and depending on your brush settings, you could ruin the sketch.

■ Finally, you can begin painting! If you have a Wacom pen tablet (`www.wacom.com`), this is a perfect time to use it. Begin painting long brush-strokes down the edges of the bottles. Paint in the label areas and in the caps of the bottles. To make the painting look consistent with the loose pen and ink sketch, brush roughly and let some of the paint flow outside the bottles.

■ After you have a light layer of paint on the image, you can darken some of the areas in several ways. You can change the blend mode, or you can change **Opacity** in the **Options** bar.

■ Besides painting directly from the digital photo in the bottom layer with the **History Brush**, you can also change to the **Brush** tool (**B**) and paint with a color found in the sketch by clicking a chosen color in the image with the **Eye Dropper** tool (**I**). As there is not much color on the surface where the bottles are sitting, select a couple of gray or tan colors with the **Eye Dropper** tool (**I**) and paint the horizontal surface with one of the large watercolor brushes using these two colors.

■ To add a bit more character to the sketch, use colors similar to those that you used on the surface below the bottles and paint horizontal and vertical lines with the brush tool around the tops of the bottles.

As your painting develops, try varying the **Flow** and **Opacity** settings. Also, try changing the **Blend Mode** in the **Layers** palette to one of the other **Blend** modes, such as: **Soft Light**, **Hard Light**, and **Darken**. Other brushes worth considering include **Oil Medium Wet Flow**, **Oil Pastel Large**, and **Charcoal Large Smear**.

My two-minute sketch is shown in Figure 32.22.

There are many, many other things you can do to this image. After you paint all that you want to paint in the **Paint Layer**, you can apply a texture by choosing **Filter ➢ Texture ➢ Texturizer** and choose a texture like **Canvas** to apply to the **Paint Layer**. You can paint on the sketch layer and mix colors directly with the black markers. Running various filters on the **Background** layer and then blending that layer with the other layers can create some interesting effects.

Likewise, you can apply filters and change colors of the paint layer by using tools, such as **Hue/Saturation**, **Levels**, **Curves**, and **Color Balance**. You can even invert the sketch layer to get an image such as the one shown in Figure 32.23. The possibilities are almost limitless. Try a few different approaches and then use one of your own photos. Pick a line drawing technique that you like and create some cool prints in just a few minutes using your own photos!

The next technique is similar to this technique in many ways, except you use the colors from the original photo and use filters to make the painting instead of using the **Brush** or **History Brush** tools. After completing both techniques, you may find combinations of the two techniques that work well, too.

32.22

32.23

CREATING A "PEN AND INK" SKETCH WITH A WATERCOLOR WASH

33.1

33.2

Of all the different art media there is, I particularly like watercolors with their often-blurry edges and transparent colors. Very loose "pen and ink" sketches with loosely defined shapes and lines with lots of character can also hold my interest. I think the looseness of these two types of artwork is what appeals to me. They can be suggestive and yet, leave enough undefined to allow your imagination to fill in the remaining parts, quite like reading a book versus seeing a movie made from the same story.

The photograph in Figure 33.1 shows an urn that I found on the front porch of a fancy home in Charleston, South Carolina. You might not think that it is possible to turn this digital photograph into a fine-art quality print on watercolor paper; but it is — try it. This is one of the many images in this book that just doesn't show well printed in the book compared to what it looks like printed full-size on quality textured fine-art paper with a photo-quality inkjet printer — it really does look quite good.

This technique shows how to transform a digital photo into a watercolor-like image and a "pen and ink" sketch, and then how the two can be combined to become a "pen and ink" sketch with a watercolor wash. Because it really is two techniques in one, it is a long technique. However, it is well worth trying on the urn image, and then on one or more of your own photos. I think you will like the results.

STEP 1: OPEN FILE

■ Choose **File** ➢ **Open** (**Ctrl+O** PC, **Cmd+O** Mac) to display the **Open** dialog box. Double-click the **\33** folder to open it and then click the **urn-before.tif** file to select it. Click **Open** to open the file.

STEP 2: DUPLICATE LAYER

■ Because both a watercolor painting and a "pen and ink" sketch are needed, you need two layers. Duplicate the **Background** layer by choosing **Layer** ➢ **Duplicate Layer**. When the **Duplicate Layer** dialog box appears, type in **pen-ink** to name the image, as shown in Figure 33.3, and then click **OK**.

STEP 3: TRANSFORM ONE LAYER INTO A WATERCOLOR PAINTING

Adobe Photoshop CS does have a watercolor filter, but in most cases, I find that it makes the images too dark with too many odd-looking brush strokes. Therefore, let's use another approach.

■ Click the **Background** layer in the **Layers** palette to make it the active layer.
■ Click the **Layer Visibility** icon in the left column in the **pen-ink** layer to hide the top layer. The **Layers** palette should now look like the one shown in Figure 33.4.
■ Choose **Filter** ➢ **Artistic** ➢ **Dry Brush** to get the **Dry Brush** filter in the **Filter Gallery** dialog box. Click in the preview window and drag the image around until you can see a few flowers. Begin experimenting with the settings for **Brush Size**, **Brush Detail**, and **Texture**. I used **2**, **8**, and **1**, as shown in Figure 33.5. Click **OK** to apply the settings.

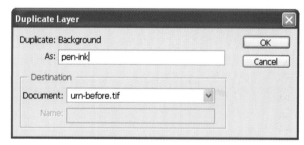

33.3

33.4

To soften the brush strokes and make them look more like a watercolor wash, use a blur filter.

■ Choose **Filter ➢ Blur ➢ Smart Blur** to get the **Smart Blur** dialog box shown in Figure 33.6. Try using a **Radius** of **10** and a **Threshold** of **50**. Also,

33.5

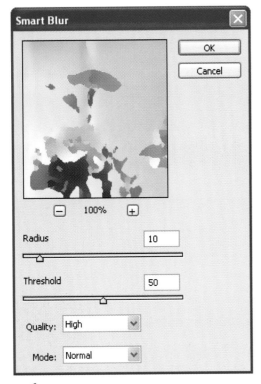

33.6

make sure you have **Quality** set to **High** and that **Mode** is set to **Normal** before clicking **OK** to apply the settings.

For this particular image, these few steps produce a realistic-looking watercolor. After using many images and trying many different techniques to create water-color paintings, I've concluded there are many vari-ables and settings for each of many different techniques; what works on one image, may work poorly on another. In general, these steps work well on images that are about 1,600 x 1,200 pixels in size and have been taken with a digital camera.

On larger files, and when photographs have been scanned with a flat-bed scanner or negatives or slides have been scanned with a film scanner, the same tech-niques work well if you first apply a light **Gaussian Blur** to the image. The larger the files, the better this technique seems to work provided that you're work-ing with a good-quality image with minimal grain. Sometimes, you may also find that an image can be made to look more like a watercolor painting if you apply some of these filters more than once. Experimentation is the key to getting what you want.

STEP 4: TRANSFORM SECOND LAYER INTO A "PEN AND INK" SKETCH

The next step is to turn the "pen-ink" layer into a "pen and ink" sketch. While most Photoshop experts use and recommend the **Find Edges** filter to make line drawings, I find I usually get much better results with a hidden option in the **Smart Blur** filter. The results, as you'll see, can be quite outstanding.

■ Click the **pen-ink** layer to make it the active **Layer**.
■ Choose **Image ➢ Adjustments ➢ Desaturate** (**Shift+Ctrl+U** PC, **Shift+Cmd+U** Mac) to remove all color.
■ Choose **Filter ➢ Blur ➢ Smart Blur** to once again get the **Smart Blur** dialog box. This time, set **Quality** to **High** and **Mode** to **Edge Only**.

Finding settings that show the vertical lines on the columns while not adding too many lines around the flowers is important. To do this, click in the preview box inside the **Smart Blur** dialog box and drag the preview image until you see the column.

- Try setting **Radius** to **25** and **Threshold** to **35**. Click **OK** to apply the settings. Have patience as the **Smart Blur** filter can take some time to process.
- You may be surprised to see what now looks like white lines on a black ink scratchboard, but this is okay — choose **Image ➤ Adjustments ➤ Invert** (**Ctrl+I** PC, **Cmd+I** Mac) and you see black lines on a white background sketch, as shown in Figure 33.7.

33.7

STEP 5: BLEND LAYERS

At this point, you have learned two techniques and you have two entirely different images made from the same digital photo — a watercolor-like image and a "pen and ink" sketch. We now want to combine these two layers.

- Click the **pen-ink** layer to make it the active layer.
- In the **Layers** palette, click in the **Blend Mode** box and choose **Multiply**. Leave **Opacity** set to **100%**. The **Layers** dialog box should now look like Figure 33.8.

STEP 6: MAKE FINAL COLOR ADJUST-MENTS AND ADD YOUR SIGNATURE

Now is the time to make a few creative color adjustments.

- To lighten the image, use an **Adjustment Layer** so that you can go back and make changes if desired. Choose **Layer ➤ New Adjustment**

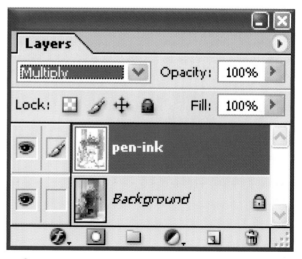

33.8

Layer ➤ Levels to get the **New Layer** dialog box. Click **OK** to display the **Levels** dialog box. Set **Input Levels** to **5**, **1.50**, and **170**, as shown in Figure 33.9. Click **OK** to apply the settings.

The final step is to adjust the colors as you'd like them. You have both Adobe Photoshop CS and an artistic license to create as you'd like to create, so try making the image turquoise, purple, and green with yellow flowers, as shown in Figure 33.2!

■ Once again, to allow you the opportunity to go back and change your settings use another **Adjustment Layer** to make changes to the colors. Click on the **pen-ink** layer and choose **Layer ➤ New Adjustment Layer ➤ Hue/Saturation** to get the **Hue/Saturation** dialog box. Set **Hue**, **Saturation**, and **Lightness** to **+120**, **+20**, and **0**, as shown in Figure 33.10.

Because we used **Adjustment Layers**, you can now go back and double-click the **Levels 1** or **Hue/ Saturation 1** layers and make changes to the settings until you get the results that you want. You may also try using some of the other color commands, such as **Color Balance** or even **Replace Colors** if you want to replace the yellow flowers with another color.

Also, don't forget to add your signature — it adds a nice touch to your painting. If you want, you could also hand paint more of the flowers yellow. Some of them seem to be lacking a bit of color on the left side of the image. A good tool for painting the flowers is one of the watercolor brushes. You also may want to put a soft edge on the image by using a soft eraser on both the ink layer and the painted layer. Save your file and it is ready to be printed.

While this image looks reasonably good on a computer screen, it *really* does look exceptional when printed on a fine-art watercolor paper with a photo-quality inkjet printer. I used an Epson 2200P printer and the Epson Watercolor Paper – Radiant White — the print is excellent and archival. Printing on quality fine-art paper is essential to getting a print that you'll be proud to frame.

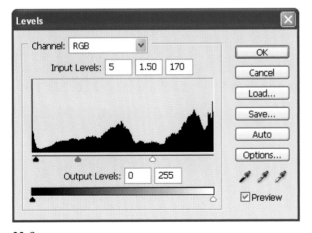

33.9

33.10

CREATING A DIGITAL PAINTING

34.1

34.2

ABOUT THE IMAGE

Egret Landing at Sunset Egret photo: Canon EOS D30, ISO 100, Fine image setting, 300mm f/2.8 with 2X tele-extender, f/9 @ 1/320, 1,440 x 2,160 pixels, 10.6MB .tif. Marsh photo: Pentax Spotmatic F, 55mm, Kodachrome, scanned with Nikon Coolscan IV, 2,222 x 1,667 pixels, 10.6MB .tif.

Admittedly, the phrase "digital painting" in the title of this technique evokes different meanings to different people. There are those who think a digital painting is a lesser "art form" than a natural media painting. Others consider a digital painting to be some kind of high-tech painting that lacks the soul that can be found in fine art painted by fine artists — instead of *computer* artists. For me, a good digital painting is just another kind of painting and it carries the same potential to be fine art. A digital painting can be as different as a watercolor painting is from an oil painting and in no way should digital painting be considered a *lesser* fine art than other media. A well-done digital painting, like those by painter Bobbi Doyle-Maher, can have the soul found in so many other types of fine art paintings (`www.rabbittwilight.com`).

In this technique, you look at how you can transform two digital photos into a "fine art" digital painting that has soul! While many digital paintings are created by carefully placing digital brush strokes on an image by using an image-editing program, this one is done by using mostly large digital brushes with soft edges and blend modes. You can successfully use this technique on all kinds of digital photos to make outstanding prints on fine art papers.

While this technique is inspiring for everyone, you need a moderate amount of traditional "painting" skills to match the painting done by Bobbi. You also need from two to four hours to complete the painting—it took Bobbi about three hours. Even if you don't have "painting" skills, you may want to quickly complete this technique as it can be used in

much simpler ways for good results, too. If you are a painter, you'll love this technique and my bet is that after you complete this painting, you'll be ready to begin exploring all the wonderful brushes in Adobe Photoshop CS.

While it is possible to complete this technique without a pen tablet and to use this approach with other digital photos, a pen tablet can make your painting more painterly, accurate, and fun. Several companies make pen tablets. Wacom (www.wacom.com) makes some of the best ones.

Before you begin this technique, if you have a photo-quality printer, print the final image file to use as a reference image. The file, egret-after.jpg, is in the \34 folder. If you do not have a color printer, you may want to open the image file anyway and choose **Image ➢ Image Size** to reduce it to a small reference image that you can keep open in your Adobe Photoshop CS work space.

34.3

STEP 1: OPEN FILE

■ Choose **File ➢ Open** (Ctrl+O PC, Cmd+O Mac) to display the **Open** dialog box. Double-click the \34 folder to open it and then while pressing **Ctrl** on the PC (**Cmd** on the Mac), click the **marsh-before.tif** and **egret-before.tif** files to select them. Click **Open** to open both files at once.

STEP 2: COMBINE IMAGES

■ Click the **Move** tool (**V**) in the **Toolbox**.
■ Click inside the **egret-before.tif** image and drag it onto the **marsh-before.tif** image to place it as a new layer in the **marsh-before.tif** file.
■ Double-click the **Layer 1** label in the **Layers** palette and the type **egret** to name the layer.
■ We will no longer need the **egret-before** image again so you may now close it.

- Select **View** ➢ **Fit on Screen** (**Ctrl+0** PC, **Cmd+0** Mac) to maximize the **marsh-before.tif** document.

STEP 3: RESIZE EGRET LAYER

- The **Layers** palette should now look like the one shown in Figure 34.4. Double-click inside the **Opacity** box inside the **Layers** palette and type **40** to lower the opacity so that you can see the marsh layer below.
- Choose **Edit** ➢ **Transform** ➢ **Scale** to get a bounding box around the **egret** image.
- To change the height and width proportionally, press **Shift** while clicking and dragging the upper-left corner handle of the bounding box to resize the image, or click the **Link** icon in the **Options** bar between the **W** and **H** fields.

- Click inside the bounding box to position the image; then, press **Shift** and click and drag one of the corner handles to size the image once again until the egret is sized, as shown in Figure 34.5. If the **Link** icon is on, you would not need to press **Shift**.

Note that a small portion of the egret's wing has been clipped in the original photo, so the egret layer ought to be positioned all the way to the right edge of the **marsh-before.tif** image.

Alternatively, you can type **85** in the **W** and **H** boxes in the **Move** tool **Options** bar (as shown in Figure 34.6) to set both **Width** and **Height** to **85%**. You can then either click the image using the **Move** tool to drag it to the correct position or type **1488.5 px** in the **X** box and **478.8 px** in the **Y** box to precisely position the egret.

- Press **Enter** (**Return** on a Mac) to set the image location and size.

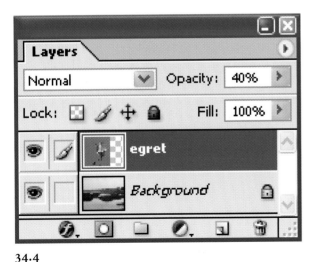

34.4

34.5

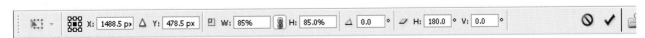

34.6

STEP 4: CROP IMAGE

■ Click the **Crop** tool (**C**) in the **Toolbox**. Delete any values in the **Height** and **Width** boxes in the **Options** bar by clicking the **Clear** button. Click just outside the bottom lower-right corner of the image and drag the **Crop** tool marquee up and to the left until you have selected a portion of the image, as shown in Figure 34.7.

■ Press **Enter** (**Return** on a Mac) to crop the image. Don't worry about the line that appears at the bottom of the image as you'll shortly mask it away!

34.7

STEP 5: MASK EGRET

In this step, you create a **Layer Mask** to mask out the entire image in the **egret** layer, except the egret. While you need to paint carefully when creating the mask, you do not need to be too precise. I would also recommend that you always use the soft round brushes and not the hard round brushes. The soft edges make it much easier for you to get the North Carolina egret to blend well into the Florida marsh!

■ Click the **egret** layer in the **Layers** palette to make it the active layer — it is now highlighted.

■ In the **Layers** palette, set **Opacity** to **60%**.

■ Choose **Layer** ➢ **Add Layer Mask** ➢ **Reveal All** to create a new **Layer Mask**.

■ Click the **Default Foreground Background Colors** icon (**D**) in the **Toolbox**. Then, click the **Switch Foreground With Background Colors** icon in the **Toolbox** to set the **Foreground** color to **Black**.

■ Click the **Brush** tool (**B**) in the **Toolbox**.

■ Click the **Brush Preset Picker** icon (the second box from the left in the **Options** bar) and select the **Soft Round 300 Pixels** brush. If you don't see a **Soft Round 300 Pixel** brush, click the menu button on the **Brush Preset Picker** palette and select **Reset Brushes** to get the default brush set.

■ Check in the **Options** bar to make sure that **Mode** is set to **Normal**. Set **Opacity** to **88%** and leave **Flow** set to **100%**.

You can now begin painting the mask. As you paint on the **Layer Mask** with black, the painted area of the **egret** layer is hidden. Painting with white removes any black paint; hence the "egret" area is once again revealed. When you paint, click often so that you can use the **Undo** feature to undo any brushstrokes that were not placed correctly, without losing too much of your work.

Start off with the **Soft Round 300 Pixels** brush and then move to increasingly smaller brushes, such as the **200, 100, 45, 21,** and **9** pixel brushes. Remember to take advantage of the **Full Screen Mode**; press **F, F,** and **Tab** to get an entire uncluttered screen of the image. Move the image around by pressing the **Spacebar** to get the **Hand** tool (**H**); then, click and drag the image where you want it. To zoom in, press **Z** to get the **Zoom** tool. Click an area and drag the selection marquee around the area that you want to view. To view the entire image, select **View>Fit on Screen** (**Ctrl+0** PC, **Cmd+0** Mac) To view at **100%**, select **View>Actual Pixels** (**Alt+Ctrl+0** PC, **Shift+ Cmd+0** Mac).

If you decide that you painted out an area that should not have been painted, toggle to white by clicking the **Switch Foreground With Background Colors** icon in the **Toolbox** to change **Foreground** to **White**. Then toggle it again to continue painting out the parts of the egret image you do not want to be visible. If needed, you can also change the **Opacity** setting in the **Layers** palette to make the egret more or less visible. Remember, your mask shouldn't be too perfect because this is to be a loose painting—not a precise photograph.

- Begin painting out the entire image except the egret by using the **Brush** tool (**B**) and an appropriate brush size. After you are done, your image should look similar to the one shown in Figure 34.8. This may take you ten minutes or more.
- I suggest that you now save your file as you have completed a considerable amount of work that you likely won't want to repeat. Choose **File ➤ Save As** (**Ctrl+Shift+S** PC, **Shift+Cmd+S** Mac) to get the **File Save** dialog box.
- Type **egret-step6** in the **Name** box. Click in the **Format** box and select **Photoshop**. In the **Save Options** box, make sure that **Layers** is checked to ensure that the layers will be saved, too!

STEP 6: CREATE NEW BACKGROUND LAYER

- Click the **Background** layer in the **Layers** palette and drag it onto the **New Layer** icon at the bottom of the **Layers** palette to create a new layer named **Background copy**.
- Click the **Layer Visibility** icon (the eye icon in the leftmost column in the **egret** layer in the **Layers** palette) to hide the **egret** layer and its **Layer Mask**.

34.8

STEP 7: CREATE SUN

■ If the **Background copy** layer in the **Layers** palette is not highlighted, click it to make it the active layer.

■ Click and hold the **Rectangular Marquee** tool in the **Toolbox** until you get a pop-up menu; choose **Elliptical Marquee** tool.

■ **Shift+click** to create a circle approximately the size of the sun shown in Figure 34.9. Click inside the circle to place it, as shown in Figure 34.9. You may want to click once on the **Layer Visibility** icon in the **egret** layer to make the egret visible. The location of the sun relative to the egret's head is important. Click inside the circle marquee and drag it where it ought to be. Then, click the **Layer Visibility** icon next to the **egret** layer to once again hide the egret.

■ To make a soft edge around the sun, choose **Select ➢ Feather** (**Alt+Ctrl+D** PC, **Opt+Cmd+D** Mac) to get the **Feather Selection** dialog box shown in Figure 34.10. Set **Feather Radius** to **9 pixels**. Click **OK** to feather the selection.

■ Just in case you later need to select the sun or everything but the sun, choose **Select ➢ Save Selection** to get the **Save Selection** dialog box. Type **sun** in the **Name** box and click **OK** to save your selection.

■ Choose **Select ➢ Inverse** (**Shift+Ctrl+I** PC, **Shift+Cmd+I** Mac) to invert the selection because we want to paint the glow around the sun.

■ Click the **Brush** tool (**B**) in the **Toolbox**.

■ Pick **Pastel Yellow Orange** from the **Swatches** palette. If the palette is not already visible, choose **Window ➢ Swatches** to get the **Swatches** palette shown in Figure 34.11.

34.9

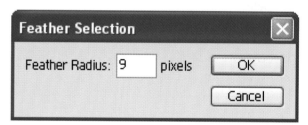

34.10

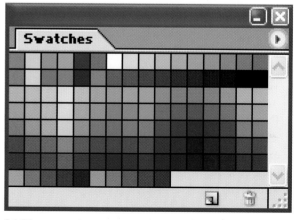

34.11

If your **Swatches** palette does not match the one in Figure 34.11, you may need to reset the palette by clicking the menu button in the **Swatches** palette and choosing **Reset Swatches** from the pop-up menu. You then are asked: **Replace current color swatches with the default colors?** Click **OK** to reset the **Swatches** palette.

■ Select the **Pastel Yellow Orange** color by clicking that color in the **Swatches** palette. If you are not sure which color box is the correct color, slowly move your cursor over the colors and the name of each color displays. If you don't get a color name displayed when hovering over a color, you will need to set **Preferences** to **Show Tool Tips** in the **General** dialog box. Or, you can set the **Swatches** palette to **Small List** mode by clicking the menu button and selecting **Small List**. All the swatch names will then be visible alongside a color sample.

■ Click the **Brush Preset Picker** in the **Options** bar to select the **Soft Round 300 Pixels** brush. Set **Opacity** to **24%**.

■ Begin painting lightly over the entire image by using a lighter touch on the ground and trees. This color helps to add a warm orange sunset glow.

■ Select **Light Cyan** from the **Swatches** palette.

■ Click the **Brush Preset Picker** in the **Options** bar to select the **Soft Round 200 Pixels** brush.

■ Paint **Light Cyan** in the water at the bottom of the image and then add some more to the top of the image in the sky area.

■ Alternate between using **Pure Yellow** and **Light Yellow** to paint around the sun and the reflection of the sun in the water. This is easy to do if you set **Pure Yellow** as the **Foreground** color and **Light Yellow** as the **Background** color and type **X** to exchange between them.

■ Choose **Select ➢ Inverse** (**Shift+Ctrl+I** PC, **Shift+Cmd+I** Mac) to select just the sun. Paint inside the selection by using **Pastel Yellow Orange**, **Light Yellow**, **Pure Yellow Orange**, **Pastel Cyan**, and **White**. Paint the yellows and

oranges in the center and to the right. Keep the blue on the left. Add a small bit of **White** as a highlight to the sun to complete it.

■ Choose **Select ➢ Inverse** (**Shift+Ctrl+I** PC, **Shift+Cmd+I** Mac) to invert the selection.

■ Click the **Brush Preset Picker** in the **Options** bar. Click the menu button to get a pop-up menu. Choose **Natural Brushes 2** and then click **OK** to replace the current brushes with the new brush set.

■ Click the **Brush Preset Picker** in the **Options** bar and pick **Pastel Dark 118 Pixels**. Mode should be set to **Normal** and **Opacity** should be set to **30%**.

■ Paint light areas around the sun **Pastel Yellow Orange**, **Light Yellow Orange**, and **Light Yellow**.

■ Paint sky and water areas that are blue with **Light Cyan**.

■ Paint foreground grass with **Dark Red Orange**, and then use **Darker Warm Brown** and **85% Gray** for the bottom of the grass.

■ Paint distant grass **Pure Yellow Green**, **Dark Yellow Green**, **Pure Yellow Orange**, and end with some more **Pure Yellow Green**.

■ Paint distant tree lines with **Light Violet** and **Pure Violet**.

■ Paint the bottom of the nearest tree line with a **Dark Blue** and **85% Gray**.

One of the keys to creating a successful digital painting when painting over a digital photograph is to use many layers of paint. As with natural media, more layers with different colors and strokes add richness and depth to the color, which helps to remove the "photograph" look. In this next step, use the same colors as before, but this time use varying brush sizes and a low opacity.

■ Click the **Brush Preset Picker** in the **Options** bar and then click the menu button to get a pop-up menu. Choose **Reset Brushes** and click **OK** to get the default brush set.

- Using the **Soft Round 300 Pixels** brush and the **200 Pixels** and **100 Pixels** sized brushes with **Opacity** set to **24%**, paint over areas to soften them. Use similar colors to what you used when you painted them before.
- Choose **Select** ➤ **Deselect** (**Ctrl+D** PC, **Cmd+D** Mac).

STEP 8: PAINT EGRET LAYER

- Click the **egret** layer thumbnail (not the **Layer Mask** icon) in the **Layers** palette to make the egret viewable. Lightly paint the right side of the wing so that it blends into the sky.
- Using the **Zoom** tool (**Z**), zoom in and lightly paint the right side of the wing so that it blends into the sky.
- Paint **Light Orange** and **Light Yellow** on the wings, neck, and top of the head by using different brush sizes as needed. These colors should be very light and add just a hint of color.

STEP 9: FLATTEN IMAGE AND BLEND

- Choose **Layer** ➤ **Flatten Image** to merge all the layers and the layer mask.

- Choose **Image** ➤ **Apply Image** to get the **Apply Image** dialog box shown in Figure 34.12.

One of the ways you can build up density and color saturation is to duplicate a layer and then blend the two layers together by using one of the **Blending Modes**, such as **Multiply**. The **Apply Image** feature works exactly the same as if you duplicated layers and then blended them with a **Blending Mode**, except you can do all this in one easy step, with one layer, and consume far less memory.

- Click the **Blending Mode** box to get a pop-up menu. Choose **Multiply**. The image then looks unacceptably dark. You can lighten the effect by

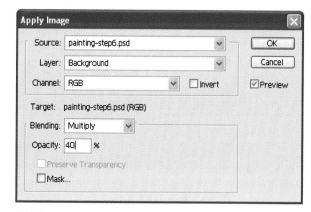

34.12

ARTIST PROFILE

Bobbi Doyle-Maher is a self-taught artist who lives in East Tennessee with her husband, three cats, and four dogs. Before stepping into the digital world, she was skilled with oil, acrylic, pastel, oil pastel, monotype, encaustic, and black and white photography. A few years ago, she began using digital image editors, such as Adobe Photoshop, MetaCreations Painter (now known as Corel Painter 8), and Right-Hemisphere's Deep Paint.

Over time, she found herself spending more time painting digitally than with traditional paints. After purchasing a digital camera and a film scanner, she began to create digital paintings by using digital photos. Her digital paint studio includes a PC, a Nikon Coolscan IV film scanner, a Wacom pen tablet, and an Epson Stylus Photo 2200 printer to make archival prints. More of her artwork may be viewed on her Web site at www.rabbittwilight.com.

reducing the **Opacity %**. Try setting **Opacity** to **40%**; click **OK** to apply the settings.

STEP 10: MAKE FINAL IMAGE ADJUSTMENTS

The image is nearly complete. At this point you can change hue and saturation by using the **Hue/Saturation** command. You can adjust overall tonal range with **Curves** or **Levels**, or apply any other effects to complete the image as you'd like it.

■ Add brush stroke effects by choosing **Filter ➢ Artistic ➢ Dry Brush** to get the **Dry Brush** dialog box shown in Figure 34.13. Set **Brush Size** to **2**, **Brush Detail** to **8**, and **Texture** to **1**. Click **OK** to apply the effects.

■ If you would like to tone down the brush effects, you can choose **Edit ➢ Fade Dry Brush** (**Shift+Ctrl+F** PC, **Shift+Cmd+F** Mac) to get the

Fade dialog box shown in Figure 34.14. Reduce the **Opacity** to **40%** and leave **Mode** set to **Normal**. Click **OK** to apply the settings.

■ Because the intent is to get an overall orange sunset glow, select the **Soft Round 300 Pixels** brush. Click the **Swatches** palette to select **Pastel Yellow Orange** and also use **Light Yellow Orange** later. Set **Opacity** in the **Options** bar to **15%**; paint over areas to soften them.

■ If there are any brushstrokes that need blending, use the **Clone Stamp** tool to remove them.

■ Make slight adjustments using **Levels** (**Ctrl+L** PC, **Cmd+L** Mac) to increase contrast to suit your own taste.

There you have it — a digital painting created from two digital photos! While there were lots of steps and we used many colors, this was not actually a painting because no detailed brush strokes were required. If you want to, you can go back and pick different brushes and actually paint this image with brush strokes — rather than soft colors that blend with the background photos.

34.13

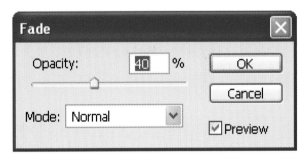

34.14

CREATIVE USE OF FILTERS AND COMMANDS

35.1

35.2

ABOUT THE IMAGE

Smith's American Fire Dept. Truck Nikon Coolpix 950 digital camera using Fine Image Quality setting, 1,200 x 1,600 pixel, 900K .jpg file

The digital photo of the two fire trucks was taken with a hand-held digital camera on an overcast day — the perfect light for taking shots of subjects such as this one. This image of a pair of old rusty fire trucks is perfect for trying all kinds of Adobe Photoshop CS filter techniques. You'll enjoy working with it, I'm sure.

Unlike most techniques in this book, where the goal is to make a cool image, our goal in this one is to edit the image in a number of ways to show you how you can get more out of Adobe Photoshop CS filters. We take a few steps, and then stop to look at the results, and then take a few more and again look at the results, and so on. At the end of the technique, you ought to be on a longer journey of your own to explore the limitless power of Adobe Photoshop CS with these tips as your guide.

In a couple of the earlier techniques in this book, you saw how you could improve the results of specific filters by doing some pre- and post-processing of an image. In this technique, you discover that you can further modify the effects of filters by:

- Blending layers (either with itself by using the **Apply Image** command or with another layer)
- Using **Layer Masks**
- Applying filters to a single channel
- Using the **Fade** command
- Changing blend **Opacity** levels
- Mixing filters or commands

STEP 1: OPEN FILE

- Choose **File** ➢ **Open** (**Ctrl+O** PC, **Cmd+O** Mac) to display the **Open** dialog box. Double-click the **\35** folder to open it and then click the **firetrucks-before.jpg** file to select it. Click **Open** to open the file.

STEP 2: APPLY CUTOUT FILTER

If you just want a good clean graphic image, then the **Cutout** filter has to be one of the best. The **Cutout** filter has three settings and you can often get better results by preprocessing the image; that is, running another command or two on it first, so that the **Cutout** filter results in a better image.

If you increase the contrast of an image before applying the **Cutout** filter, you will have better control over the level of detail in an image. For the purposes of this technique, assume that we want a sharp, high contrast image with strong colors.

- To increase contrast, choose **Image** ➢ **Adjustments** ➢ **Curves** (**Ctrl+M** PC, **Cmd+M** Mac) to get the **Curves** dialog box.
- Click the **Set White Point** eye dropper (it is the third eye dropper in the bottom-right corner of the **Curves** dialog box). Click once inside the nearly white lettering on the side of the Smith's truck to set the **White** point. If you don't get the results you want and you want to try another

place, press **Alt** on the PC (**Option** on the Mac) and the **Cancel** button turns into a **Reset** button; click **Reset** to start all over again.

- Do the same thing with the **Set Black Point** eye dropper (the first eye dropper on the left), but make sure to click inside a part of the image where you think it should be the blackest, such as inside the front left wheel well where it is all shadow. After you click, you should notice that the darks (or blacks) get slightly blacker, which is good.
- Click **OK** to apply the settings. The image now has much more contrast.
- Choose **Filter** ➢ **Artistic** ➢ **Cutout** to get the **Cutout** filter in the **Filter Gallery** dialog box shown in Figure 35.3. To meet our initial objectives, set **Number of Levels** to **8** to maximize the number of colors. Set **Edge Simplicity** to **0** as we want detail, not simplified edges. Set **Edge Fidelity** to **3** to maximize the edge detail. Click **OK** to apply the filter.
- Try bumping up color saturation by choosing **Image** ➢ **Adjustment** ➢ **Hue/Saturation** (**Ctrl+U** PC, **Cmd+U** Mac) dialog box. Set **Hue** to **+15**, **Saturation** to **+40**, and **Lightness** to **0**. Click **OK** to apply the settings. Your image should look something like the one shown in Figure 35.4.
- Create a duplicate layer by choosing **Layer** ➢ **Duplicate Layer**; click **OK**. You now have two layers in the **Layers** palette and the top layer (now named **Background copy**) should be highlighted.

35.3

STEP 3: USE QUICK MASK

No doubt about it—the easiest and most frequently used filter effect for those new to any of the Photoshop family of products is the **Poster Edges** filter. If you use it, odds are good someone will look at your work and say, "Oh, you used the **Poster Edges** filter!" If you don't mind this—and I sometimes don't because I admit to liking the **Poster Edges** filter as there are times and places where it is okay to use it—you can use this filter to make some wonderful inkjet prints when a textured fine-art paper is used.

■ Because we want to apply the **Poster Edges** filter on the **Background**, click once in the thumbnail in the **Background** in the **Layers** palette to set it as the active layer.
■ Click the **Layer Visibility** icon in the left column of the **Background copy** layer to hide that layer.

One of the problems with the **Poster Edges** filter is that some images (such as this one) need to have different settings applied to different parts of the image. The solution is to use the wonderful and quick-to-use **Quick Mask**. Using the **Quick Mask** you can apply the optimal settings to each part of the image. In this image, we want to use one setting for the trucks as they are smooth, and a second setting for areas covered by grass and tree leaves, as they have lots of edges and shadows.

The **Quick Mask** is what it sounds like—a mask that you can create quickly. After you turn on the **Quick Mask**, anything that you paint with black is masked, while everything that is not painted is not masked. When it is turned on, you paint the mask. When you turn it off, it automatically creates a selection for you from the mask you painted, thereby allowing you to affect only the areas that were not masked.

■ To edit in **Quick Mask** mode, click the **Quick Mask Mode** button (**Q**), which is near the bottom of the **Toolbox**, as shown in Figure 35.5. Before painting, make sure that the **Foreground** color is **Black** by clicking the **Set Default Foreground and Background Colors** (**D**) icon,

35.4

35.5

which is located just to the bottom of the **Foreground** and **Background** color boxes in the **Toolbox**.

■ Select the **Brush** tool (**B**) by clicking it in the **Toolbox**.

■ Click the **Brush Preset Picker** box (the second brush box from the left) in the **Options** palette to select an appropriate brush. I suggest selecting the **Soft Round 300 Pixels** brush by clicking on it in the **Brush** palette shown in Figure 35.6.

The **Options** bar should now show **Mode** as **Normal**, **Opacity** as **100%**, and **Flow** as **100%**. As you click and drag your cursor, you paint with a red color, much like a Rubylith — the default color of the mask. Keep clicking and dragging until you paint all of the leaves and the grass. After you are done, your mask should look similar to the one shown in Figure 35.7.

■ To turn off **Quick Mask** mode and once again edit in **Standard mode**, click the **Standard Mode** button in the **Toolbox** or type **Q**. You now see a

selection marquee showing you where want to apply the **Poster Edges** filter.

■ Choose **Filter ➤ Artistic ➤ Poster Edges** to get the **Poster Edges** filter in the **Filter Gallery** dialog box shown in Figure 35.8. If you click inside the image preview box inside the **Poster Edges** dialog box, the cursor turns into the **Hand** tool. You can now click and drag the image to pick an area where you can best judge the settings. Because we are going to set the filter for the truck, click and drag until you can view the Mack emblem on the side of the hood.

35.7

35.6

35.8

Assuming that we agree that we want a nice level of posterization with medium heavy lines, try the settings of **4**, **3**, and **6** respectively for **Edge Thickness**, **Edge Intensity**, and **Posterization**. To turn the **Poster Edges** filter on and off to view the changes, click the **Layer Visibility** icon at the left of the **Poster Edges** layer at the bottom-right of the **Filter Gallery** dialog box. Click **OK** to apply the settings.

■ Invert the selection by choosing **Select ➢ Inverse** (**Shift+Ctrl+I** PC, **Shift+Cmd+I** Mac).

■ Choose **Filter ➢ Artistic ➢ Poster Edges** to get the **Poster Edges** filter in the **Filter Gallery** dialog box once again. Click inside the image preview box and drag the image until you see the bottom-left corner of the image. Try setting **Edge Thickness**, **Edge Intensity** and **Posterization** to **0**, **0**, and **5** respectively.

■ Click **OK** to apply the settings. The areas covered with grass and leaves will have similar, but less strong, characteristics as the portion of the image where there are fire trucks.

■ If the **Poster Edges** effect is too strong for you, you can fade the effect by choosing **Edit ➢ Fade Poster Edges** (**Shift+Ctrl+F** PC, **Shift+Cmd+F** Mac) to get the **Fade** dialog box shown in Figure 35.9. Not only can you adjust the "fade factor" by adjusting **Opacity**, but you can also change the

Blending Mode! Using the **Preview** feature, you can see the changes in the image as you make them. After you are done experimenting, click **Cancel**. I just wanted to show you how the **Fade** command works — not actually use it.

■ Choose **Select ➢ Deselect** (**Ctrl+D** PC, **Cmd+D** Mac) to remove the selection marquee.

■ To further enhance the filter you just applied, choose **Image ➢ Adjustments ➢ Levels** (**Ctrl+L** PC, **Cmd+L** Mac) to get the **Levels** dialog box. Set **Input Levels** to **20**, **100**, and **235** respectively, and then click **OK**.

STEP 4: BLEND LAYERS

In the **Background** layer, we now have an image created with the all-too-common **Poster Edges** filter. On the **Background copy** layer, we have an image created with the **Cutout** filter. Now blend them to get a hybrid that will keep most people guessing as to how the image was created.

■ Click the **Background copy** layer in the **Layers** palette to make it the active layer. Click the **Blend Mode** box and choose **Lighten** as the blend mode. Reduce **Opacity** to about **60%**.

The image now looks entirely different. Try other **Blend Modes** and vary the **Opacity** setting. By doing this, you get a good idea of the vast number of combinations possible. After you find a **Blending Mode** that you like, you can get the exact effect you want by adjusting the **Opacity**. Should you want, you can even add a third or fourth layer and another filter or two to the stacked layers. Adobe Photoshop CS's new **Filter Gallery** is an excellent feature to use to create stacked layers. Notice that you can click the **New Layer** button at the bottom of the **Filter Gallery** dialog box and add additional layers, each created with different filters from the **Filter Gallery**.

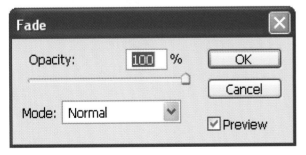

35.9

STEP 5: APPLY FILTER TO JUST ONE CHANNEL

In this step you'll learn how you can apply a filter to a single **Channel** instead of all three **Channels** at once.

- Choose **Layer** ➢ **Flatten Image**.
- If the **Channels** palette is not displayed, choose **Window** ➢ **Channels** to get the **Channels** palette shown in Figure 35.10. At this point, all the channels are highlighted, meaning that any edits that you do are done to all three channels. To edit just the **Red** channel, click the **Red** channel.
- Choose **Image** ➢ **Adjustments** ➢ **Posterize** to get the **Posterize** dialog box shown in Figure 35.11. Set **Levels** to **4** and click **OK**.
- To view all channels, click the **RGB** thumbnail in the **Channels** palette. The effect of this step is to posterize just the red colors in the trucks and to make them even more posterized.

Remember that you can use the **History** palette to easily move back and forth between steps to view differences in effects. For example, you can click back one step to see what your image looked like before applying a filter to just the **Red** channel. Then click to

the last step to once again see the effect of the filter. Be aware that if you run another command or filter after having looked at a past history state, all future history from that state forward will go away. You do have one chance to get it back — you can select **Undo** (**Ctrl+Z** PC, **Cmd+Z** Mac) once to get back the old history.

The final image is probably not one you want to print out, but with these tips, you are on your way to being a master of using filters. Use these tips as "starter" ideas for coming up with your own ideas on how you can get the most from Adobe Photoshop CS filters. Before going on to the next technique, see if you can create several cooler looking images of the two fire trucks. Then check the gallery on this book's companion Web site to see if your images are substantially different from those in the gallery at www.reallyusefulpage.com/50pscs/firetrucks.htm. If they are, please e-mail a small JPEG file to ggeorges@reallyusefulpage.com. I'd like to display your work in the gallery to show how different users use the same tool differently. Please make sure that the longest side of the image is 400 pixels and that it is a JPEG file.

This technique concludes this chapter. In the next chapter, we'll use some of the best plug-ins on the market to edit more digital photos.

35.10

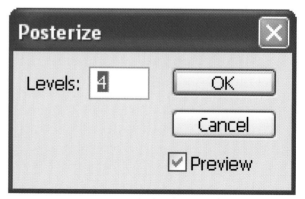

35.11

7

j. georges '02

USING
PLUG-INS

Adobe Photoshop CS is such a powerful software tool that you can use it to do just about anything you want to do to digital images—but doing it easier and better is often the claim made by software vendors that make plug-ins. In this chapter, you learn about five plug-ins that are useful to almost all photographers.

Capture One DSLR is a RAW image file conversion tool that offers "work flow" features that make it easy to edit batches of digital images with or without Adobe Photoshop CS, and the converted images are outstanding. Convert to B&W Pro provides you with incredible control over how color images are converted to black and white images. You discover how to transform a digital photo into a painterly image by using buZZ.Pro 2.0—one of the more fun plug-ins on the market. PhotoKit Sharpener is a tool that gives you all the power you need to sharpen any image for any output—this is one tool that everyone ought to at least try. The last technique shows you how to use Dfine to remove the dreaded digital noise from images.

Before you begin each of these techniques, you should download a trial version of the appropriate plug-in if you don't already have it. As vendors continuously update their products and make updates available on the Internet, a Web page has been created on this book's companion Web page, which will provide a list of current "clickable" links to take you to the most current software. All of the plug-ins in this chapter are available as downloadable "trial versions." It's wise to use these trial versions as you work through each of these techniques. You can then determine if the plug-ins will work for you and the work you do. You can find the links page at www.really usefulpage.com\50pscs\plug-ins.htm.

CONVERTING RAW IMAGES WITH CAPTURE ONE DSLR

36.1

36.2

Iris in Early Morning Canon EOS D60 mounted on a tripod with 550EX flash, 300mm f/2.8 IS, ISO 100, f/5.6 @ 1/125, RAW image setting, 2,048 x 3,072 pixels, 6.1MB .CRW RAW file

Technically, Phase One's Capture One DSLR is not a plug-in. However, it may be configured so that you can convert RAW images from any of the supported cameras and have the images be automatically opened in Adobe Photoshop CS. Therefore, it effectively acts as a RAW file conversion plug-in in addition to being a stand-alone image editor with image management capabilities. If you frequently need to convert large batches of RAW images, Capture One DSLR has wonderful workflow features that will save you a tremendous amount of time and you will get outstanding images. Trial versions of both Capture One DSLR Professional Edition and Capture One DSLR Limited Edition may be downloaded from the Phase One Web site at: www.phaseone.com.

STEP 1: LAUNCH CAPTURE ONE DSLR AND CHOOSE RAW FILE TO CONVERT

- After launching **Capture One DSLR**, the application window should look similar to the one shown in Figure 36.3 with four different windows: a folder explorer, thumbnail and information window, an image preview, and a five-tabbed settings window.

- After finding the \36 folder in the folder explorer window, click the image named **CRW_0166.CRW** to show it in the preview window. You can now close the folder explorer window to get a larger preview window.

STEP 2: SELECT CONVERSION SETTINGS

- Click the **Exposure Warning** (**F5**) icon to display a color overlay on any area of the image that has exceeded user-selectable settings for under- and over-exposure. In this case, you can see a slight amount of blue mask in the middle of the iris in the preview image shown in Figure 36.4 indicating that that area is under-exposed.

> **NOTE**
>
> Capture One DSLR can only be used to convert RAW images from specific camera models as is the case with most RAW image converters. There is a limited version called Capture One DSLR Limited Edition, which has less functionality and it supports an even more limited set of camera models, mostly the lower-end digital SLRs. Before you purchase either of these products check to see if your camera model is one of the supported models; if so, download and try a trial version.

- To the right in the settings window you can see the **Capture** tab, which is primarily used when you have a camera tethered to the computer.

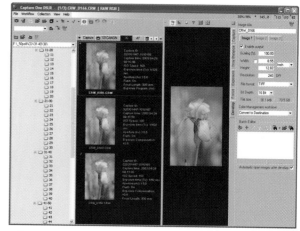

36.3

36.4

At the bottom of the tab you can find some shot information such as ISO speed, exposure time, flash, and so on.

■ Click the **Gray Balance** tab to see the choice of settings you see in Figure 36.5. If this image had a neutral color in it, you could select the **eyedropper** tool and instantly correct the color. In this case, however, we will use subjective judgment to choose settings. Note that you can choose between any of the camera's default color balance settings such as **Daylight**, **Cloudy**, **Tungsten**, and so on by selecting a setting from the drop-down color balance menu. This is one of the reasons to shoot in RAW as you have a choice of any white balance setting *after* you've taken a photo.

Drag the **Color Temperature** slider to **4125K** and set **Tone Balance** to **–6**. You can make very finely tuned color adjustments with the **Color Cast** wheel and the **Hue** and **Sat** sliders.

■ Now click the **Exposure** tab to get a window like the one shown in Figure 36.6. To lighten the image, click the **EC** (Exposure Control) slider and set it to **0.35** — about one-third of a stop. To add some contrast to the image, slide the **CC** (Contrast Control) slider to **4**. You can make further adjustments using the **Levels** and **Curve** tools, which work like the comparable tools in Adobe Photoshop CS. At the bottom of the window, there is a **Color Saturation** slider; slide it to boost color by **5.0%**.

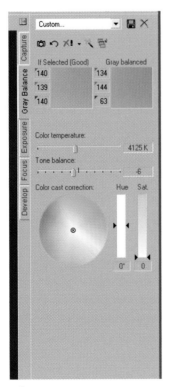

36.5

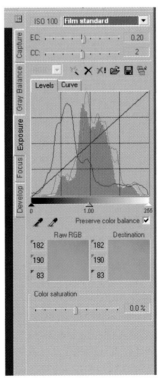

36.6

■ The last settings you need to make can be found by clicking the **Focus** tab, which allows you to sharpen your image. There is a preview image window that shows the image at 100 percent. To select a specific area to view, click inside the image preview and drag the marquee to where you want it. Figure 36.7 shows the **Focus** tab preview window set to show the beard of the iris so that you can view the results of the sharpen settings.

36.7

You can now choose from a **Soft Look** or **Standard Look** sharpening method and then set **Amount** and **Threshold**. In this case, choose **Soft Look** and set **Amount** to **50** and **Threshold** to **3**. If you plan on using one of many other sharpening techniques later in your editing process, you will want to set **Amount** to **0**.

STEP 3: CONVERT IMAGE

You are now ready to convert the RAW image to a TIFF or JPEG file. Before beginning the conversion process it is worth noting that all of the settings you have chosen for this image are saved. This means that you can at any time go back and preview this image with these same settings or even make a print, without having to go through this editing process all over again. An additional benefit of these saved settings is that you do not need hard drive space to store images that have been converted because you are just saving settings. Anytime you want to tweak settings, you can make your changes and once again they will be saved.

Another workflow benefit of Phase One's Capture One DSLR is that you can now select one or more images in the thumbnail view and apply all of the settings you have chosen for one image — to any of the other images. This is an incredible time-saving feature if you have taken a number of photos in the same light, or you have taken many photos of the same subject using lots of camera settings. You simply edit one image and apply the settings to the others. Each image may then be edited separately. Okay, now let's convert the image.

■ Click the **Develop** tab to get the **Develop** window shown in Figure 36.8. Here you have options to increase scaling by a percentage amount or by entering specific image dimensions. You can also choose the **TIFF** or **JPEG** format as well as **8-BIT** or **16-BIT** formats.

36.8

■ If you need to make two or three different images during the conversion process, you click the **Image 2** and **Image 3** tabs and choose appropriate settings for the additional images. This feature makes it easy to convert, for example, one image for print in 16-bit format, a second image for a Web page, and a third image in 8-bit TIFF format for use on a contact print.

■ To begin the conversion process, click the **Develop** icon in the **Batch Editor**. If the **Automatic Open Images After Develop** box is checked and you have chosen Adobe Photoshop CS as the target editor in the preferences, the image will be opened inside Adobe Photoshop CS once it has been converted. The results of these settings may be seen in the photo shown in Figure 36.2.

Once you have chosen settings for one image, you can begin the conversion process and continue viewing, selecting, and editing images while the conversion is done in the background. Anytime you want to convert an image, you simply add it to the conversion list and the images will be converted in order and to your exact specifications. Capture One DSLR offers many advantages over the Adobe Camera RAW plug-in in terms of work flow. If you manage and convert large batches of RAW images, this is a most useful tool to have!

CONVERTING COLOR TO BLACK AND WHITE USING CONVERT TO B/W PRO

37.1

37.2

Purple Iris Canon EOS D30 mounted on a tripod, 100mm macro f/2.8, ISO 100, RAW setting, ¹/₄ @ f/14.1, 2,160 x 1,440 pixels, edited and converted to 8.9MB .tif

I n Technique 14, you learned about four different approaches to converting a color image to a black and white image. In each case, only Adobe Photoshop CS filters and commands were used to make the conversions. While one or more of these approaches can be used on any image to make a wonderful black and white image, finding the optimal settings to get the image you want takes time and considerable experimentation — and comparing one setting to another is difficult.

In contrast, several Adobe Photoshop CS plug-ins have been specifically designed for converting color to black and white. They not only make it easier to compare different settings, but some of them even mimic the processes of conventional black and white photography. One of my very favorite plug-ins is The Imaging Factory's Convert to B/W Pro plug-in.

To learn more about Convert to B/W Pro and to get a free downloadable trial version, visit `www.the imagingfactory.com` or `www.reallyuseful page.com\50pscs\plug-ins.htm` to get a clickable link to The Imaging Factory Web page and read any notes and updates about this and many other Adobe Photoshop CS–compatible plug-ins.

STEP 1: OPEN FILE

■ After installing the **Convert to B/W Pro** plug-in, choose **File ➤ Open** (**Ctrl+O** PC, **Cmd+O** Mac) to display the **Open** dialog box. Double-click the **\37** folder to open it and then click the **iris-before.tif** file to select it. Click **Open** to open the file.

This close-up photo of an iris is a good photo to use to learn about the Convert to B/W Pro plug-in settings. Part of the image has a considerable area that has very subtle tonal changes (the top white part of the iris) and other parts of the image show red, yellow, green, blue, and magenta — every color except cyan.

STEP 2: RUN CONVERT TO B/W PRO PLUG-IN

■ Choose **Filter ➤ theimagingfactory ➤ Convert to B/W Pro** to get the plug-in dialog box shown in Figure 37.3.

Getting the *right* settings for this image with this plug-in is strictly a matter of aesthetics — what you like will be the *right* setting for you. For this image, you may want to find a setting that shows detail in the bottom part of the flower, but offers excellent contrast in the entire image. Also, see if you can pick settings that maximize blacks, while making sure that

you can still see detail in all parts of the image, especially in the dark parts of the flower at the bottom of the image.

■ Click the **Pre Filter Color** check box to turn pre-filtering on if a checkmark is not already there. Click in the **Pre Filter Color** box to select a filter color from the pop-up menu. Your choices are **Red**, **Orange**, **Yellow**, **Green**, **Cyan**, **Blue**, and **Magenta**. Using these filters is similar to using color lens filters on a camera lens; they help to increase image contrast and differentiate colors with the same gray values. Click on each of the choices in sequence to see which ones meet your objectives.

Figure 37.4 shows a series of images for all of the preset color settings, plus the original color image. Besides being able to select from the presets, you can select any one of 360 colors across the color range, plus adjust the color saturation from **0** to **100 %** by using the **Pre Filter Color** sliders.

■ Click in the **Pre Filter Color** box and select **Blue**.

■ Click the **Color Response** check box if a checkmark is not already there. Click in the **Color Response** box to get a pop-up menu giving you

37·3

a choice of **Linear**, **Photoshop**, **Agfa PAN APX**, **Ilford DELTA**, **Ilford FP4**, **Kodak T-MAX**, and **Kodak TRI-X**. These settings determine the relationship between colors of the original image and the shades of gray on the final image as they might occur when using specific brands of film.

Once again, I suggest that you experiment to see which setting best meets our objectives. Select **Kodak TRI-X**. If you are not happy with any of the preset **Color Response** settings, you can adjust the ten sliders just below the **Color Response** box to create your own color response.

Red

Orange

Yellow

Green

Cyan

Blue

Magenta

37·4

■ Click the **Tonal Response** check box if a checkmark is not already there. Click in the **Tonal Response** box to get a pop-up menu giving you a choice of **Linear** or a custom setting. Click **Linear**. In the **Tonal Response** area, you can use sliders to adjust **Neg. Exp. Exposure**, and **Multigrade**. You should try each of these sliders, especially the **Multigrade** slider as it mimics the multigrade exposure system developed by Ilford.

After experimenting with the **Tonal Response** sliders, check in the **Tonal Response** box to once again select **Linear** to restore the default settings.

■ The last area in the **Convert To B/W Pro** dialog box is for tinting or toning with colors. Click the **Sepia Tone Color** check box if a checkmark is not already there. Click in the **Sepia Tone Color** box to get a pop-up menu giving you a choice of **Blue** or **Tobacco**. Click **Tobacco** to get an image, such as the one shown in Figure 37.5. If you don't like

37·5

either of the preset tones, you can select any color you want by clicking in the color box; then you can also select the intensity of the color as well.

Clicking **Tint** tints your image, thereby leaving the whites a pure white. Clicking **Tone** tones the entire image including the white areas so that there are no pure whites.

■ Click in the **Sepia Tone Color** box to switch off toning. The final image shown in Figure 37.6 was created with the settings shown in Figure 37.7.

While several other good color-to-B&W conversion plug-ins are available, Convert to B/W Pro offers more user-selectable settings than any other plug-in that I know of, and it can be used with 16-bit RGB files — which is one of the strengths of Adobe Photoshop CS. This means that minute detail available in the original color file can be made visible in the resulting black and white file as accurately as is possible. If you edit 16-bit images such as the RAW image files taken with many digital cameras, you will love the results of this plug-in. My bet is that you won't want to convert color images to black and white images without this plug-in after you use it a few times.

37.6

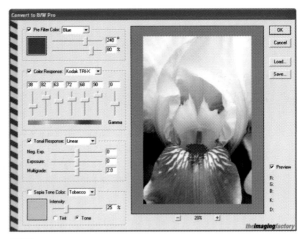

37.7

CREATING ARTWORK
WITH BUZZ.PRO 2.0

38.1

38.2

As I enjoy airbrush and watercolor painting I have also enjoyed transforming digital photos into images that look like a "painting" without having to apply lots of brush-strokes. Very early on, I learned that to create a successful digital painting, most digital photos need to be simplified; that is, many of the finer details need to be removed or simplified. Then those simplified areas need to once again be simplified only this time just in terms of color as brushstrokes are usually painted with a single color. Finally, those stroke-like marks need additional effects, such as texture, softness, or thickness to make an image look like a painting.

The Segmentis Limited buZZ.Pro 2.0 is a PC-only plug-in that offers 19 different effects that make it easy for you to create a variety of painting effects. The filters range from very powerful simplifiers, to blurs, screens, lines, and more. Each of these effects can be loaded into a stack; some of the effects allow further settings to be made. After some experimentation, buZZ.Pro 2.0 can be used to create many different painted effects. In this technique, you transform a photo of a farm house into a painting by using buZZ.Pro 2.0.

STEP 1: OPEN FILE

■ Choose **File ➤ Open** (**Ctrl+O** PC, **Cmd+O Mac**) to display the **Open** dialog box. Double-click the **\38** folder to open it and then click the **farmhouse-before.tif** file to select it. Click **Open** to open the file.

STEP 2: LOAD BUZZ.PRO 2.0 PLUG-IN

A downloadable trial version of buZZ.Pro 2.0 is available at www.fo2pix.com, or you can visit www.reallyusefulpage.com\50pscs\plug-ins.htm to get a clickable link to the download page and to learn more about many other Adobe Photoshop CS–compatible plug-ins.

■ After installing **buZZ.Pro 2.0**, choose **Filter ➤ buzzPro ➤ buzz.Stack** to get the two interdependent dialog boxes shown in Figure 38.3 and Figure 38.4.

■ To begin the simplification process, click **Simplifier Two** in the **Available Effects** box in the **Custom** dialog box to select it; click the **Add** button to add the effect to the **Current Stack**. The

buzz.Pro 2 preview dialog box should now look similar to the one shown in Figure 38.5.

■ Click in the preview image to drag the image to the left corner of the roof.

■ Slide the **Remove Large** and **Add-back Small** sliders all the way to the left. Begin sliding the **Remove Large** slider toward the right until the preview image is simplified as much as you want. Try using a setting of **96**.

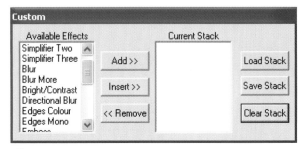

38.4

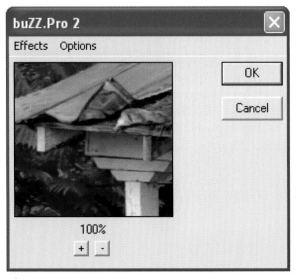

38.3

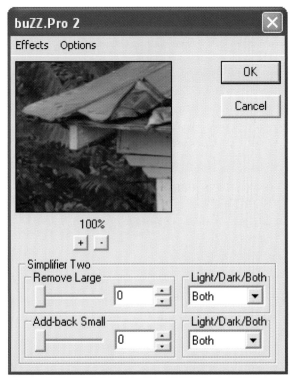

38.5

To add back some of the important small detail, slide the **Add-back Small** slider toward the right. A setting of **5** is good.

■ Click in the preview image once again and drag the image around to view the effects on the important parts of the image. Make sure the settings that you choose are good settings for the roof, the eaves, the orange daylilies, and the white flowers in the foreground.

■ To add contrast, click **Bright/Contrast** in the **Available Effects** box in the **Custom** dialog box; click **Add** to add that filter to the **Current Stack**. The **Custom** dialog box should now look like the one shown in Figure 38.6 and the **buzz.Pro 2** dialog box should look like the one in Figure 38.7.

Slide the **Brightness** slider to the right to get a setting of **15**. Slide the **Contrast** slider to the right until it shows **40**. These settings increase the brightness and contrast levels of the image Click **OK** to apply the settings.

STEP 3: MAKE FINAL ADJUSTMENTS

■ After making a few additional adjustments with **Levels** and **Hue/Saturation** to suit my taste, the image looks like the one shown in Figure 38.8. Now, try making your own adjustments by using **Levels** and **Hue/Saturation** to suit your tastes.

■ To add the final touch, use the **Adobe Photoshop CS Text** tool to add a signature.

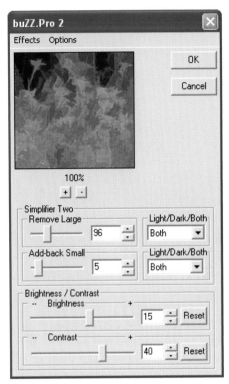

38.7

38.8

38.6

Because of the way that buzz.Pro 2.0 simplifies images, it can be used to create very large, high-quality images. Figure 38.9 shows an image of some

38.9

mountains in Sedona, Arizona that was taken with a Nikon 950 digital camera. The original image was a mere 1,600 x 1,200 pixels. Using the Adobe Photoshop CS **Image Size** command, the image was increased to 3,840 x 2,880 pixels—a 31.6MB image, which when printed at 240 dpi makes an excellent 16" x 12" print.

Besides creating painted effects, buZZ.Pro 2.0 can also be used to create various line or ink drawings. Stacking the 19 different filters in different combinations and in different orders allows you more flexibility than you would ever need. Some experimentation is required, but with some time, you can create some very nice effects. When you get a combination of filters that you like, you can save them as a **Stack** so that they can be easily applied again. You can also use one of the 16 preset **Stacks** that come with the software.

Segmentis offers several other products similar to buZZ.Pro 2.0. You can learn more about them on their Web site at `www.fo2pix.com`.

SHARPENING AN IMAGE WITH PHOTOKIT SHARPENER

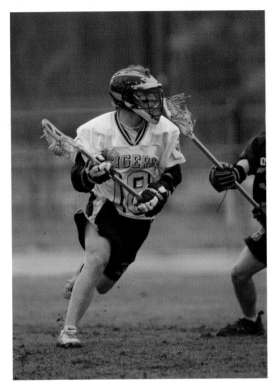

39.1

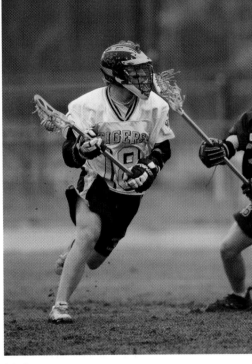

39.2

Getting Ready to Shoot Canon EOS 1D, 300mm f/2.8 IS with 1.4 tele-extender, ISO 800, f/4.0 @ 1/320, Fine Image File setting, edited and cropped to be a 5.8MB .tif (5" x 7" @ 240 dpi)

Sharpening an image well is nearly always a challenge. Despite the fact that there are many sharpening plug-ins, **Actions**, and techniques available, all of them fail on more images than they succeed on because optimal sharpening depends on so many factors and it is very difficult to provide a "one size fits all" approach to the wide range of images that you will want to sharpen. So, how do you sharpen an image well? It all depends on the image, the desired "sharpening" effect, the source of the image, and the intended output.

The good news is a talented group of Photoshop experts (Martin Evening, Bruce Fraser, Seth Resnick, Andrew Rodney, Jeff Schewe, and Mike Skurski) at Pixel Genius, LLC. have created an incredible sharpening tool they call

PhotoKit Sharpener that can be used to sharpen just about any image for any output. If there is bad news, it is that you must spend considerable time reading the excellent documentation and learning how to use PhotoKit Sharpener. It will be worth your time— that I promise you. Anytime I feel it is important to sharpen an image, I always use PhotoKit Sharpener; whether it is for sharpening images that are to be used for making prints or for images that will be displayed on a Web page.

In this technique we look at how you can use PhotoKit Sharpener to sharpen an image of a lacrosse player taken in early evening using an ISO 800 setting. This challenging image was selected to show you how PhotoKit can be used to sharpen an image to be printed on an inkjet printer (Epson 2200 using Premium Glossy Photo Paper) and how one can be sharpened for use on a Web page too.

To get a copy of PhotoKit Sharpener or to learn more about it visit `www.pixelgenius.com/sharpener`, or you can visit `www.reallyusefulpage.com\50pscs\plug-ins.htm` to get a clickable link to the download page and to learn more about many other Adobe Photoshop CS–compatible plug-ins. Trial versions are available and there are versions for both PC and Mac. You may also want to download and read the PDF user manual from that site as it is one of the best resources you will find on image sharpening.

TIP

To get the best results from PhotoKit Sharpener when shooting with a digital camera, you should turn off any sharpening or smoothing features in your camera. You should also turn off any sharpening or smoothing features when converting an image from a RAW file. Otherwise, you may get unpredictable results from sharpening an already sharpened image.

STEP 1: OPEN FILE

■ Choose **File ➤ Open** (**Ctrl+O** PC, **Cmd+O** Mac) to display the **Open** dialog box. Double-click the **\39** folder to open it and then click the **lax18-before.tif** file to select it. Click **Open** to open the file.

■ Select **View ➤ Actual Pixels** (**Alt+Ctrl+0** PC, **Option+Cmd+0** Mac) or double-click the **Zoom** tool in the **Toolbox**. Viewing the image at **100%** makes it easier for you to judge the effects of sharpening settings.

STEP 2: APPLY PHOTOKIT CAPTURE SHARPENER

■ PhotoKit Sharpener has been designed to address sharpening in three stages: capture sharpening to restore sharpness lost during the digital capture process, creative sharpening to enhance specific parts of an image, and output sharpening designed for specific output size and output device. To apply capture sharpening, select **File ➤ Automate ➤ PhotoKit Capture Sharpener** to get the **Capture Sharpener** dialog box shown in Figure 39.3.

■ Click in the **Sharpener Set** box and select **Digital Low-Res Smoothed Sharpen**, which has been designed for digital captures up to about 4 megapixels with the need for some smoothing due to a high ISO setting.

■ Click in the **Sharpener Effect** box and select **Medium Edge Sharpen**. This setting is for

39.3

"normal" images without fine detail or wide smooth areas that may require a "wider edge" sharpening effect. Click **OK** to apply.

If you take a look at the **Layers** palette you will find that you now have a layer set with a **Light Contour** and **Dark Contour** layer as shown in Figure 39.4. If you click either of these layers you will find that **Opacity** has been set to a default value of **66%**. You can make adjustments to the layers at once, or either of these layers independently to increase or decrease the strength of this initial sharpening.

■ After you have made any adjustments you want you can flatten the image to conserve memory by selecting **Layer ➢ Flatten Image** or keep the layers as they are.

STEP 3: APPLY PHOTOKIT SELECTIVE SHARPENER

■ Now you can apply some localized sharpening or smoothness to the image to meet your artistic intent. In this case, let's sharpen the players in the

image along with their equipment. Click on the **Background** layer to make it the active layer. Select **File ➢ Automate ➢ PhotoKit Creative Sharpener** to get the **Creative Sharpener** dialog box shown in Figure 39.5. Click in the **Sharpener Set** box to select **Sharpening Brushes** and then click in the **Sharpener Effect** box to select **Sharpen Brush Narrow Edges 1**. Click **OK** to apply the settings and to automatically create a layer mask set to hide all.

■ The **Brush** tool is now active and you can begin painting on the mask with white to reveal the layer with the sharpening effects. I suggest that you paint over both players with the **Brush** tool while varying the size by pressing the [key to increase brush size, and the] key to reduce brush size. You may want to avoid painting on the player's legs. Don't forget to paint across the ground in a horizontal line where there is an "in-focus" patch of grass.

If you paint where you should not have painted, just change the color to **Black** (**X**) and paint the mask back. Switch back to **White** (**X**) and continue painting until you are finished.

■ Once you have completed your painting, you can modify the strength of the sharpening effect by adjusting the **Opacity** level in the **Layers** palette. To strengthen the effect, slide the slider up from **50%**. Conversely, you weaken the sharpen effect by sliding the slider back down from **50%**. I chose to set **Opacity** to **25%**. While it looks a bit too sharp on the screen, it will look good when it is printed on the target inkjet printer.

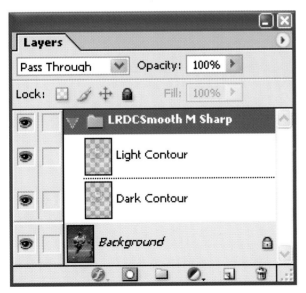

39.4

39.5

■ Another way of making part of the image look sharp is to soften the area next to it. So, now let's smooth the area around the players using a PhotoKit **Smoothing Brush**. Click on the **Background** layer to make it the active layer. Select **File ➢ Automate ➢ PhotoKit Creative Sharpener** to once again get the **Creative Sharpener** dialog box. This time select **Smoothing Brushes** by clicking in the **Sharpener** box; then, click in the **Sharpener** box and select the magical **Edge-Protected Smoothing Brush 2**. This magical brush allows you to smooth non-edge areas of an image without using layer masks to protect important edges! Click **OK** to apply the action.

■ Once again you can paint the mask to smooth the image where you want to smooth it. This smoothing effect has the added advantage of reducing the digital noise caused by the **800 ISO** setting. Once you have completed the painting of the mask, the **Layers** palette should look similar to the one shown in Figure 39.6.

STEP 4: COMPLETE EDITING AND SAVE FILE

Now is the time to do any additional editing you might like to do such as applying **Curves**, **Levels**, **Hue/Saturation**, and so on. Just to add a little punch to this image I added a slight adjustment with **Curves** to increase image contrast. Once your editing is complete, you can save the file with the layers, or flatten the image and then save the file if you don't plan on going back to do any further tweaking of settings.

STEP 5: SHARPEN IMAGE FOR USE ON A WEB PAGE

■ As our original goal was to create a well-sharpened image for both the Web and an inkjet printer, select **Image ➢ Duplicate** to make a duplicate image. Select **Image ➢ Image Size** to get the **Image Size** dialog box. Make sure there is a checkmark in the box next to **Constrain Proportions** and next to **Resample Image**. Click in the **Resample Image box** and select **Bicubic Sharper**. Type **600** in the **Height** box in the **Pixel Dimensions** area and click **OK** to resize the image to 401 x 600 pixels.

■ Select **View ➢ Actual Pixels** (**Alt+Ctrl+0** PC, **Option+Cmd+0** Mac) or double-click the **Zoom** tool in the **Toolbox**. This will make it easier to judge the effect of the sharpen settings.

■ Select **File ➢ Automate ➢ PhotoKit Output Sharpening** to get the **Output Sharpening** dialog

39.6

box. Set **Sharpener Set** to **Web and Multimedia Sharpeners**. Notice that the dialog box shows the current image size as being 480 pixels wide. Click in the **Sharpener Effect** box and select **400-pixel Wide Edge Sharpen**. Click **OK** to sharpen the image. As was the case with the sharpeners we applied earlier, you can make choose the level of the sharpening effects by varying **Opacity** in the **Layers** palette after choosing sharpening settings.

The image now looks perfect for display on a Web page. Save it using **File ➢ Save for Web** so that you can pick optimal JPEG setting. If you use the **JPEG Medium** setting, the image is only 30K! If you want to view this image you may find it in the **\39** folder. It is named **lax18-web-after.jpg**.

STEP 6: SHARPEN IMAGE FOR PRINTING ON AN EPSON 2200 INKJET PRINTER

■ Now let's return to the original image to make a print using an Epson 2200. Click on the lax18-before.tif image to make it the active image. Before we apply any sharpening we need to check the image size to make sure it is properly sized for a 5" x 7" print at 240 dpi. Select **Image ➢ Image Size** to get the **Image Size** dialog box shown in Figure 39.7. It is sized as it ought to be sized.
■ Select **View ➢ Actual Pixels** (**Alt+Ctrl+0** PC, **Option+Cmd+0** Mac) or double-click the **Zoom** tool in the **Toolbox**. This will make it easier to judge the effect of the sharpen settings.
■ Select **Layer ➢ Flatten Image**.
■ Select **File ➢ Automate ➢ PhotoKit Output Sharpening** to get the **Output Sharpening** dialog box. Set **Sharpener Set** to **Inkjet Output Sharpeners**. Notice that the dialog box shows

the current image size as 240 dpi. Click in the **Sharpener Effect** box and select **Inkjet 240 Glossy** because we intend to print this **240** dpi image on glossy paper. Click **OK** to sharpen the image. Once again, you have the option to adjust the level of the sharpening effects by varying **Opacity** in the **Layers** palette. For this image, set **Opacity** to **60%** and you are ready to print the image. Remember that you do not have to save this image if you saved the earlier image with the **Capture** and **Creative Sharpeners** applied as this image can easily be created from that image or another one can be created for any other output.

Just imagine — when you need to automate an entire batch of images like the lacrosse action photo we just sharpened, you can do so with little effort if you use these PhotoKit Sharpeners in a Photoshop **Action** or **Droplet**.

39.7

REMOVING DIGITAL NOISE WITH DFINE

40.1

40.2

ABOUT THE IMAGE

Eastern Box Turtle in Orange Canon EOS 1D hand-held with 520EX flash, 100mm f/2.8 Macro lens, Fine Image Quality setting, ISO 3200, f/7.1 @1/90, 2,464 x 1,648 pixels, 2.7MB .jpg

A heavy downpour can often set turtles out walking as was the case with this handsome Eastern Box turtle in North Carolina. There was heavy cloud cover and the trees in the forest blocked most of the sunlight, so there was little light to shoot the turtle. Yet the rich orange and brown colors of the turtle set against the oranges and browns of autumn made the turtle an attractive subject. In an effort to not overpower the existing light, a small amount of fill flash was used from a flash mounted high above the camera to bring out important details. To get adequate light, an ISO 3200 setting was used, which added considerable digital noise to the image.

Of all the tradeoffs in photography, I personally would love to see the tradeoff between ISO settings and digital noise go away with the introduction of new technology. The challenge of removing unwanted detail (digital noise) and keeping wanted detail (important photographic detail) is a difficult one — unless you are using a digital noise removal tool such as nik multimedia's digital noise reduction plug-in Dfine 1.0.

Dfine 1.0 has been developed for Windows 98/ME/ 2000/XP, and Mac OS 9 and Mac OS X systems. It supports both 8-bit and 16-bit digital images, with the software utilizing full 16-bit image capabilities. When it is used on 8-bit images, Dfine uses an internal conversion procedure that allows the image to be processed with the advantages of a 16-bit image, thereby eliminating the histogram "gapping" that can occur on an 8-bit image. If you need to remove digital noise, this is a valuable plug-in. Dfine 1.0 can be used to remove digital noise without the use of camera-specific profiles; however, you will get much better results if you purchase the camera profiles for your camera. Depending on your camera model, the cost of camera profiles is between $30 and $50.

STEP 1: OPEN FILE

■ Choose **File** ➢ **Open** (**Ctrl+O** PC, **Cmd+O** Mac) to display the **Open** dialog box. Double-click the **40** folder to open it and then click the **turtle-before.jpg** file to select it. Click **Open** to open the file.

STEP 2: DUPLICATE LAYER

It is often a good practice when applying a filter such as Dfine 1.0 to create a new layer so that you can easily compare the "before" and "after" results by turning on, or turning off, the layer with the effects applied. It also makes it easy to discard the results because you can just simply delete the layer.

■ To create a duplicate layer, choose **Layer** ➢ **Duplicate Layer** to get the **Duplicate Layer** dialog box. Type **Dfine** in the **As** box and click **OK**.

Before loading **Dfine**, increase the image size to **100%** and then **200%** using the **Navigator** to study the amount of digital noise and JPEG artifacts that need to be removed. A quick analysis will reveal that

different areas require varying levels of noise removal. The background is in obvious need of digital noise removal as is the part of the turtle's back that is out-of-focus. In contrast, the sharply focused parts of the turtle including his face and the in-focus parts of his back look pretty good as they are. If we can't find one "global" setting to remove sufficient digital noise without loosing detail, we can selectively apply noise reduction in varying ways to those areas that are most in need of noise reduction. This strategy will leave us with an optimal image with all the important picture detail remaining and in condition for later sharpening if such steps are to be taken.

STEP 3: LOAD DFINE PLUG-IN

■ To load Dfine 1.0 choose **Filter** ➢ **Define 1.0** ➢ **Dfine 1.0** to get the **Dfine 1.0** dialog box shown in Figure 40.3.

STEP 4: CHOOSE DFINE SETTINGS TO REDUCE DIGITAL NOISE

■ To get a large preview of the image, click the **mode** button and select the **one view** mode.

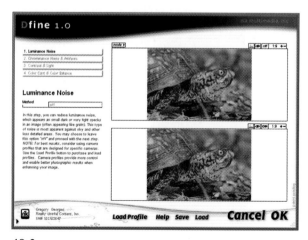

40.3

Increase the zoom by clicking the + icon until zoom shows as being **3:1**. Click in the preview and drag the image until you can see the background area and part of the top of the turtle's head, as in Figure 40.4. You can now clearly see the noise and more easily identify characteristics that will help you remove it.

■ The best way to use Dfine to remove digital noise is to use a camera-specific profile. As this image was taken with a Canon 1D and it was shot at ISO 3200, we will select the **Canon 1D – ISO 3200** profile. Click the box beneath **Luminance Noise** to get a pop-up menu.

If the appropriate camera-specific profile is now shown, you can select it. If one does not show and you have already purchased one and have installed it, click on **Load Profile** to get a menu that will allow you to load profiles. If you don't have a camera profile you can purchase one online from the nik multimedia, Inc. Web site by selecting the **Get Profile From Web** menu item after clicking on **Load Profile**.

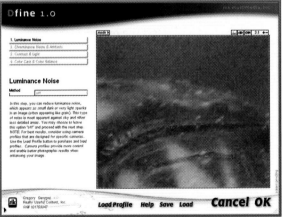

40.4

■ In this case, we will select the **Canon 1D – ISO 3200** profile. You now need to pick five colors from the image and adjust each of the **Camera Profile Controller** sliders to get the optimal results. When you are picking the colors, you will need to change zoom level and you will need to click and drag the image around in the preview window.

We now want to pick five different colors in the image where there is digital noise so that we can adjust each of those colors to remove the noise while retaining image sharpness and detail. First, click the **eyedropper** to the left of the **first slider** and then click in the image on one of the lighter colors in the background above the turtle.

■ Click the **eyedropper** to the left of the **second slider**; then click in the image on one of the darker colors in the background above the turtle.

■ Click the **eyedropper** to the left of the **third slider**; then click in the image on an orange part of the turtle.

■ Click the **eyedropper** to the left of the **fourth slider**; then click in the image on the turtle's skin where it is nearly black.

■ Click the **eyedropper** to the left of the **fifth slider**; then click in the image on the turtle's shell where it is a dark gray.

■ Now that you have picked five different colors from the image, you are ready to adjust the sliders to remove digital noise. Getting these five sliders set optimally can take some time. Remember that you want to keep the sliders as low as possible to ensure image sharpness. You may even find that you will end up with one slider set to **0**. Click each slider while carefully watching the zoomed preview. Once you have set each slider, go back and see if you can make any further adjustments to improve the image. You can see the colors and slider values that I selected in Figure 40.5.

■ Now that you have set the **Luminance Noise** settings, it is time to set the **Chrominance Noise and Artifacts** settings. Click the **2. Chrominance Noise & Artifacts** menu item. Click in the box to the right of **Method** and select **Protected Reduction**.

The two sliders under **Protected Reduction** are for removing both chrominance noise and artifacts. Chrominance noise appears as small off-colored "specks." JPEG artifacts look like little squares in the image.

■ I used the setting of **11** for **Chrominance Noise Level** and **90%** for **Protect Color Details**, as shown in Figure 40.6. To apply these settings click **OK**. If you were wondering why we only completed two of the four steps in the **Dfine** dialog box, it is because the last two steps (**3. Contrast & Light** and **4. Color Cast & Color Balance**) are better done in Adobe Photoshop CS.

STEP 5: EVALUATE RESULTS AND MAKE ADJUSTMENTS

■ You can now evaluate the results to make sure you have not removed important detail, that the image is not too soft, and that you have removed sufficient digital noise by clicking the **Layer Visibility** icon to the left of the **Dfine** layer, as shown in Figure 40.7. Turning this layer on and off at **100%** zoom lets you clearly see the effects.

If the effects are too strong, you can adjust the **Opacity** level to reduce the effects globally. If there are areas where important detail has been lost or where the image is overly soft, you can create an **Adjustment Layer** and use the **Brush** tool to selectively paint back in the original image.

■ To complete this image I chose to create an **Adjustment Layer** and selectively paint back in the sharply focused area of the turtle's head, leg, and shell. I then created a duplicate layer and changed it to **Multiply** and reduced the **Opacity** to about **25%**. Using an **Adjustment Layer**, I was able to tone down the bright reflections on the turtle's back. One quick adjustment with **Curves** to increase contrast and the image was complete, as shown in Figure 40.2.

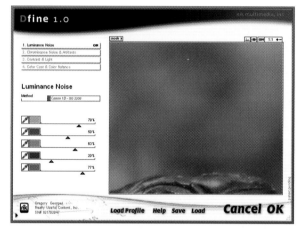

40.5

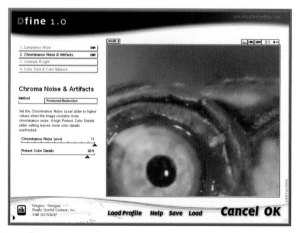

40.6

When you install Dfine, you also install the **Dfine Selective** tool, which can be accessed by selecting **File ➤ Automate ➤ Define**. The **Dfine Selective** tool offers ten different types of noise reduction tools, as shown in Figure 40.8. Each of these tools can be applied selectively by painting with a brush tool. This is an excellent tool to use when you need to remove noise in specific areas such as sky in a landscape photo, or to smooth or soften digital noise in a smaller area such as a face in a portrait. Notice that this tool has specific settings for sky, skin, shadow, background, and so forth.

> **TIP**
>
> In order to get the best effects from Dfine, you should avoid using in-camera noise reduction and sharpening features. You should also avoid using above-average contrast settings in your digital camera. In low light situations, digital noise can often be reduced when a flash is used because the light often helps to reduce the amount of noise that will be generated.

You have now read about and possibly used some of the best Photoshop-compatible plug-ins on the market. If you want to learn about other useful plug-ins, visit `www.reallyusefulpage.com\50pscs\plug-ins.htm`. Next up is a chapter on making digital prints.

> **TIP**
>
> When using Dfine on an image that will be printed, reducing noise is often better than removing it entirely. Reducing noise in high-detail areas will generally lead to better results with less loss of detail. To make the best decision on how well you have removed noise and how much detail you have kept you must print out the image on the target printer.

40.7

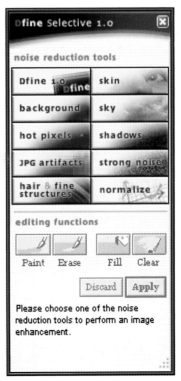

40.8

CHAPTER 8

MAKING PHOTO-GRAPHIC PRINTS

Chapter 1 through Chapter 7 covers 40 techniques to help you create digital images that you can use to make fantastic photographic prints that you can enjoy, share with others, or sell to make a profit. In this chapter, you discover how you can turn those digital images into a variety of photographic prints to suit your needs, whether you want the "one-hour" style of print or fine-art prints printed on fine art paper suitable to be hung in a gallery or museum.

The first technique covers myths, realities, and techniques you'll want to know about when you need to increase the size of an image to make a large print. The next technique covers step-by-step instructions on how to use an ICC profile and soft-proofing to get the best possible print when using a desktop inkjet printer such as the Epson 2200. Another technique tells you what you need to know to get reasonably priced, yet high-quality Fuji Frontier prints made from a local print service. If you want the convenience of uploading and ordering prints online, the next technique shows you some important steps and tips on how to get prints made by using the Shutterfly online printing service. The final technique covers steps to take to get the ultimate photographic print — a Lightjet 5000 print from Calypso, Inc. No matter what kinds of prints you want to make, this chapter will help you get them made well.

INCREASING IMAGE RESOLUTION TO MAKE LARGE PRINTS

41.1

41.2

ABOUT THE IMAGE

Swift Long-Winged Skimmer
Canon EOS 1D, 180mm f/3.5 Macro with 24mm extension tube, ISO 200, RAW image setting, f/8 @ 1/25, 3.3MB 2,488 x 1,656 pixel .crw file has been converted to an 8-bit 12.4MB .tif using Capture One DSLR

Since Adobe Photoshop 7 was released, there have been many affordable technological innovations that make it easier for you to get quality prints made in the sizes you want without worrying about image degradation due to interpolation (a mathematical process to estimate pixel values). If you want quality large prints, there are several ways to get them including:

■ Shoot with a large megapixel camera. Capturing the resolution you need to begin with is always superior to any other approach that requires interpolation. As 6-, 8-, 11-, and 14-megapixel cameras become more common and affordable, the whole issue of increasing image size to gain sufficient resolution becomes less of an issue unless you have plans for very large prints.

■ Use the "new and improved" interpolation algorithms in Adobe Photoshop CS to get excellent results. Adobe Photoshop CS's algorithms include Bicubic Smoother, Nearest Neighbor, Bilinear,

Bicubic (new and improved since Adobe Photoshop 7), and Bicubic Sharper.

■ Use software specifically designed for increasing image resolution. Camera RAW found in Adobe Photoshop CS allows you to increase image size as does Phase One's Capture One DSLR. There are also plug-ins such as LizardTech's Genuine Fractals Print Pro, Extensis's pxl SmartScale, and S-Spline from Shortcut Software to name just three. Other software products including image viewers and editors contain interpolation algorithms that are often touted as being superior (but may or may not be) to the original Bicubic found in earlier versions of Photoshop. These programs include Qimage Pro and IrfanView 32, and Photo Cleaner.

■ Keep your images at their captured resolution and leave any necessary resampling to the driver of the target printer. In Technique 45 you will learn that the Lightjet 5000 printer can print exceptional images as large as 30" x 40" from a 3-megapixel or larger camera if the photo is an excellent photo. Many of the new under-$1,000 photographic printers made by Canon, Epson, HP, and other printer vendors are quite capable of increasing image size with minimal image degradation. If you want to improve the results you get from such printers, you can purchase RIP software such as ImagePrint (www.colorbytesoftware.com), which in some cases can even improve on image quality when image resolution is increased.

With all those choices, the multi-million-dollar question remains: How should *you* increase the size of an image without causing unacceptable image degradation? There are many answers (and opinions) to that question and in *my* opinion, each *good* answer always starts with "it depends." How far you can "res-up" an image *depends* on a number of image characteristics and how critical it is to have a sharp, in-focus image instead of one with the dreaded (or sometimes desirable) pixelization or softness that comes from adding pixels in places where there were previously no pixels.

While there are many rules or recommendations about when and how to use different techniques and software products to increase the size of an image, I *strongly* recommend that you learn to get the best results you can with the features found in Adobe Photoshop CS and with any capabilities that might be found in your target printer. Without question, many of the new digital SLRs and prosumer-level digital cameras have greatly changed my view of how far you can res-up an image. Many digital cameras create nearly noise-free digital photos when lower ISO settings are used. If a digital picture is in focus and it is noise-free, it can be enlarged much more than a scanned image that contains both film grain and digital noise that gets created during the scanning process. Soft blurred digital photos can also have a remarkable smoothness to them that allows such a photo to be increased many times its original size. A good example of a soft image is the iris found in Technique 45. Good editing techniques can be used to make 30" x 40" prints and larger from this image that was taken with a 3-megapixel Canon D30.

One other factor that can limit how large an image can be increased is how much the image needs to be sharpened. In Technique 11, you learned that an image should not be sharpened until it has been sized for its intended use. The process of up-sampling an image will at some point create visible pixelization; sharpening an image with moderate pixelization can result in a wholly unsatisfactory image. Likewise, up-sampling an image that has already been sharpened can cause an even nastier problem—up-sampled sharpening! Remember that you can't actually sharpen an image; you can only increase the perception that an image is sharp by creating more contrast along the "edges" of an image and this increase in contrast normally does not res-up well.

Okay—enough talk; it is time to increase the size of the digital photo of a dragonfly to make a print to fit on Super B-sized paper, which is 13" x 19". Super B paper is the largest paper that can be used in most of the desktop inkjet printers such as the Epson 1280 and 2200.

The dragonfly photo is a good one to use to learn about increasing image size as some of the areas of the image are sharply focused and other areas are soft and out of focus due to the extremely shallow depth of field.

STEP 1: OPEN FILE

■ Choose **File** ➢ **Open** (**Ctrl+O** PC, **Cmd+O** Mac) to display the **Open** dialog box. Double-click the **\41** folder to open it and then click the **dragonfly-before.tif** file to select it. Click **Open** to open the file. This image has been converted from a RAW file without any sharpening and without increasing resolution. Some basic image enhancement has been done with Adobe Photoshop CS. No sharpening has yet been applied.

STEP 2: INCREASE IMAGE SIZE

■ Choose **Image** ➢ **Image Size** to get the **Image Size** dialog box shown in Figure 41.3. Make sure there is a checkmark in the box next to **Constrain Proportions** to keep the proportions of the image the same when the image size is changed.

Click in the box next to **Resample Image** if there is not already a checkmark; then select **Bicubic Smoother** as the interpolation algorithm. **Bicubic Smoother** is almost always the best method to select for enlarging images and it is superior to the "step or stair interpolation" in which you increase an image by a small percent many times until you get the image size you want. **Bicubic** in Adobe Photoshop CS is a new version, but it generally produces poorer results than **Bicubic Smoother**. If you are in need of down-sampling an image, you should try **Bicubic Sharper**.

To get a ½" border on 13" x 19" paper, type **18** in the **Width** box in the **Document Size** area. Notice that the 11.8MB file is now a 35.5MB file with dimensions of 4,320 x 2,875 pixels. While we have only increased the width and height about 175 percent, we have increased the total pixel count by 300 percent (35.5/11.8 = 300 percent).

■ Click **OK** to increase image size by **300%**.

If you are planning on making a print on a specific printer, then make any judgment calls on how far you can increase image resolution by *making prints* — not by looking at the image on your computer screen. After you make a few prints, go back and look at the images on your screen and you are likely to be surprised to see that what looks like a "not so good" image makes a beautiful print.

STEP 3: SHARPEN IMAGE

Now — and only after the image has been sized to its final size — should you sharpen the image. You can learn more about sharpening images in Techniques 11 and 39.

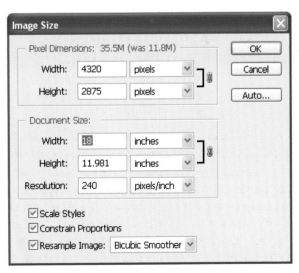

41.3

Next time you need to increase the size of an image remember: the best approach to increasing image resolution "depends" on the quality and characteristics of your image. Experiment and don't judge the effects of up-sampling or sharpening by looking at your monitor if you are printing the image. Print it — then judge the results. My bet is that you will more often than not get the best results using Adobe Photoshop CS's new **Bicubic Smoother** algorithm found in the **Image Size** box; plus, it is so fast compared to just about any other approach or software product you may use. Try it — I'm betting you'll be happy with the results you get.

USING AN ICC PROFILE AND PROOF COLORS WHEN PRINTING WITH AN INKJET PRINTER

42.1

42.2

ABOUT THE IMAGE

Red and Orange Iris on Green Canon EOS D60 mounted on a tripod, Canon 550 EX flash mounted above lens on Really Right Stuff B91 Flash Arm, 300mm f/2.8 IS, ISO 100, RAW image quality setting, f8.0 @ 1/30, 2,052 x 3,076 pixels, 9.4MB .tif (RAW) converted to 8-bits per channel 18.9MB .tif

For me, to a very great extent, photography is *the* print! No matter what subject I shoot, what kind of camera I use, what image editor or plug-in I use, or what fancy editing techniques I apply, if the print is no good — neither is the rest of the process I used to create it. Consequently, the printer is a very important part of photography for me, and probably for you, too. For this reason, I will be bold and speak my opinion. At the time this book went to press, the Epson Stylist Photo 2200 printer was and may still be arguably the best photographic printer on the market that costs less than $1,000 if you want an archival print; the 2200 is best in terms of image quality and print longevity when used with the correct inks and media.

Henry Wilhelm, *the* recognized expert on print longevity has considerable information about print permanence on his Web site at `www.wilhelm-research.com`. Using the Epson 2200 and the Epson UltraChrome ink sets, he says you can expect prints made on certain kinds of papers when framed and displayed under glass to last from nearly 60 years to well over 80 years. He also rates one of my favorite fine art papers, Crane's Museo, at 85 years when used with UltraChrome Inks. In this technique, you will learn how to set up and use an ICC profile created by Crane to get the best possible print from an Epson 2200 inkjet printer using the UltraChrome ink sets with the Photo Matte ink and Crane's Museo fine art paper.

Before beginning this technique, I should mention that we will be using Adobe Photoshop CS's soft-proofing feature to get a good idea of what the image will look like when it is printed, by looking at a computer screen. There are several advantages to this approach over just using the **Print Preview** and **Print dialog** boxes.

To complete this technique exactly as it is written you will need to use an Epson 2200 printer, a Crane Museo paper printer profile, and Crane Museo paper. If you don't have Museo paper, you can order it online from the Crane Web site at `www.crane.com`. You can buy a trial pack of Museo paper or full packages in a variety of sizes. If you don't have Museo paper and you don't want to buy Museo paper, you can still follow this technique — but use a color profile for your chosen printer and ink/media combination. The overall process is the same for Epson printers as well as most of the other photographic desktop printers. If you want to print on a fine-art paper though, I highly recommend that you try this paper, providing you have an appropriate printer profile for Museo paper and your printer. Contact Crane to see if they have printer profiles for your printer if you are not using an Epson 2200 — they may have, or maybe will create a profile for your printer and their paper.

STEP 1: INSTALL ICC COLOR PROFILE

You can find two Museo color profiles that have been created by Crane in the **\42** folder on the companion CD-ROM. These color profile files are named **EPSON Stylus Photo 2200_Museo_8-5-2003.icc** and **EPSON Stylus Photo 2200_Museo_PhotoBlack.icc**.

■ Before you can use color profiles, you must first install them in the right folder so that Adobe Photoshop CS can find them. On Windows XP, you can install color profiles by selecting the two Museo profiles in the **\42** folder on the companion CD-ROM and then right-clicking them. Select **Install Profile** from the pop-up menu to install the profiles in the correct folder.

On a Mac, the profiles need to be installed into the **Profiles** folder of the **ColorSync** folder, which can be found in the **System Folder** folder. Drag and drop the Museo paper profiles from the **\42** folder on the companion CD-ROM to the **ColorSync Profiles** folder (HD:Library:ColorSynch:Profiles).

STEP 2: OPEN FILE

■ Choose **File ➢ Open** (**Ctrl+O** PC, **Cmd+O** Mac) to display the **Open** dialog box. Double-click the **\42** folder to open it and then click the **red-iris-before.tif** file to select it. Click **Open** to open the file.

STEP 3: INCREASE IMAGE RESOLUTION

■ Select **Image** ➢ **Image Size** to get the **Image Size** dialog box. As we want the largest image that we can print on Super B paper, which is 13" x 19", make sure **Constrain Proportions** is checked and that **Resample** image is checked with **Bicubic Smoother** set as the method of interpolation.

Type **18** in the **Height** field in the **Document Size** area with **Inches** set as the measurement. The image should now be 35.6MB and 2,882 x 4,320 pixels in size. Click **OK** to increase image resolution.

STEP 4: SET UP SOFT-PROOFING

■ Select **View** ➢ **Proof Setup** ➢ **Custom** to get the **Proof Setup** dialog box shown in Figure 42.3. Click in the **Profile** box and choose **EPSON Stylus Photo 2200_Museo_8-5-2003.icc**. **Preserve Color Numbers** should not be checked, **Intent** should be set to **Perceptual**, and **Use Black Point Compensation** should not be checked.

To save these settings for future use, click the **Save** button and save the setup as **MuseoMatteBlack**; click **OK** to apply the settings. You should immediately see a difference in how the image looks. To swap back and forth between "before" and "after," press **Ctrl+Y** on the PC and **Cmd+Y** on the Mac.

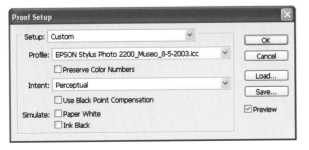

42.3

STEP 5: COMPLETE ANY NEEDED EDITS WHILE USING SOFT PROOFING

When you use Adobe Photoshop CS's **Proof Setup**, you can do more than simply set up the proper ICC profile for your printer. You, in fact, are also changing the way you see the image on the screen. As soon as you turn on **Proof Setup** as you did in Step 3, the image you see on your screen will simulate the way the print will look because the screen view will now reflect the smaller gamut of the target printer — not the wider gamut of your computer screen. You can even choose **View** ➢ **Gamut Warning** (**Shift+Ctrl+Y** PC, **Shift+Cmd+Y** Mac) to see what, if any, parts of your image are out of gamut and won't print properly on the target printer.

If you have a properly calibrated monitor and you have accurate profiles of your printer, you can use soft proofing to get better prints than you can in any other way. The significant advantage here is that you

NOTE

If you are using an Epson 2200, you may also want to try using the second Museo color profile that can be found on the companion CD-ROM. It is named **EPSON Stylus Photo 2200_ Museo_PhotoBlack.icc** and it has been created for use with Epson's Photo Black UltraChrome Ink. While the documentation with the printer suggests using the Matte Black UltraChrome Ink when printing on fine art papers such as Crane's Museo, some photographers have found that they can at times get better prints using the Photo Black ink. So, Crane was kind enough to create this second profile to use.

are more likely to avoid trying to print colors that are out of gamut as you can see them on your screen and you can edit while seeing the likely results on your printer.

STEP 6: SET UP PRINTER AND MAKE PRINT

■ Choose **File ➢ Print with Preview (Alt+Ctrl+P** PC, **Opt+Cmd+P** Mac) to get the **Print** dialog box. Click in the **Show More Options** box to get the **Print** dialog box shown in Figure 42.4. Click next to **Proof Setup** in the **Source Space** area to select the Museo color profile we selected in Step 3. Set **Print Space Profile** to the **EPSON Stylus Photo 2200_Museo_8-5-2003.icc** profile; set **Intent** to **Relative Colorimetric** and make sure that **Use Black Point Compensation** remains unchecked.

■ Click **Page Setup** to get the **Page Setup** dialog box. Click in the **Size** box and select **Super B 13x19**. **Orientation** should be set to **Portrait**.

Because of the thickness of the Museo paper, you should set **Source** to **Manual Paper Feed** and feed the paper in from the back of the Epson 2200 printer to ensure proper paper feeding. Click **OK** to apply the settings. Click **Print** to get the **Print** dialog box shown in Figure 42.5.

■ Click in the **Name** box to select the **Epson Stylus Photo 2200**; then, click **Properties** to get the **Epson Stylus Photo 2200 Properties** dialog box shown in Figure 42.6. First select **ICM** in the **Color Management Area** and then click next to **No Color Adjustment** in the **ICC Profile** area.

■ Click in the first box in the left column under **Paper & Quality Options** and select **Manual** to handle the thickness of the Museo paper. Choose **Enhanced Matte Paper**. While we are using Museo paper, not **Enhanced Matte Paper**, Crane used this setting while creating the color profiles so it is the right choice now. Choose **Photo – 1440 dpi** and **Super B (13x19)**. Set **Orientation** to **Portrait**.

High Speed should be checked; **Black Ink Only** should not be checked. **Edge Smoothing** and **Print Preview** should both be checked.

42.4

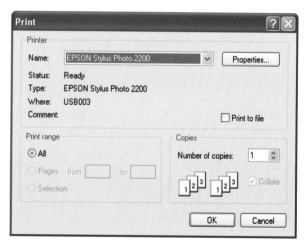

42.5

■ Click on the **Page Layout** tab and click in the box next to **Centered** to center the image in the middle of the page. Click **OK** to close the **Properties** dialog box and then click **OK** to begin the printing process. Because we have checked **Print Preview**; once the computer has created the print file, you will get a **Print View** dialog box showing how the print fits on the page. If it looks correct, select **Print** — otherwise, click **Cancel** and you can go back and change settings (and you avoid wasting paper and ink due to the wrong settings).

Getting the best results from the Epson 2200 printer or any other photographic quality inkjet printers can be challenging. If you are not getting the results you want, consult one or more of the resources listed in the material that follows.

■ There are more than a dozen e-mail groups with a focus on making digital prints and for users of specific models of inkjet printers at Yahoo!Groups. You can get a listing of the groups by typing in keywords related to digital prints at `http://groups.yahoo.com`. These e-mail groups can be wonderful places to get quick answers to questions you may have. One of the more active groups is `http://groups.yahoo.com/group/EPSON_Printers`.

■ Alan Womack's FAQ (Frequently Asked Questions) Web page is based upon postings made to several of the largest Epson Printer e-mail groups. You can find the FAQ Web page at `http://home.att.net/~arwomack01`.

■ Ian Lyon's Web site, Computer Darkroom, offers lots of useful information, tutorials, product reviews, and links to various color profiles. You can find this site at `www.computer-darkroom.com`. He is one of the internationally

recognized experts on color management and digital print technologies.

■ If you want personal access to some of the best color management experts (there are nine of them) that can be found, you may want to consider subscribing (for a small fee) to *Imaging Revue* at `www.imagingrevue.com`. *Imaging Revue* was created to be *the* source for information that specifically pertains to the world of professional digital imaging. Imagine having the foundation of collective knowledge offered by these and other experts whenever, and wherever, you need it!"

■ Harald Johnson's book, *Mastering Digital Printing: Photographer's and Artist's Guide to Digital Output,* is an excellent book that covers all kinds of topics on the subject of digital printing and it offers a wonderful history of digital printing. His Web site at `www.dpandi.com` is also worth checking occasionally for useful and interesting articles and for a well-maintained resources page.

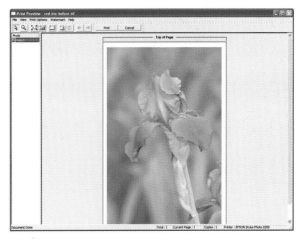

42.6

GETTING FUJI FRONTIER PRINTS MADE

43.1

43.2

Driving Through the Lane and on to #1 Canon EOS 1D digital camera, 200mm f/2.8 (260mm effective focal distance), ISO 200, Fine image setting, F/5.6 @ 1/500, 1,648 x 2,364 pixels, 2.0MB .jpg

If you like to get your photos processed at a nearby one-hour photo lab and you now want quick turnaround on inexpensive prints made from images that you have on a CD-ROM or other digital image storage media, you should look for a nearby photo lab that has one of the Fuji Frontier printers. An increasing number of one-hour labs and independent film labs are using these printers, which are high-capacity machines that can produce prints from conventional films, digital still cameras, and computer manipulated images. Fuji Frontier printers may be found at some drug stores that process film, discount stores such as Costco, some of the Wolf camera stores, and so on. Taking the time to find one nearby can be worthwhile as prints made from a Fuji Frontier printer are generally excellent value. Typical prices at discount stores are: 4" x 6" $0.40, 5" x 7" $2.50, 8" x 10" $5.00, and 10" x 15" $13.00.

The objective of this technique is to make an 8" x 10" print of the excellent NCAA basketball photo that was taken by Mark McIntyre during a game between NC State and the soon-to-be 2002 NCAA basketball champions — Maryland.

STEP 1: OPEN FILE

■ Choose **File** ➢ **Open** (**Ctrl+O** PC, **Cmd+O** Mac) to display the **Open** dialog box. Double-click the **\43** folder to open it and then click **basketball-before.jpg** to select it. Click **Open** to open the file.

STEP 2: CROP AND SIZE IMAGE

Fuji Frontier printers automatically crop images to fit within standard photo sizes. If you want to make a print that does not have the same width to height proportions as one of the standard size prints, you must add more canvas by using the Adobe Photoshop CS **Image** ➢ **Canvas Size** command. However, before using the **Canvas Size** command, set the background color to any color other than white so that when you add more canvas it will have some color to it — then when the print is made, you simply cut the colored background part of the photo off.

■ To crop the image to the proportions of an 8" x 10" print, click the **Crop** tool (**C**) in the **Toolbox**. Type **8 in** in the **Width** box, **10 in** in the **Height** box, and delete any values in the **Resolution** box in the **Options** bar.

■ Choose **View** ➢ **Fit on Screen** (**Ctrl+0** PC, **Cmd+0** Mac) and click the maximize icon in the upper-right corner or the image window if the document window is not already maximized and you are using a PC. Click just outside the bottom-right corner of the image and drag the **Crop** marquee up and to the left to include as much of the image as possible. Click the checkmark in the **Options** bar or press **Enter** to crop the image.

■ The image is now **1,648** x **2,060** pixels, which is **206DPI** for an 8" x 10" print. To view this information choose **Image** ➢ **Image Size** to get the **Image Size** dialog box. Click **Cancel** to close the dialog box.

When getting prints made with a Fuji Frontier printer, you generally get a better print if you do not up-sample the image — just crop it and let the Fuji Frontier re-size it.

STEP 3: SHARPEN IMAGE

■ The image can now be sharpened. As selecting **Unsharp Mask** settings when viewing an image at

MARK MCINTYRE

Mark McIntyre has been shooting sports photos since the late 1970s. He has shot basketball, baseball, bowling, field hockey, football, fencing, golf, lacrosse, rugby, track and field, soccer — and the Olympics. Over the years, he has been the official photographer for Penn State, Temple, NC State, and Wake Forest's basketball teams and his photos have been printed in many newspapers and most of the major sports magazines, including *Sports Illustrated*. The inset photo shows Mark shooting an ACC game from the best place on the court using two hand-held cameras and customized remote controls for two other stationary cameras, which allows him to get great photos of key plays anywhere on the court. Mark McIntyre may be contacted by telephone at (336) 545-4450.

100% is best, choose **View** ➤ **Actual Pixels** (**Ctrl+0** PC, **Opt+Cmd+0** Mac). Choose **Filter** ➤ **Sharpen** ➤ **Unsharp Mask** to get the **Unsharp Mask** dialog box shown in Figure 43.3. Try setting **Amount** to **175%**, **Radius** to **1.0**, and **Threshold** to **1**. Click **OK** to sharpen the image. These settings work pretty well with this image; however, if you want to do an even better job of sharpening this photo read Technique 11 and Technique 39.

STEP 4: SAVE FILE AND WRITE TO CD-ROM

Fuji Frontier printers only accept JPEG files, so make sure you save your file as a JPEG.

■ You can now save your file by choosing **File** ➤ **Save As** (**Ctrl+Shift+S** PC, **Shift+Cmd+S** Mac) to get the **File Save** dialog box. After selecting an appropriate folder, type a name in the **File Name** box so you don't save it to the original file.

■ Click in the **Format** box and select **JPEG** if it is not already selected. Click **OK** to get the **JPEG Options** dialog box, as shown in Figure 43.4. Type **12** in the **Quality** box or slide the slider all the way to the right to get to **12**. Using this setting, you will get the highest quality JPEG file that is possible. Click **OK** to save the file. You now have a 2.9MB JPEG file ready to be printed.

Your file is now ready to be written to a CD-ROM or other removable storage media and to be taken to a local photo lab where there is a Fuji Frontier printer. You may save yourself some time by calling the photo lab before visiting to learn more about what storage media is acceptable to the lab, available print sizes, turnaround time, and additional ordering information.

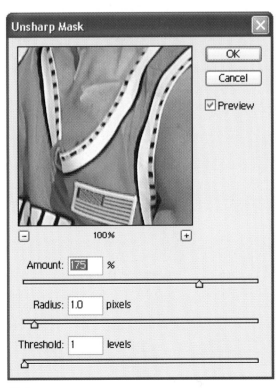

43.3

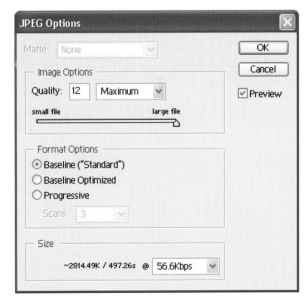

43.4

USING SHUTTERFLY'S ONLINE PRINTING SERVICE

44.1

44.2

ABOUT THE IMAGE

Variety of Photos These five photos have been edited and saved as JPEG files to conserve space on the companion CD-ROM. No image sharpening has been done, nor has image resolution been increased. They have all been cropped to desired print sizes.

One of the great benefits of shooting with a digital camera if you have a high-speed Internet connection is that you can easily upload digital photos from your computer and order prints online. One of the better and more competitively priced online printing services is Shutterfly. In this technique, you learn how to quickly and easily order prints online from Shutterfly. If you are using a Mac, you can order prints from Shutterfly as described in this technique, or you can use Apple's iPhoto application, which offers a comparable and excellent Kodak print service.

Shutterfly was selected as the service to use for this technique for three important reasons. First, Shutterfly's online service is excellent for getting "one-hour" style prints made from your digital images. Shutterfly uses state-of-the-art digital printers designed for professional photofinishers. These printers expose Fuji's Crystal Archive photographic paper by using red, green, and blue lasers to produce some of the sharpest prints available. The exposed photographic paper is chemically processed in the same way as in traditional photo labs. Second, Shutterfly has an option that allows you to turn off all their "intelligent processing" features so that your prints may be printed as you intended to have them printed — rather than being further manipulated for color, contrast, and image sharpness. Finally, Shutterfly's online services have been "built-in" to Adobe Photoshop CS, which makes it an easy service to use.

While I offer strong praise for the Shutterfly service, please be aware that this is a low-cost, high-volume automated service. Do not expect to get the same results that you will get from premium photo-printing services, such as those offered by Calypso, Inc., which you will read about in the next technique.

At the time this book went to press, the cost for printing photos at Shutterfly was: $0.39 for a 4" x 6", $0.79 for a 5" x 7", and $3.19 for an 8" x 10". Besides offering online photo printing services, Shutterfly also offers a large assortment of photo objects and additional photography services including their innovative Snapbook. You can even order 16" x 20" or 20" x 30" poster prints. To learn more about Shutterfly and their offering, visit `www.shutterfly.com`.

Anyone with an Internet connection can use the Shutterfly online services; however, having a fast Internet connection, such as a DSL line or cable modem enables you to upload your images much faster than slower Internet services. If you have a slow connection, you may want to consider lowering the quality setting when saving your files as JPEG files.

STEP 1: COPY THE IMAGES YOU WANT TO PRINT INTO A NEW FOLDER

The easy way to upload images and order prints online is to place a copy of all the photos you want prints made from, into a new folder. For example, you could create a folder named **\shutterfly** and then each time you place a new order, you should create subfolders named **\order1**, **\order2**, and so on. Once you have selected and copied all of the images you want to use to get prints made into a new folder, you are ready to edit them.

■ Click the **File Browser** icon in the **Options** bar to open the **File Browser**. In the **Folders** window in the **File Browser**, click the folder where you saved the chosen image files. Figure 44.3 shows the **File Browser** with five images that have been selected to be used for ordering prints; in this case, the five images found in the **\44** folder have been selected.

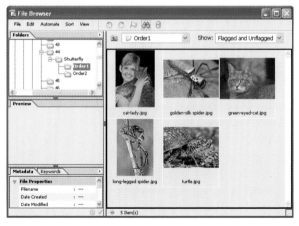

44.3

■ Because Shutterfly offers you an option to print the filename on the back of each photo, you may want to consider renaming the files with names, places, dates, or other identifying text.

Ideally, the images you will have copied into the folder for ordering prints will be images that have been edited and saved in a non-lossy image file format such as TIFF, PSD, or BMP as it is best not to save as a JPEG and then edit and once again save as a JPEG. The images can even be RAW files if you plan on converting them and editing them before placing the orders. To learn more about converting RAW files, read Techniques 8 and 36.

STEP 2: PREPARE THE IMAGES FOR UPLOADING

Any time you use an automated printing service, you must submit images that can be printed on "standard sized" papers (4" x 6", 5" x 7", 8" x 10", or 11" x 14") or you may get prints back that have been cropped in ways that you did not want. As we have chosen to use Adobe Photoshop CS to edit the images, we will do all the editing and sizing before we upload the image and order prints. This approach is much easier and better than using the cropping and editing features that are available in the "upload" software or on Shutterfly's Web page.

The Shutterfly service only works with JPEG images so you must convert them if they are not already in the JPEG format. You also must properly crop, or add "canvas" to your prints as needed to avoid getting back prints that were printed in a way other than what you wanted.

If you have images that are cropped as you want them, but the length and width proportions do not match standard prints sizes, you must first add canvas to them. For example, let's assume that we want to make an 8" x 10" print from the **golden-silk spider.**

jpg image found on the companion CD-ROM in the **\44** folder.

■ Choose **File** ➣ **Open** (**Ctrl+O** PC, **Cmd+O** Mac) to display the **Open** dialog box. Double-click the **\44** folder to open it and then click **golden-silk spider.jpg** to select it. Click **Open** to open the file.

■ Before adding canvas, you should first set the **Background** color to any color other than **White**; preferably a color that contrasts with the edge of the image. A color other than white will be recognized as part of the print and the automatic printing feature will not force the image to be cropped in an undesirable manner. Click **Background** color in the **Toolbox** and select any color other than **White**.

■ Check image size by selecting **Image** ➣ **Image Size** to get the **Image Size** dialog box shown in Figure 44.4. Make sure there is a checkmark next to **Constrain Proportions** and then type **10** in the **Width** box in the **Document Size** area; Click **OK**.

■ To add canvas to the image, select **Image** ➣ **Canvas Size** to get the **Canvas Size** dialog box

44.4

shown in Figure 44.5. Uncheck **Relative** to view the size of the image. In this case, the image is **10** inches wide and **6.688** inches tall. To make this print as an 8" x 10" print, click in the **Height** box and type **8**. Then, click either the **Up** or **Down Anchor** box to create new canvas above or below the image. Click in the **Canvas Extension Color** box and select **Background**. Click **OK** to apply the settings. The image should now look similar to the one shown in Figure 44.6.

STEP 3: MAKE ANY FINAL EDITS AND SHARPEN THE IMAGE

Your image is now sized and cropped as desired. If you have any additional edits to make to the image—now is the time. Once all the edits have been made you can sharpen the image. To learn more about sharpening images, read Techniques 11 and 39.

STEP 4: SAVE THE FILE AS A JPEG FILE

■ You can now save the file by choosing **File** ➢ **File Save As** (**Shift+Ctrl+S** PC, **Shift+Cmd+S** Mac) to get the **File Save As** dialog box. Choose your

output folder. Check to see that **Format** is set to **JPEG** and click the **Save** button to get the **JPEG Options** dialog box shown in Figure 44.7. If you will be uploading the images with a high-speed Internet connection, you should select either **Maximum** or **High Quality** setting in the **Image Options** area. If you have a slow-speed Internet connection, you can select a lower quality setting to decrease upload time, while at the same time decreasing the quality of the print somewhat. Click **OK** to save the file.

TIP

If you want to make a variety of different size prints of the same photo, you can do so easily by using Adobe Photoshop CS's Picture Package feature by selecting **File** ➢ **Automate** ➢ **Picture Package**. This feature allows you to choose from preset package layouts, or you can even design your own. Once you have created an image, save it to the folder you use to order prints from Shutterfly and place your order. You may want to check the price list to see if it costs you more money or less money to print several prints on a single larger print.

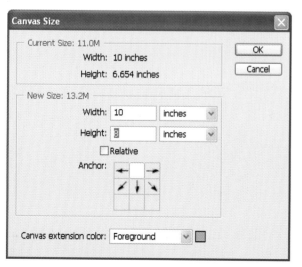

44.5

44.6

You should now repeat Steps 2 through 4 for each of the other images you want to upload. If you have more than just a few images you want to upload, you should consider creating an **Action** to automate the opening, editing, and saving of image files. To learn more about using Adobe Photoshop CS's automation features read Technique 6.

STEP 5: SELECT AND UPLOAD THE IMAGES

You are now ready to upload the images to Shutterfly.

■ Select each of the images in the **File Browser** that you want to upload. You can select all of them in the folder by selecting **Edit ➤ Select All** (**Ctrl+A** PC, **Cmd+A** Mac) from the **File Browser** menu, or by clicking on each image you want while pressing the **Ctrl** key on the PC or the **Cmd** key on the Mac.

■ To begin the upload process, choose **Automate ➤ Online Services** from the **File Browser** menu to get the **Online Services Wizard** shown in Figure 44.8. Continue the upload

process by completing each of the steps in the **Online Services Wizard.**

■ When all the images have been uploaded, you will be presented with a dialog box where you can click on a **View at Shutterfly** button, which opens up your Shutterfly account to the **Album** page as is shown in Figure 44.9. Click the album that contains the photos you just uploaded and then click **Next** to open the album.

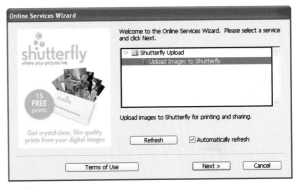

44.8

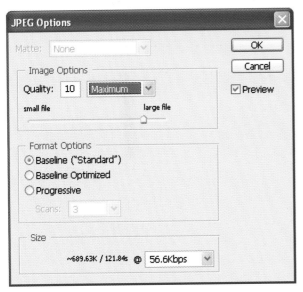

44.7

44.9

STEP 6: TURN OFF IMAGE ENHANCEMENTS

Shutterfly has created and uses a proprietary image processing system called VividPics. VividPics reads the metadata (embedded information/EXIF data) in an image file to see if it can identify what kind of digital camera was used and what settings were used so that Shutterfly printers can make the prints with the best sharpness, clarity, and consistency of color. If you upload unedited photos straight from a digital camera, VividPics can read this metadata and use it to make better photos than you would get from a system that does not have a similar kind of feature. However, if you have spent time editing your images with an image editor such as Adobe Photoshop CS and then you save the file — not only might you lose the metadata, but you probably do not want the VividPics feature to make more corrections to your already corrected images. In this case, you should turn the VividPics feature off.

■ To turn off **VividPics**, you first must select the photo or photos that you do not want **VividPics** to further enhance. Click **All** to select all images, and then click **Enhance and Fix Pictures**. Then, click the **Effects** tab and place a checkmark in the **"Don't apply automatic corrections to picture"** box. To turn off **VividPics** for all the other selected pictures, click **Apply this effect** to other pictures and follow the dialog boxes.

STEP 7: PLACE ORDER

■ After you have turned off **VividPics**, you are ready to place your order. To specify order details, scroll back to the top of the Web page and click **Order Prints**. Click the **Order Prints** button on the right side of the Web page to get a Web page similar to the one shown in Figure 44.10. Here you can indicate how many prints you want made in each of the available sizes for each image. You can even see how the image will be cropped when selecting different sizes by clicking **Print Preview**.

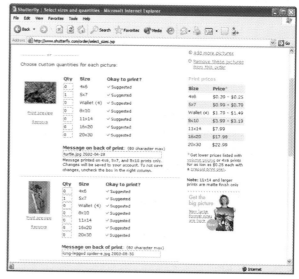

44.10

■ After specifying the quantity of each size you want to print, continue with the ordering process by clicking the **Select Recipients** button to specify the address where the photos are to be sent. After selecting a mailing address, continue on to **Checkout** to complete your order.

Ordering dozens or even hundreds of photos is just as easy as it is to order a single photo, as shown in this example, which makes this a good choice for event photographers.

TIP

In addition to ordering prints for your own use, Shutterfly also offers Shutterfly Pro Galleries and a "pro" printing service. Those who do event photography, such as sports and wedding photographers, can use it to sell their photos from online photo galleries. This service allows you to "mark-up" your photos and to charge a different amount of money for each offering for each event you shoot. All you have to do is upload the photos and receive payment from Shutterfly for any photos you've sold. Shutterfly takes care of all the order handling, the printing, packaging, shipping, customer service, and so on. It is a great service if you want to just take photos and sell them online. There is a small annual fee for this service.

GETTING LIGHTJET 5000 PRINTS FROM CALYPSO, INC.

45.1

45.2

Purple & Yellow Iris on Green Canon EOS 1D digital camera on tripod, 300mm F/2.8 IS with 25mm extension tube, ISO 200, RAW image quality setting, F/8.0 @ 1/25, 1,648 x 2,464 pixels, slightly edited and converted to 8-bits per channel, 12.2MB .tif

I f you want the ultimate print made from one of your image files, then you want a Lightjet 5000 print made on Fuji Crystal Archive photographic paper. These continuous tone photographs are known for their rich blacks, print permanence, and excellent color range. Such prints are the preferred prints of many artists and professional photographers all over the world.

While there are over 400 sites worldwide that have Lightjet printers, only a few of those sites keep their printers properly color-managed so that you get consistent prints that match the images on your monitor. Calypso, Inc. (www.calypsoinc.com), in Santa Clara, California is one company that I recommend due to the efforts they take to provide you with color-managed prints. Their focus is on nature, landscape, wildlife, fine art, and

303

travel markets, and they have a list of customers that includes many of the finest photographers in the world.

To get prints made at Calypso, you can either upload image files to their FTP site or you can write the image files to a CD-ROM and send them via mail or a courier service. Calypso offers two different pricing plans. The "preferred" pricing plan is for images that have been prepped, color-managed, and profiled directly to the Calypso Lightjet 5000. In this case, you take all the responsibility for color management. Or, you can pay more and have them do some of the work for you and they will be responsible for color-management. Please visit the Calypso Web site and read Calypso's Guide to Color Management on the Lightjet 5000.

This technique covers the steps you need to take to enjoy the "preferred" pricing plan. In this technique, you take a 3.1 megapixel photo of an iris taken with a Canon EOS D30 digital camera and follow steps to size the image and sharpen it so that it can be used to make an 11" x 14" Lightjet 5000 glossy print at Calypso, Inc.

I had Calypso print a series of increasingly larger prints with the intent of stopping once the image began to show some degradation. Much to my surprise and jubilation, they stopped printing when they got to a 30" x 40" print due to shipping problems and the costs of shipping larger prints — not because of image degradation! If you take into account the distance that you view an image, there was no visible difference between the 11" x 14" print and the 30" x 40" print. Obviously, you stand back a couple of feet when you are looking at a print as large as 30" x 40", which is much further back than if you were looking at

an 8" x 10" print. Digital cameras make great images for making large prints — test one of your images.

STEP 1: DOWNLOAD CALYPSO'S LIGHTJET 5000 ICC COLOR PROFILE

In order to get a print from Calypso that matches the image on your screen, you *must* have a properly calibrated monitor and the color of your image file *must* be converted to the appropriate ICC color profile for the media you want. To learn more about how to calibrate your monitor read Technique 1.

■ To get Calypso's Lightjet 5000 ICC color profile, go to www.calypsoinc.com. In the left frame, click **Colorsync Profiles**. In the frame on the right, you find both **PC** and **Mac** profiles. Click the appropriate profile to begin downloading a ZIP file containing three color profiles: one for CD II paperMatte, Gloss, and newSupergloss paper. Additional files may be added when new media becomes available and on occasion, new profiles are substituted for those listed here.

■ After the files have been unzipped, they need to be copied to the appropriate directory for your operating system. If you are using Windows XP, use Windows Explorer to locate and open the folder where the unzipped files were saved. Press **Ctrl** while clicking each of the three files to select them all. Right-click one of the files to get a pop-up menu; choose **Install Profiles**. Windows XP automatically installs the color profiles for you. If you are using a Mac, the profiles will need to be copied into the ColorSync Profiles folder (HD\Library\ColorSync\Profiles).

STEP 2: OPEN FILE TO BE PRINTED

■ Choose **File** ➢ **Open** (**Ctrl+O** PC, **Cmd+O** Mac) to display the **Open** dialog box. Double-click the **\45** folder to open it and then click **iris-before.tif** to select it. Click **Open** to open the file.

To order prints from Calypso, the file must be either a Photoshop `.psd` file or a `.tif` file and starting with an Adobe RGB (1988) profile is best if you have a choice. As the iris-before.tif file is already tagged as Adobe RGB 1988 and it is a TIFF file, the file is ready for the next step.

STEP 3: CROP AND SIZE IMAGE

■ To crop the image to the proportions of an 11" x 14" print, click the **Crop** tool (**C**) in the **Toolbox**. Type **11 in** in the **Width** box and **14 in** in the **Height** box in the **Options** bar.

While it is possible to also enter **150** in the **Resolution** box to resize the image to the Lightjet 5000's minimum recommended DPI setting after the **Crop** command is applied, it is best to first crop the image. Then up-sample with the **Image Size** command as you can then choose the more appropriate **Bicubic Smoother** method of interpolation.

■ Choose **View** ➢ **Fit on Screen** (**Ctrl+0** PC, **Cmd+0** Mac) and click the maximize icon in the upper-right corner or the image window if the document window is not already maximized if you are using a PC (press **F** if you are using a Mac to change to **Full-Screen** mode). Click just outside the bottom-right corner of the image and drag the **Crop** marquee up and to the left to include as much of the image as possible.

To move the **Crop** marquee up to include more space above the iris, press the **up arrow** to move up one pixel at a time or press **Shift** and the **up arrow** to move the selection marquee up **10 pixels** at a time. Once you have selected the part of the image you want you can click the checkmark in the **Options** bar or press **Enter** to crop the image.

■ Now select **Image** ➢ **Image Size** to get the **Image Size** dialog box shown in Figure 45.3. Make sure that **Constrain Proportions** and **Resample Image** is checked. **Resample Image** should be set to **Bicubic Smoother**. Type **150** in the **Resolution** in the **Document Size** area and then click **OK** to resize the image slightly.

■ The image should now be **1,650 x 2,100** pixels, which is **150 dpi** for an 11" x 14" print. To view this information, choose **Image** ➢ **Image Size** to get the **Image Size** dialog box. Click **Cancel** to close the dialog box.

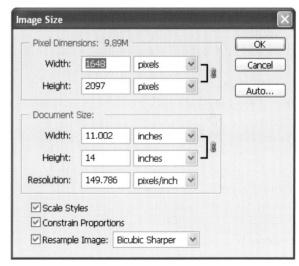

45.3

STEP 4: SHARPEN IMAGE

■ As the image is now sized for the intended output size, you can now sharpen it. Because it is best to select **Unsharp Mask** settings when viewing an image at **100%**, choose **View ➢ Actual Pixels** (**Ctrl+0** PC, **Opt**+**Cmd**+**0** Mac). Choose **Filter ➢ Sharpen ➢ Unsharp Mask** to get the **Unsharp Mask** dialog box shown in Figure 45.4. Try setting **Amount** to **250%**, **Radius** to **0.3**, and **Threshold** to **0**. Click **OK** to sharpen the image.

45.4

To learn more about sharpening images read Technique 11 and Technique 39.

STEP 5: CONVERT PROFILE TO CALYPSO LIGHTJET 5000 COLOR PROFILE

■ To convert the profile to the Calypso Lightjet 5000 color profile that was downloaded in Step 1, choose **Image ➢ Mode ➢ Convert to Profile** to get the **Convert to Profile** dialog box shown in Figure 45.5. Click in the **Profile** box to get a pop-up menu. You find three profiles named with "**Calypso**"; these are the three Calypso Lightjet files. Select **Calypso LJ5 Glossy v2.icc** to select the glossy media profile. (Later versions or new color profiles may have different names.)

  Make sure **Engine** is set to **Adobe (ACE)** and that **Intent** is set to **Perceptual**. **Use Black Point Compensation** and **Use Dither** should both be switched off.

■ Click **OK** to convert the profile.

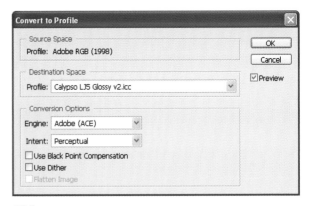

45.5

STEP 6: SAVE FILE AND SEND OR UPLOAD TO CALYPSO

■ You can now save your file by choosing
File ➤ **Save As** (**Ctrl+Shift+S** PC, **Shift+Cmd+S**
Mac) to get the **File Save** dialog box. After selecting
an appropriate folder, type a name in the **File
Name** box so that you don't save it over the original file. Make sure that the **ICC Profile** box is
checked in the **Color** area — it should show the
Calypso LJ5 Glossy v2.icc profile that you selected
earlier. Also make sure you are not saving layers.

■ Click **OK** to save the file.

Your file is now ready to be written to a CD-ROM or
other removable storage media and be sent to Calypso
or be uploaded to the Calypso FTP Web site. Please
visit the Calypso Web site to learn more about what
storage media is acceptable to Calypso, about getting an
FTP site set up for your image files, and additional
ordering information. Also, feel free to e-mail Michael
Chambers at Calypso to ask questions and to request
that an FTP account be set up for your use. His e-mail
is `m_chambers@calypsoinc.com`.

To get more recommendations and tips on how to
get Lightjet 5000 prints, visit this book's companion
Web page at `www.reallyusefulpage.com\`
`50pscs`. This technique concludes the chapter on
making prints. In the next and final chapter you learn
how to create and display your photographs online in
a Web-based photo gallery.

CHAPTER **9**

CREATING AN ONLINE PHOTO GALLERY

Ｉf you want to share your work on the Internet, you should find the five techniques in this chapter to be both useful and fun. The first technique covers all that you need to know to create excellent images for use on a Web page. The next technique shows you how you can use those images along with Adobe Photoshop CS's Web Photo Gallery feature to create a Web photo gallery. Next, you learn how to create an image map. If you don't know what an image map is or how it can be used — this is surely a technique you should read. An image map can be used to create viewer-friendly navigation between Web pages and it can be used to creatively display your photography, too. You then learn how to create rollover images that are wonderful for showing "before" and "after" images. The final technique covers the steps you can take to create an animation to spice up your Web gallery.

PREPARING IMAGES FOR DISPLAY ON A WEB PAGE

46.1

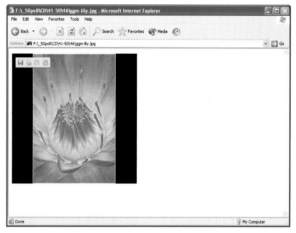

46.2

General George Moore Tropical Lily Canon EOS 1Ds mounted on a tripod, MT-24EX Macro Twin Lite, 180mm f/3.5, ISO 100, RAW image quality setting, f11.0 @ 1/25, 2,704 x 4,064 pixel, 9.4MB RAW converted to 8-bits per channel, 800 x 533 pixel 1.2MB .tif

N o doubt about it — you can quickly and easily create an image to be placed on a Web page using commands such as **Save for Web**, or even **Save As**. But, there is much more to creating excellent images that display well on a Web page than merely saving them as a JPEG image using one of these commands. In this technique, you'll learn all the steps you need to take to make excellent images that have been optimized specifically for viewing on a Web page and, if you like, the images can include information that identifies them as *yours* as well as titles, shooting information, and so forth.

For this technique, we will be using a photo of a brilliantly colored tropical lily. This image has been converted from a RAW format file to a TIFF format and it has been resized so that the longest side is 600 pixels. No significant editing was done to it. When the image was converted using Adobe Camera RAW, care was taken *not* to sharpen the image as you can get better results by applying sharpening once the image has been sized for the Web page. Once you have been through this technique, you will have learned how the images that you will use in the next technique were prepared.

STEP 1: OPEN FILE

■ Select **File** ➤ **Open** (**Ctrl+O** PC, **Cmd+O** Mac) to display the **Open** dialog box. After locating the **\46** folder, double-click it to open it. Click **ggm-lily.tif** and then click **Open** to open the file.

STEP 2: SIZE IMAGE

■ The first step is to resize the image to the final size needed for the Web page, which is an image that will fit within a 350 x 350 pixel square. Select **Image** ➤ **Image Size** to get the **Image Size** dialog box shown in Figure 46.3. Make sure that **Constrain Proportions** is selected. Click in the **Height** box under **Pixel Dimensions** and type **350**. New to Adobe Photoshop CS is a new interpolation algorithm for downsizing images that helps maintain image sharpness when the image size is reduced. Make sure there is a checkmark next to **Resample Image** and click in the box to select the new algorithm: **Bicubic Sharper**. Click **OK** to resize the image.

STEP 3: SHARPEN IMAGE

■ Now that the image is at its final size, we can sharpen it. Select **Filter** ➤ **Sharpen** ➤ **Unsharp Mask** to get the **Unsharp Mask** dialog box. As this is a soft image, not much sharpening is needed. Try setting **Amount** to **100%**, **Radius** to **0.7**, and **Threshold** to **0** to bring out the highlights on the tips of the lily. Click **OK** to apply the settings. To learn more about sharpening an image, read Technique 11 and Technique 39.

STEP 4: ADD FRAME OR OTHER IMAGE ENHANCING FEATURES

Depending on how you want your photos to look, the design of the Web gallery, and the Web page's background color, you may want to add a frame or just a simple line around your image. When you use Adobe

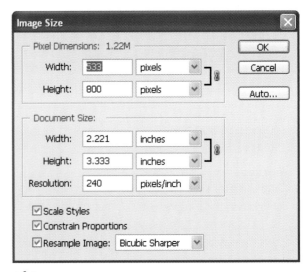

46.3

Photoshop CS's Web Gallery feature, you will find that there is an option to automatically add a line around each image. However, if you plan on adding extra canvas as described in the next step, you will need to add a line before you run Web Gallery.

■ If you want to add a single colored line around your image, select **Select** ➤ **All** (**Ctrl+A** PC, **Cmd+A** Mac) and then **Edit** ➤ **Stroke** to get the **Stroke** dialog box shown in Figure 46.4. In this dialog box you can choose the **Width** of the stroke in pixels and the **Color** of the line. Let's set **Width** to **1px**. Make sure to set **Location** to **Inside** so the entire line with will show on the image. In this case, the image will be placed against a black background, so let's choose **White** as the color and click **OK** to add the line around the image.

STEP 5: ADD CANVAS TO PREVENT "IMAGE JUMPING"

If you have viewed a Web photo gallery where the height and width sizes vary between images you may have noticed text, images, and navigation features that "jump" as you move between images. To avoid this, you simply need to add each of your images to a background image that has the width of the widest image, and the height of the widest image. As we will be using a Web page design for images that fit in a 350 x 350 pixel square, we need to add this image to a black 350 x 350 pixel canvas.

■ Select **Image** ➤ **Canvas Size** to get the **Canvas Size** dialog box shown in Figure 46.5. Type **350** in the **Width** and **Height** boxes after setting the increment to pixels. Leave the **Anchor** set to the default center box. Click in the **Canvas extension color** box and select **Black**. Click **OK** to add **Black** canvas. Your image should now look like the one

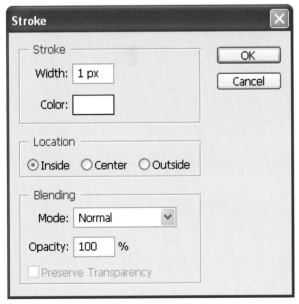

46.4

46.5

shown in Figure 46.6. If you have a horizontal image, it would like the one shown in Figure 46.7.

STEP 6: ADD COPYRIGHT AND OTHER INFORMATION TO THE IMAGE FILE

Anyone with even limited experience of sharing photos on the Internet will be aware that images do get copied and used by others without permission. While it is nearly impossible to stop such action, you can at least add your copyright and contact information to each image you post on a Web site.

> **TIP**
>
> To improve the way your images are displayed on a Web page you can add matte borders and even frames that look like real picture frames. Check out the framing choices found in the Frames Action set. You will find Drop Shadow Frame, Strokes Frame, Photo Corners, and even Wild Frame.

- Select **File ➤ File Info** (**Alt+Ctrl+I** PC, **Option+Cmd+I** Mac) to get the dialog box shown in Figure 46.8. Here you can add all kinds of information. Many of these fields contain information that can be used with the **Web Photo Gallery** feature making it easy to add information to an image once and then have **Web Photo Gallery** automatically place it on a Web page. You can add any information you'd like at the top, but each time you post images to a Web site you ought to set **Copyright Status** to **Copyrighted** and type copyright information in the **Copyright Notice** box. To insert a © symbol, press and hold **ALT** while typing **0169** on a PC; on a Mac, press **Option+G**. Add a year and your name. It may also be a good idea to add your Web site address if you

46.6

46.7

have one so that you may be contacted if need be. Click **OK** to place this information into the image file.

When you set the **Copyright Status** to **Copyrighted**, many imaging applications will indicate that the image is copyrighted by showing the © symbol in the title bar as you can see in Figure 46.6 and Figure 46.7.

STEP 7: ADD A VISIBLE WATERMARK OR COPYRIGHT TEXT TO THE IMAGE

There are two types of watermarks that you can add to your images: invisible and visible. An invisible watermark is embedded into the image, in some cases by the Digimarc plug-in (**Filter ➢ Digimarc ➢ Embed Watermark**). To learn more about the Digimarc service, visit `www.digimarc.com`. Or, you can also add a visible watermark or text to your image. Adobe Photoshop CS's Web Gallery has a feature that automates the process of placing text on each image. However, this automated feature does not let you change text color or text location. Therefore you may find that the text either distracts the viewer from

viewing your image or it is not visible because it is a color that blends in with the image color.

- To add text to an image use the **Horizontal Type** tool (**T**) and choose text color and text placement to suit each image. Should you prefer vertical type, select the **Vertical Type** tool instead of the **Horizontal Type** tool. If you are using an **Action** to place text, make sure to stop the **Action** so that you can choose text color and place the text when the **Action** is running. See Technique 6 to learn more about creating and using **Action.**

STEP 8: SAVE THE IMAGE AS A JPEG FILE

- Before you can save an image as a JPEG image, you must first flatten the image if you have layers such as those that you may have created when adding type. Select **Layer ➢ Flatten Image**.
- Select **File ➢ Save for Web** (**Alt+Shift+Ctrl+S** PC, **Option+Shift+Cmd+S** Mac) to get the **Save for Web** dialog box shown in Figure 46.9. The **Save for Web** feature not only gives you lots of options for optimizing your images, but it also provides you with "before" and "after" so that you can get the best balance between image size

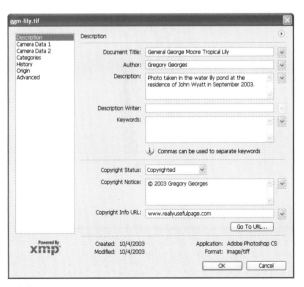

46.8

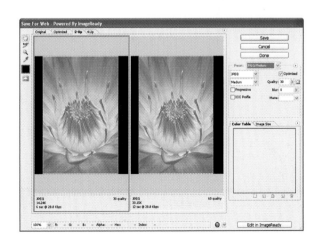

46.9

and image quality. Click in the **Preset** box and choose **JPEG Medium** to use as a good starting point Click the **2-Up** tab if it is not already selected. The image on the left is the original image. The image on the right shows how the image looks with the settings you've chosen. Below the second image you can read file size. This image is now 30.15K — a good size for quick downloading. Click **Save** to save the image and then click **Save** again to save the image in the folder you want. If the file size is larger than about 35K you may want to consider reducing the level of compression. If the image quality decreases too much, you can increase the compression level until you are happy with the image.

Remember that all the steps you need to take to create Web images can be automated and saved as either an **Action** or a **Droplet**, which will save you tremendous time and increase accuracy. To learn more about creating **Actions** and **Droplets**, read Technique 6. Making an **Action** is simple — you just record the steps you take when you edit the first image. Then, run the **Action** against the rest of the images in **Batch** mode. Try it out — **Actions** are wonderful timesavers!

> **WARNING**
>
> No matter how hard you work or what techniques you use to protect images you display on the Internet from being used without your permission or knowledge, you will not be successful if someone really wants the images. Many photographers take great effort and expend lots of time trying all kinds of techniques to prevent the copying and use of their images without their permission. Such techniques include adding a rollover image with text to each image, placing each image as the background image, adding expensive digital copyright "signatures," or using one of many Java scripts in an attempt to prevent use. In *all* these cases, the use of a free or inexpensive screen capture utility will give anyone quick access to your images.
>
> If you truly do not want to have your images downloaded and used by unauthorized users, there are really only two reasonable choices. Place images on your Web site that are too small to be useful for other purposes, or simply do not upload your work to the Internet. If you want to make it possible for visitors to your Web site to enjoy your work, you should make it as easy as possible for them to navigate and view your images. Otherwise, they are likely to leave and never return and the image thieves will have won!

CREATING AN ONLINE GALLERY USING WEB PHOTO GALLERY

47.1

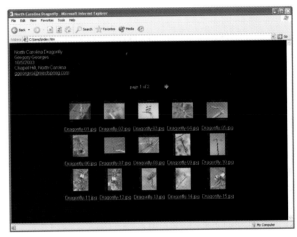

47.2

North Carolina Dragonfly
Canon EOS 1D digital camera, 180mm f/3.5 macro or 300mm f/2.8 with extension tubes and a 1.4x tele-extender, various camera settings. All 20 images have been converted from RAW to JPEG, cropped, resized, and edited as suggested in Technique 46.

One significant benefit of using digital photos is that they can easily be shared online. As more and more people have access to the Internet, displaying your photographs online makes them available to a large worldwide audience. Adobe Photoshop CS makes it remarkably easy to create an online photo gallery as most of the repetitive and tedious tasks are all automated when you use the Web Photo Gallery feature. Although Web page designs are limited to 11 preformatted styles, the use of any HTML editor makes it possible for you to modify the style sheets or the completed HTML pages to suit your own design requirements.

In this technique, you use Web Photo Gallery to create an online gallery for the set of 20 North Carolina dragonfly photos shown in Figure 47.1. Before you start creating the Web gallery, you may want to take a quick look at the completed gallery so that you can understand more about the many options that are available when using the Adobe Photoshop CS Web Photo

Gallery feature. Assuming that you copied the contents of the companion CD-ROM to your hard drive as recommended in the Introduction, you can find the Web gallery in the **\47\gallery** folder. On a PC, use Windows Explorer; on a Mac, use the Finder to locate the **\47\gallery** folder. Double-click on the file **index.htm** to view the completed Web gallery. The gallery should now be viewable in your default Web browser, as shown in Figure 47.2.

STEP 1: RUN WEB PHOTO GALLERY

Web Photo Gallery can be run from either the main Adobe Photoshop CS menu, or from the menu found in **File Browser**. Using the **File Browser** makes it easy for you to select the images you want, so for this technique let's use the **File Browser**.

- Click the **File Browser** icon on the **Options** bar (or select **Window ➤ File Browser**) to display the **File Browser** if it is not already showing. Click in the **Folders** window to find and select the **\47** folder to display the 20 dragonfly images. Click the first image; then, while pressing **Shift**, click the last image to select all 20 images and highlight them, as shown in Figure 47.3.
- In the menu found in the **File Browser**, select **Automate ➤ Web Photo Gallery** to get a dialog box similar to the one shown in Figure 47.4. Yours may be slightly different if the **Options** box shows a setting other than **General**.
- Click in the **Styles** box to get a pop-up menu listing 11 different Web page styles. If you click any one of these styles, a small thumbnail image displays on the right side of the dialog box. This thumbnail shows how the completed Web page will look. Let's choose **Simple** as the **Style** for this technique.

47.3

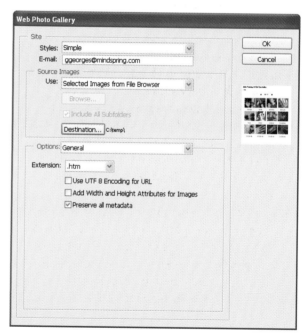

47.4

If you want to display a clickable e-mail address on your Web page, click in the **E-mail** box and type an e-mail address. This address will be displayed in the upper left-hand corner of each Web page.
As we have already selected the images we want to use in the **File Browser**, set **Use** to **Selected Images from the File Browser** if it is not already shown. To set the destination folder, click **Destination** to get the **Browse for Folder** dialog box. Select the folder you want to use. If you need to, you can also create a new folder. Once you have selected a folder, click **Choose**.

Click in the **Options** box if **General** is not shown and choose **General**. Make sure there is a checkmark in the box next to **Preserve all metadata** so that we can keep the metadata in the image files.

■ Click in the **Options** box and select **Banner**. You can now type in any information you want displayed on your Web page in the banner area.

■ Click in the **Options** box and select **Large Images**. These settings allow you the option of having Web Gallery automatically resize your images. As we have already sized the dragonfly images as we want them (read Technique 46), click to remove a checkmark if there is one next to **Resize Images**. The images already have a border line, so set **Border Size** to **0**.

If you want to include **Filename**, **Title**, **Description** or other information that has been written to the image files, you can place a checkmark next to each type of information that you want Web Gallery to put on the Web pages. To learn more about how you can add this kind of information to an image, read Technique 13 and

Technique 46. You can also set the **Font style** and **Font size**.

■ Click in the **Options** box and select **Thumbnails**. Here you can determine the way the thumbnail images are displayed. Set **Size** to **Medium** and use **5** and **3** in the **Columns** and **Rows** boxes, respectively. Make sure to set **Border Size** to **0** as we don't want a border line around the thumbnail images.

■ Click in the **Options** box and select **Custom Colors**. For a simple black and white Web gallery set **Background** and **Banner** to **black** and all other colors to **White** as shown in Figure 47.5.

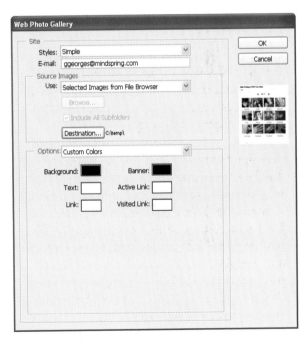

47.5

- Click one final time in the **Options** box and select **Security**. Click in the **Content** box to choose from the settings: **None, Custom Text, File Name, Copyright, Description, Credits,** and **Title.** You can choose from these types of information to use as text on your image if you want to print directly on the images. In this case, select **None**.

- Click **OK** to begin creating the photo gallery. As the Web pages are being created, you see all the images that are loaded, edited, and closed, showing you the incredibly tedious and time-consuming task it has saved you from! Once the Web page has been completed, the new Web page should be loaded and displayed in your default Web browser. It should look similar to the one shown in Figure 47.2. Once you click one of the images, you will get a Web page with an enlarged image, as shown in Figure 47.6. It has navigation buttons that allow you to move between images or the thumbnail pages.

STEP 2: CUSTOMIZE THE WEB GALLERY

The Adobe Photoshop CS **Web Photo Gallery** feature has done a tremendous amount of work for you, but you may not want your gallery to look like it was created with a standard Adobe Photoshop CS style template. Or, you may not like the colors, or the location of the large images, or one of a vast number of other possible details — and that is okay.

You have three ways to customize Web pages created by the **Web Photo Gallery** feature. First, you can use an HTML editor to edit each of the HTML pages so that they are exactly as you want. Second, you can copy the Adobe Photoshop CS **Web Photo Gallery** style folder you choose to use and rename it — then edit the style templates and run **Web Photo Gallery**. This approach lets you use your own customized template any time that you want with no additional HTML editing required. Third, you can create your own HTML pages using an HTML editor and use all the thumbnails and images automatically created with **Web Photo Gallery**. You can find out more about customizing **Web Photo Gallery** style sheets by reading the Adobe Photoshop CS Help and the documentation that comes with Adobe Photoshop CS.

47.6

CREATING AN IMAGE MAP
FOR SITE NAVIGATION

48.1

48.2

ABOUT THE IMAGE

Photo Gallery Navigation Page 640 x 480 pixel .jpg image created in Adobe Photoshop CS, 50K .jpg file

No doubt about it — this technique is an exceedingly useful technique for anyone interested in creating an online photo gallery, even if you don't know what an image map is! If you want a simple navigation page, consider creating an image map with thumbnail-size versions of your photos. You won't need to create buttons or navigation bars, or have one of those text menu navigation bars like those that are created by so many Web page creation tools.

The navigation image shown in Figure 48.1 was created by dragging and dropping thumbnail images onto a black background — it was then saved as an optimized JPEG file that is small in size and can quickly download even when using a slow Internet connection. In this technique, you discover how to create a link to a Web page for each of the thumbnail photos that ought to be linked to another Web page. Adobe ImageReady CS, which comes with Adobe Photoshop CS is all you need to complete the work.

STEP 1: OPEN FILE

■ Launch Adobe ImageReady CS.

■ Choose **File** ➢ **Open** (**Ctrl+O** PC, **Cmd+O** Mac) to display the **Open** dialog box. Double-click the **\48** folder to open it and then select the **link-graphic.jpg** file. Click **Open** to open the file.

■ To reset all of the Adobe ImageReady CS palettes, choose **Window** ➢ **Workspace** ➢ **Default Palette Locations**. The Adobe ImageReady CS workspace should now look similar to the one shown in Figure 48.3.

STEP 2: CREATE SLICES

■ Click the **Slice** tool (**K**) in the **Toolbox**, which is shown in Figure 48.4.

■ If the image is not zoomed to **100%**, choose **View** ➢ **Actual Size** (**Ctrl+Alt+0** PC, **Cmd+ Option+0** Mac). Viewing the full-size image makes it easier to use the **Slice** tool.

■ Using the **Slice** tool (**K**), click the upper-left corner of the black and white thumbnail image of a farm house and clouds and drag the selection marquee box down and to the right until you surround the entire image, as shown in Figure 48.5. If

48.4

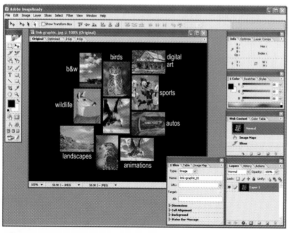

48.3

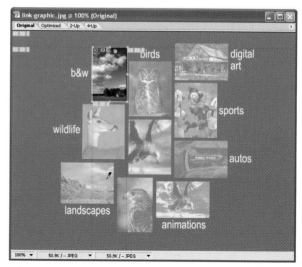

48.5

your selection marquee is not perfect, you can click one of the selection handles and drag the marquee to where it ought to be to make it perfect. You have now created your first image slice!

■ As you may have guessed, you now need to do the same thing to each of the other images that need to be linked. To make some of your later work easier, I suggest that you create slices for all the images in a sequential clockwise fashion. Do not be concerned that other slices are being created (meaning that the numbers for the slices increase faster than you select thumbnail images) as these "automatic" extra slices are necessary. You can tell the difference in what you created and what Adobe ImageReady CS created; solid lines indicate user-created slices and the automatically created slices are indicated by dotted lines.

■ After you create all the slices for the thumbnails that need links, your image should look like the one shown in Figure 48.6. Note that you do not need to create a slice for the two images that do not have text near them — they are just filler images. If you need to delete a slice, select the **Slice Select** tool (**O**) in the **Toolbox**; click on the slice you want to delete and press **Delete**.

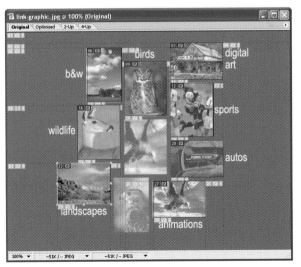

48.6

STEP 3: CREATE LINK FOR EACH SLICE

Now that you have created slices for all the thumbnails that need a link to a Web page, you need to type in the URL for each thumbnail. You have two easy ways to do this. You can open the **Web Content** palette (Figure 48.7) and then sequentially click each thumbnail to select a slice. Or, you can click the **Slice** tool (**K**) in the **Toolbox** and wait until you get a pop-up menu, and then click **Slice Select** tool (**O**). Using the **Slice Select** tool (**O**), you can then click each thumbnail in the image to select a slice. In either case, the goal is to sequentially select each image that needs to be linked, and then type in the appropriate URL in the **Slice** palette.

■ After selecting the **Slice Select** tool (**O**), click once in the **b&w** thumbnail image to select it.
■ If the **Slice** palette is not open, choose **Window** ➤ **Slice** to get the **Slice** palette shown in

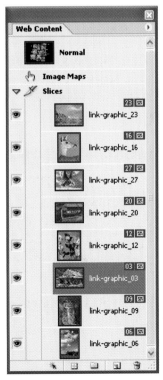

48.7

Figure 48.8. Type **linked-page.htm** in the **URL** box. For convenience and testing purposes, a Web page called **linked-page.htm** is in the **\48** folder. This process allows you to test your links and see how easy it is to create image slices.

■ Select each slice in a clockwise fashion. To easily enter **linked-page.htm** in the **URL** box in the **Slice** palette, you can click the **down arrow** at the right side of the **URL** box and select it from the list of recently used URLs — and if you type the link correctly the first time, you won't make an error. Life is good! Continue on until you have linked all the slices.

STEP 4: SAVE IMAGE AND HTML CODE

You're now just about done. Just save the image and the Adobe ImageReady CS-created HTML code and you're ready to test it in a Web browser.

■ Click **File** ➤ **Save Optimized As** (**Ctrl+ Shift+Alt+S** PC, **Option+Shift+Cmd+S** Mac) to get the **Save Optimized As** dialog box shown in Figure 48.9.

■ Assuming that you followed the recommendations in the Introduction about copying the contents of the companion CD-ROM, select the **\48** folder. If you did not follow these recommendations, you need to make sure that you copy the file

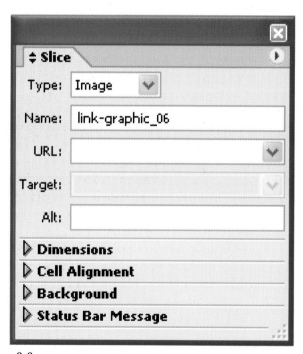

48.8

48.9

linked-page.htm from the \48 folder on the companion CD-ROM to the same folder you select to save the image and HTML files. This file allows you to test each link.

■ Click in the **Save as type** box and select **HTML and Images**. The **File Name** box must now show **link-graphic.html**.

■ Click **Save** to save the image and create the HTML page.

STEP 5: VIEW IMAGE AND TEST LINKS

■ Using Windows Explorer if you are using a PC or the Finder if you are using a Mac, open the **\48** folder and double-click the **link-graphic.html** to load it in your default Web browser. If you

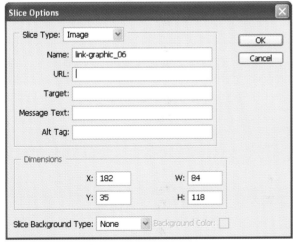

48.10

use Microsoft Internet Explorer, your Web browser should look similar to the one shown in Figure 48.2.

■ As you move your cursor across any of the thumbnail images that have been linked, the cursor changes to a hand cursor indicating a clickable link is there. Click a linked thumbnail and you are taken to **linked-page.htm** where you can click to return to the **link-graphic.html** page. If you created and linked all the slices correctly, you should be able to click each image that is associated with a text title and get **linked-page.htm**.

While we have done all of this work in Adobe ImageReady CS, getting the same results by using just Adobe Photoshop CS is also possible. Adobe Photoshop CS offers considerably fewer features for creating Web graphics than does Adobe ImageReady CS so that is why we used Adobe ImageReady CS. As you gain experience with Adobe ImageReady CS, it will be your choice for Web image creation. Should you want to try completing this technique in Adobe Photoshop CS, you need to enter the URL in the **Slice Options** dialog box shown in Figure 48.10. To access this dialog box, click the **Slice Select** tool (**K**) on a slice.

My hope is that you have learned how you can use image maps and how to create them, and that you will create one for your own Web photo gallery. If you do, and you'd like to share your work with other readers of this book and visitors to the companion Web page, please send an e-mail with a link to `ggeorges@ reallyusefulpage.com` and tell me about your Web gallery.

CREATING ROLLOVER IMAGES WITH IMAGEREADY

49.1

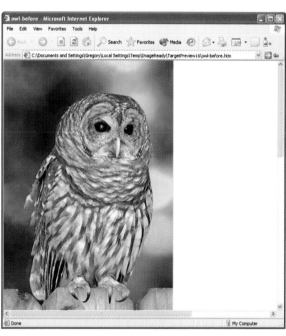

49.2

ABOUT THE IMAGE

Rehabilitated Barred Owl Canon EOS D30, 300mm f/2.8, ISO 100, f/4.0 @ 1/60, RAW setting, 2,160 x 1,440 pixels, edited and converted to 640 x 427 .jpg files

If you have viewed a Web page that features an image that changed to another image when you rolled your mouse over it, you've seen a rollover image. Rollover images are very commonly used as navigation buttons on Web pages. However, they can also be used to *layer* "before" and "after" images as well. Using a rollover image is a much better way to compare two images than having them placed next to each other on a Web page. In this technique you will learn how to use features found in Adobe ImageReady CS to create a "before" and "after" rollover image for use on a Web page.

Creating a rollover image and the necessary HTML code (a special programming code used by Internet browsers) needed to display a rollover image is easy when using Photoshop and ImageReady as you will learn in this technique. However, in order to use this code and the rollover image in a Web page with other content, you will need an HTML editor and you will need to have some basic understanding of how to cut and paste HTML code in an editor, and where it ought to be pasted. Two of the more feature-rich HTML editors are found in Macromedia's Dreamweaver and in Microsoft's FrontPage. You can also accomplish what you need to with the free or inexpensive editors that can be found on CNET's `www.download.com`. Just search for "HTML editors." Most of the software found on CNET's Web page is available as 30-day trial versions. You can also use Netscape's Composer, which is a simple, but free HTML editor that comes with Netscape 7.0.

STEP 1: OPEN FILE

- Using Adobe Photoshop CS, select **File** ➢ **Open** (**Ctrl+O** PC, **Cmd+O** Mac) to display the **Open** dialog box. After locating the **\49** folder, double-click it to open it. Press **Ctrl** (**Cmd** on the Mac) and click the files **owl-after.jpg** and **owl-before.jpg** to select them both. Click **Open** to open the files.

Our goal is to create an image for a Web page that features the final edited image (**owl-after.jpg**), but when you move your mouse over the image, the original converted, but not edited RAW image (**owl-before.jpg**) is displayed.

STEP 2: ADD THE "AFTER" IMAGE TO THE "BEFORE" IMAGE AS A LAYER

- Click the **Move** tool (**V**). Click the **owl-after.jpg** image to make it the active image. While pressing the **Shift** key (to align the images), drag the image onto the **owl-before.jpg** image and release the mouse button.
- You can now close the **owl-after.jpg** image.
- Click the **owl-before.jpg** image to make it the active image. Your **Layers** palette should now look like the one shown in Figure 49.3. To view the **Background layer**, click the **Layer Visibility** icon to the left of **Layer 1**. Click the **Layer Visibility** icon once again to turn it back on.

STEP 3: CREATE A "SLICE" AND SEND TO IMAGEREADY CS

You now need to create a "slice," which tells a Web browser where the mouse needs to be to initiate a "rollover" image to be displayed.

■ Select **Layer ➢ New Layer Based Slice**. You should now see a small blue line around the image and a tiny "01" in the upper-left corner of the image indicating the area of **slice 1**.

■ You are now ready to use Adobe ImageReady CS to finish your image rollover. Select **File ➢ Edit in ImageReady** (**Shift+Ctrl+M** PC, **Shift+Cmd+M** Mac) to send the file to Adobe ImageReady CS. Alternatively, you can click the **Edit in ImageReady** button at the very bottom of the

Toolbox to load Adobe ImageReady CS and to display the image we've been working on.

Adobe ImageReady CS is an image-editing tool similar to Photoshop except it has a tremendous number of features that are specifically for working with Web images. Depending on which palettes you have opened and how they are displayed, your Adobe ImageReady CS screen should now look somewhat like the one shown in Figure 49.4.

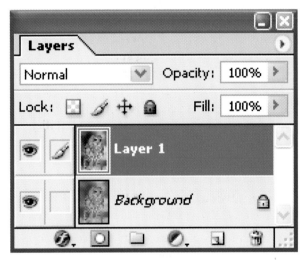

49.3

49.4

STEP 4: USE IMAGEREADY TO CREATE ROLLOVER AND HTML CODE

- If the **Layers** palette or the **Web Content** palette is not visible, choose **Window ➢ Layers**, or **Window ➢ Web Content** to display them.
- Beneath **Slices** in the **Web Content** palette you should now have one image and it should be highlighted in a blue color. Click the **Create Rollover State** button (the one just to the left of the **Garbage Can** icon) at the bottom of the **Web Content** palette to create a new slice. The **Web Content** palette should now look like Figure 49.5.
- To correctly set the rollover state to be the original "before" image, you need to click the

Background Layer in the **Layers** palette to make it the active layer and you need to click the **Layer Visibility** icon just to the left of **Layer 1** to hide that layer. The **Layers** palette should now look like the one shown in Figure 49.6. The document window will now show the "before" image with less tonal range and less saturated colors. This will be the rollover image.

STEP 5: OPTIMIZE IMAGES AND TEST ROLLOVER IMAGE

- To choose the type of file and the level of compression, click in the **Preset** box in the **Optimize**

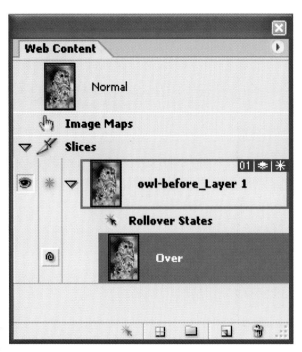

49.5

49.6

palette and select **JPEG Medium**. The **Optimize** palette should now look similar to the one shown in Figure 49.7.

If you want more control over how your image will be optimized, you can click the **Quality** and **Options** icons in the **Optimize** palette to get more setting controls.

■ To view the rollover, click the **Preview Document** icon (**Y**) near the bottom of the **Toolbox** as shown in Figure 49.8. Now when you move your mouse over the image you will see the rollover effect as intended. Move your mouse off

the image and it will return to the "after" image. To turn off the preview, once again, click the **Preview Document** icon (**Y**) in the **Toolbox**.

STEP 6: CREATE WEB PAGE

■ To view the new rollover image in Microsoft Internet Explorer click the **View in iexplore** icon (**Ctrl**+**Alt**+**P** PC, **Cmd**+**Option**+**P** Mac) at the bottom of the **Toolbox**. Adobe ImageReady CS will then create the HTML text and load the

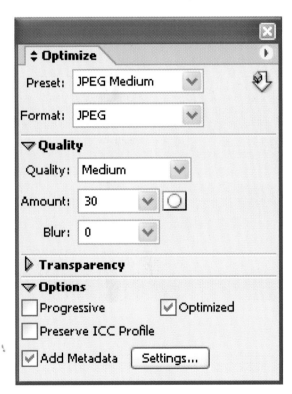

49.7

49.8

rollover image into Microsoft Internet Explorer, as shown in Figure 49.9.

As you move your mouse over the image, the "before" image should appear; move your mouse off the image and it will once again display the "after" image. Below the image you will find some information on the image, and below that you will find all the

HTML code needed to properly display the rollover image.

You can now copy the HTML code from the Internet Explorer window and paste it into the source code for the Web page where you intend to display the rollover image. Or, you can select **File ➢ Save Optimized As** to get the **Save Optimized As** dialog box shown in Figure 49.10. Type the filename you want in the **File name** box. Click in the **Save as type** box and select **HTML and Images**. Click **Save** to save the images plus a Web page. You can now view the rollover image by clicking the HTML file found in the folder where you saved it.

49.9

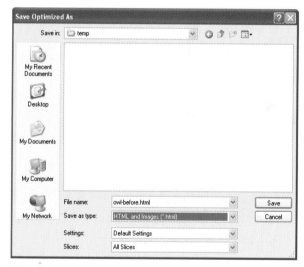

49.10

CREATING ANIMATIONS USING DIGITAL PHOTOS

50.1

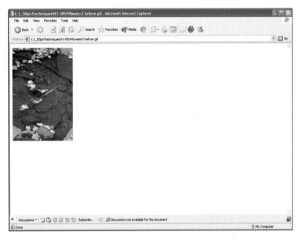

50.2

ABOUT THE IMAGE

Seeing Through the Fall Colors Canon EOS D30 digital camera mounted on a tripod, 100mm f/2.8 macro with circular polarizer, ISO 100, Fine image setting, 1/8 @ f/2.8, images have been edited and resized to be 214 x 320 pixel .jpg images (41K and 49K)

The two photos shown in Figure 50.1 were taken with a Canon EOS D30 digital camera and a circular polarizer on a 100mm lens. The photo on the left shows the results of rotating the circular polarizer so that all reflections were removed from the surface of the water. Without the surface reflections, it was possible to see all the way to the bottom of the stream. The second photo shows the results of rotating the circular polarizer so that the reflections were maximized.

The goal of this technique is to create an animation for a Web page that shows what it looks like when the circular polarizer is rotated. To accomplish this seemingly difficult objective, the images will be combined into one image as separate layers; then **Opacity** will be varied on the top layer and the animation will be created by using the **Tween** feature in Adobe ImageReady CS.

STEP 1: OPEN FILES AND COMBINE THEM INTO ONE FILE

Completing this technique is possible with just Adobe ImageReady CS, the Adobe Photoshop CS companion "Web image tool." However, its tight integration with Adobe Photoshop CS offers so many benefits to those with computers that have sufficient resources to run both applications simultaneously that we will use both applications. If your computer struggles to load and run both applications, close Adobe Photoshop CS and just run and use Adobe ImageReady CS. Adobe ImageReady CS uses for the most part, the same menu commands and shortcuts as Adobe Photoshop CS.

■ Using Adobe Photoshop CS, choose **File ➢ Open** (**Ctrl+O** PC, **Cmd+O** Mac) to display the **Open** dialog box. Double-click the **\50** folder to open it. Press **Ctrl** on a PC or **Cmd** on the Mac while clicking the **water1-before.jpg** and **water2-before.jpg** files to select them both; click **Open** to open both files in Adobe Photoshop CS.
■ To create a layer containing the **water1-before.jpg** image in the **water2-before.jpg** image, click the **water1-before.jpg** image to make it the active image. Click the **Move** tool (**V**) in the **Toolbox**. Press **Shift** on a PC or **Cmd** on a Mac while clicking in the **water1-before** image and drag the cursor onto the **water2-before.jpg** image. When you release the mouse button, the **water2-before.jpg** image now has a second layer, as you can see in the **Layers** palette shown in Figure 50.3.

Alternatively, you can click the **water-before1.jpg** image to make it the active image and then press **Shift** (**Cmd** on a Mac) while clicking the image's thumbnail in the **Layers** palette and draging it onto the **water-before2.jpg** image. In both cases, pressing **Shift** on a PC (**Cmd** on a Mac) forces the new image to be perfectly aligned to the image where it is dragged.

■ You can now close the **water1-before.jpg** image as it is no longer needed.

STEP 2: SEND IMAGE TO ADOBE IMAGEREADY CS

■ The image is now ready to be edited with Adobe ImageReady CS. To open Adobe ImageReady CS (if it is not already open) while sending the two-layered version of the **water2-before.jpg** image, click the **Edit in ImageReady** button (**Shift+Ctrl+M** PC, **Shift+Cmd+M** Mac), which is at the bottom of the **Toolbox**, as shown in Figure 50.4.

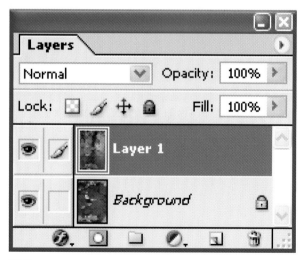

50.3

■ You should now see the **water2-before.jpg** image in the Adobe ImageReady CS workspace. As you will need quite a few palettes, I suggest that you arrange the palettes in one of the default positions by choosing **Window ➢ Workspace ➢ Interactivity Palette Locations**. The Adobe ImageReady CS workspace should now look similar to the one shown in Figure 50.5.

STEP 3: CREATE ANIMATION

To create an animation, you now need to carefully define the first and last image and apply the **Tween** command to automatically create all the transitional states in between. That's it — it is that simple! Because we want the beginning of the image to look as if no polarizer was used (the image with the rich fall colors), we set it as the first image. Then we create a second image in the **Animation** palette and carefully set it to look like the image where the circular polarizer's full capability of removing reflective light has been used (the image showing the bottom of the shallow stream).

■ Click the **menu button** in the upper-right corner of the **Animation** palette to get a pop-up menu; click **New Frame** to create a second frame

50.4

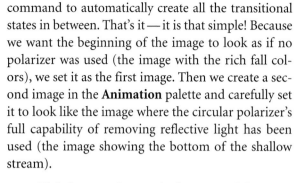

50.5

50.6

in the **Animation** palette, which should now look like the one shown in Figure 50.6. The second animation cell is now highlighted indicating that it is the active cell. The **Layers** palette now reflects the settings for the active cell, as does the **water2-before.jpg** image.

■ Click the **Layer Visibility** icon to the left of the **Layer 1** layer in the **Layers** palette to hide that layer. The **Layers** palette should now look like the one shown in Figure 50.7. This now changes the look of the second cell in the **Animation** palette to look like the image where the bottom of the stream may be seen.

■ Press **Shift** and click cell **1** in the **Animation** palette to select both cells. Click the bottom of either cell to get a pop-up menu giving you options for setting the amount of time each cell is displayed; click **0.2** to set each cell to display two-tenths of a second.

■ With both cells still highlighted, click the menu button in the upper-right corner of the **Animation**

palette to get the pop-up menu shown in Figure 50.8. Click **Tween** to get the **Tween** dialog box shown in Figure 50.9. This dialog box allows you to set the characteristics of the tween effect — the way the images are made "between" each cell.

■ Click in the **Frames to Add** box and type **18**, which results in a total of 20 cells — the starting and ending cells, plus 18 "tweened" cells. **All Layers** should be selected in the **Layers** area. In the **Parameters** area, only **Opacity** should be selected. Click **OK** to begin the tweening process.

■ The **Animation** palette should now look like the one shown in Figure 50.10. To see the entire animation, you have to use the scroll bar at the bottom of the **Animation** palette.

■ At the bottom-left corner of the **Animation** palette, there is a **Looping Option** setting box; click it to get a pop-up menu. Then, click **Once**

50.7

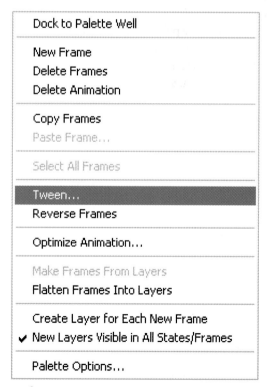

50.8

to have the animation play a single time without looping.

■ To view the **Animation**, click the **Plays/Stops Animation** button in the **Animation** palette — the button with a single triangle on it. You now see the 20-cell animation play in the **water2-before.jpg** image window. Pretty cool, don't you think?

■ It is way beyond the scope of this book to cover the many intricate details of Web images, but you should be aware that Adobe ImageReady CS is doing some pretty sophisticated manipulation of the images based upon defaults or your chosen settings. Take a quick look at the **Optimize** palette. If it isn't showing, select **Window ➢ Optimize**. Click the **Quality**, **Transparency**, and **Options** icons to view the many options that are available. Because animations must be GIF files and because we want the best quality of animation for our stream image animation while making it an easy download, select **GIF 128 Dithered** in the **Preset** box. The **Optimize** palette should now look similar to the one shown in Figure 50.11.

■ To find out how large the image has become, click on the **Optimized Tab** in the **water2-before.**

jpg document window. If you click the down arrow at the bottom of the document window you get a pop-up menu; choose **Original/Optimized File Sizes**, which will show the entire 20-cell GIF image file is **556.3K**. While that is small for what is essentially a file containing 20 different images, the file is a bit large to download from a Web page and just fine to use as a CD-ROM-based image. To make it smaller, you can change GIF settings, make the image smaller, or tween with fewer than 20 cells.

50.10

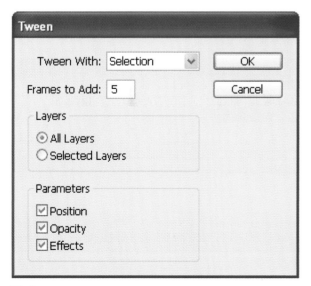

50.9

50.11

STEP 4: SAVE AND VIEW ANIMATION FILE

■ To optimize and save the newly created
animation, choose **File** ➢ **Save Optimized As**
(**Ctrl**+**Shift**+**Alt**+**S** PC, **Option**+**Shift**+**Cmd**+**S**
Mac) to get the **Save Optimized As** dialog box.
After selecting a folder where you want to store
the image, click **Save** to save the file.
■ To view the animation, open up a Web
browser; then using Windows Explorer (Finder
for Mac users), find and then click and drag the
water2-before.gif file onto the open Web browser,
as shown in Figure 50.12. As soon as it displays,
the animation begins to play. As we set the looping
option to play once, it plays once. To view it again,
click the Web browser's **Refresh** or **Reload** button.

STEP 5: RETURN TO PHOTOSHOP CS

■ You can now close Adobe ImageReady CS, or
you can click the **Jump** button at the bottom of
Adobe ImageReady CS's **Toolbox** to return to
Adobe Photoshop CS.

Admittedly, this animation is very simple and we
avoided looking at the many other features that allow
you to further control how the animation displays.
But, this example gives you a good idea of what can
be done with animations. Well-thought-out animations can enhance Web pages, but they also can repeat
too often, be distracting, and ultimately lower user
experience if you have not used them appropriately.

You may now want to consider other ways that you
can use animations. How about having a moon float up
toward the top and off of a late evening photo as if it
were rising in the sky? Or, you can create an animation
where the sky gets darker and darker until it is almost
totally black as it does each evening when the sun sets.
You can take ideas such as these and turn them into
interesting features on a Web page in just a few minutes

using Adobe ImageReady CS. For example, the **sunset-
in-the-forest.gif** image that can be found in the **\50**
folder was easily created by using the image as the first
cell. Reducing **Lightness** with **Hue/Saturation** created
the second cell. 28 new cells were then tweened to create the final GIF. To view the results, drag it onto an
open Web browser. The image loops three times. What
animation do you want to create?

You have now reached the end of the last technique
and the end of the book. I hope you have enjoyed the
techniques and the digital photos that you used to
complete the techniques. If you have any questions
about these techniques, ideas for new techniques,
comments about how one or more of them may be
improved, or you have some work you would like to
share on the companion Web page, please send me an
e-mail—I would enjoy hearing from you. I can be
reached at `ggeorges@reallyusefulpage.`
`com`. See you out there shooting!

50.12

APPENDIX A
WHAT'S ON THE CD-ROM

This appendix provides you with information on the contents of the CD that accompanies this book. For the latest and greatest information, please refer to the ReadMe file located at the root of the CD. Here is what you will find:

- System Requirements
- CD-ROM Installation Instructions
- What's on the CD
- Troubleshooting

SYSTEM REQUIREMENTS

Make sure that your computer meets the minimum system requirements listed in this section. If your computer doesn't match up to most of these requirements, you may have a problem using the contents of the CD.

FOR WINDOWS 9X, WINDOWS 2000, WINDOWS NT4 (WITH SP 4 OR LATER), WINDOWS ME, OR WINDOWS XP:

- PC with a Pentium processor running at 120 Mhz or faster
- At least 32 MB of total RAM installed on your computer; for best performance, we recommend at least 64 MB
- Ethernet network interface card (NIC) or modem with a speed of at least 28,800 bps
- A CD-ROM drive

FOR MACINTOSH:

- Mac OS computer with a 68040 or faster processor running OS 7.6 or later
- At least 32 MB of total RAM installed on your computer; for best performance, we recommend at least 64 MB

CD-ROM INSTALLATION INSTRUCTIONS

To install a particular piece of software, open its folder with My Computer or Internet Explorer. What you do next depends on what you find in the software's folder:

1. First, look for a ReadMe.txt file or a .doc or .htm document. If this is present, it should contain installation instructions and other useful information.

2. If the folder contains an executable (.exe) file, this is usually an installation program. Often it will be called Setup.exe or Install.exe, but in some cases the filename reflects an abbreviated version of the software's name and version number. Run the .exe file to start the installation process.

WHAT'S ON THE CD

The following sections provide a summary of the software and other materials you'll find on the CD.

IMAGES FOR THE 50 TECHNIQUES

All of the images for the techniques are on the CD in the folder named "Techniques". There is a sub-folder for each technique. For example, you can find the images for Technique 12 in the folder \techniques\11-20\12.

- 50 sets of original "before" photos for completing each of the fifty step-by-step techniques and 50 "after" images showing the final results. Most of the "before" images are digital photos created with professional digital SLR cameras and quality lenses including the Canon EOS 1Ds, 1D, D60, and D30 cameras; and, the Fuji FinePix S2 Pro.
- Internet browser-based slide show featuring "before" and "after" images. To run the show, use Windows Explorer or Mac Finder to locate the folder **/show**. Double-click **index.htm** to run the slide show in your Internet browser. You can also view this slide show online at www.reallyusefulpage.com/50pscs/show.

TROUBLESHOOTING

If you have difficulty installing or using any of the materials on the companion CD, try the following solutions:

- **Turn off any anti-virus software that you may have running.** Installers sometimes mimic virus activity and can make your computer incorrectly believe that it is being infected by a virus. (Be sure to turn the anti-virus software back on later.)
- **Close all running programs.** The more programs you're running, the less memory is available to other programs. Installers also typically update files and programs; if you keep other programs running, installation may not work properly.
- **Reference the ReadMe.** Please refer to the ReadMe file located at the root of the CD-ROM for the latest product information at the time of publication.
- **Image files.** When working with image files from the CD-ROM if you receive a message that you are working with a "Read-Only" file, read the Introduction to learn more about how to change file attributes.

If you still have trouble with the CD-ROM, please call the Wiley Product Technical Support phone number: (800) 762-2974. Outside the United States, call (317) 572-3994. You can also contact Wiley Product Technical Support at www.wiley.com/techsupport. Wiley Publishing will provide technical support only for installation and other general quality control items; for technical support on the applications themselves, consult the program's vendor or author.

To place additional orders or to request information about other Wiley products, please call (800) 225-5945.

APPENDIX B
COMPANION WEB SITE

A companion Web site has been created especially for this book at `www.reallyusefulpage.com/50pscs`.

WHAT IS ON THE SITE?

- Updates and corrections to this book
- *50 Techniques* Readers' Image Gallery: View the work of other readers and share your best work, too! If you have created an outstanding image that you would like to share with others, please e-mail a .jpg file version to `curator@reallyusefulpage.com`. Make sure that the images fit within a 640 x 640 pixel square and that they are under 75K. Future editions of this book may contain images submitted to this gallery. Permission will be requested and credit will be given to those who submit images.
- A really useful list of online photography and image editing resources including Photoshop plug-ins
- FAQ (Frequently Asked Questions) section for getting answers to common questions
- Recommended book reading list to further your skills
- List of online galleries that you might like to visit

JOIN AN ONLINE FORUM

The author of this book has created and hosts an online forum at Yahoo! Groups for readers of his books, as well as anyone else that has an interest in digital photo editing. To join, visit `http://groups.yahoo.com/group/digital-photo-editing`. Alternatively, visit this book's companion Web site (`www.reallyusefulpage.com/50pscs`) and click on Join an E-mail Group.

Subscribe to the e-mail service to participate. You can post images and share tips and techniques with other readers of this book. There will even be an occasional online chat session, which you will be invited to.

CONTACT THE AUTHOR

Gregory Georges welcomes comments from readers. He may be contacted by e-mail at `ggeorges@reallyusefulpage.com`, or occasionally on AOL IM under the Buddy Name, DigitalGregory. His Web site is `www.reallyusefulpage.com`. While he reads all e-mail, the heavy volume makes it difficult to respond to all messages immediately, so please have patience.

INDEX

Z

ABOUT THE AUTHOR

Gregory Georges has been an active photographer for more than 25 years. In 1999, his passion for photography finally took priority over his work in the software industry when he decided to undertake photography full-time and to work to achieve another lifelong goal — to become an author. Having continuously used computers for his work and personal life since he took his first computer programming class in 1969, Gregory was able to excel in the new world of digital photography.

After writing his first book on digital cameras in late 1999, Gregory became the founding author for the "50 Fast" book series for Wiley Publishing, Inc. with *50 Fast Photoshop 7 Techniques*. His second book, *50 Fast Digital Photo Techniques* quickly became an Amazon "Top 50" bestseller, and his books have been translated into more than ten languages. Gregory has also written *50 Fast Digital Camera Techniques*, *Digital Photography: Top 100 Simplified Tips & Tricks*, and *Digital Camera Solutions*. Gregory also writes for *eDigital Photo* and *Shutterbug* magazines. His Web site ReallyUsefulPage.com is a really useful Web page for learning more about how to get the most from new digital photography.

COLOPHON

This book was produced electronically in Indianapolis, Indiana. Microsoft Word 2000 was used for word processing; design and layout were produced using QuarkXPress 4.11 and Adobe Photoshop 7.0 on Power Macintosh computers. The typeface families used are: Chicago Laser, Minion, Myriad, Myriad Multiple Master, Prestige Elite, Symbol, Trajan, and Zapf Dingbats.

Acquisitions Editor: Michael Roney
Project Editor: Amanda Peterson
Technical Editors: Dennis Short, John Wyman
Copy Editor: Roxane Marini
Editorial Managers: Rev Mengle, Robyn Siesky
Permissions Editor: Laura Moss
Production Coordinator: Maridee Ennis
Cover Art: Gregory Georges
Quality Control Technicians: John Greenough, Susan Moritz, Brian Walls
Production: Elizabeth Brooks, Sean Decker, Lauren Goddard, Jennifer Heleine, LeAndra Hosier, Lynsey Osborn, Melanie Wolven
Proofreading: Joanne Keaton
Indexing: Sherry Massey